A GRANDER VISION

To my wife, Sheila, and my daughters, Lisa, Susie, and Amanda, and grandchildren, Kiyara, Ava, and Callum

To my brothers and sisters Mike, Deirdre, Frank, Yvonne, Ken, Sean, and Sharon

In memory of my parents, Danny and Maureen, and my brothers Noel and Don

CONTENTS

FOREWORD

In this autobiography, Sid Ryan traces his life from working-class roots in Dublin to the presidency of the Ontario Federation of Labour. Sid's passion for social justice and international solidarity comes across as we follow him from the barricades at the 2001 Quebec Summit of the Americas, through his visits to Ireland and the Middle East, and on to his years at the pinnacle of the Canadian labour movement.

Sid's story of growing up in Ireland during the fifties and sixties shares features many can identify with: a weak economy forcing his dad to work in England for lengthy periods of time, with his mom staying at home to raise the kids on a tight budget. Sid's father was influential; Sid took an interest in politics, sport, and rebel music from him. We share a passion for hurling, with Sid embracing his father's support for Tipperary. Father Alec Reid — the Sagart, who played a central role in the peace process — was also from Tipp and shared the same passion for hurling. Sid worked in Belfast in the 1960s and details his memories of the civil rights era at that time and its violent repression. It is this Irish connection that would eventually lead to our meeting.

Over the centuries, Ireland's freedom struggle benefitted greatly from the support of its sons and daughters dispersed throughout the world. The Irish diaspora stood with us through the good times and the bad times. It played a vital role in helping us develop the peace process, in the face of a hostile British government and Irish establishment.

Irish emigrants to Canada and their descendants, including members of my own family, played a prominent role in that international solidarity. As elsewhere, trade unionists were key backers of our struggle. It was the great Irish revolutionary James Connolly who coined the phrase: "The cause of Ireland is the cause of labour; and the cause of labour is the cause of Ireland." We were blessed with many trade unionists, like Sid, who share that vision. Sid is one of our friends.

As our nascent peace process developed in the 1980s, our Canadian friends lobbied hard for the government to issue me a visa to enter Canada in my role as uachtarán (president) of Sinn Féin. Sid supported the campaign and used his good offices to press for a visa. Eventually, a visa was won and I got to visit Toronto in 1994. Sid joined me on stage for a massive rally at Convocation Hall, University of Toronto. During the visit, Sid also helped organize a very well-attended meeting for trade union leaders and activists, where I was able to brief them on the peace process and the struggle for Irish reunification.

With Gerry Adams in 1994 at the Delta Chelsea Hotel, Toronto.

With Gerry Adams, president of Sinn Féin, when he visited Toronto in 2009.

Sid took up the challenge to support the peace process. He visited the north of Ireland three times in the late 1990s as part of Canadian observer delegations at controversial, and sometimes violent, Orange marches in Portadown and Belfast. On each of these visits, I had the pleasure of thanking Sid and his colleagues, including the late Warren Allmand, for their interest and support.

We are in a better place in Ireland today. I have visited Canada as president of Sinn Féin on many occasions since the nineties. On each and every visit, Sid has been there to offer support and encouragement.

It was, therefore, an honour to be asked by Sid to write this foreword. Sid played his part in helping making Ireland a better place today. I know he will continue showing support for our cause and that of oppressed people everywhere in the years ahead. *Go raibh maith agat*, Sid — thank you.

Gerry Adams, Teachta Dála, Louth; former leader of Sinn Féin
Belfast, Ireland
May 2018

QUEBEC CITY, APRIL 2001

I knew there was a chance that there would be some kind of confrontation — maybe even violence — but I would never have guessed the melee would be so fitting. The toughs who blocked our path tried to make us turn to the right. We knew the road to the left was the way to go. It was perfectly symbolic.

The incident occurred at the Summit of the Americas in April 2001. I was pretty sure the burly men trying to thwart our demonstration were union members, and their interference, sadly, indicative of a fissure in the labour movement that I had struggled with throughout my years as a union leader. The things that divided us were complicated, but the effects of the rift were simple: it distanced us from our philosophical roots and from our members, and it made us less effective — or worse — against an opponent that wasn't divided at all.

The Quebec City summit was one in a series of high-level meetings convened over a period of years by corporations and politicians to tie nations together in a web of global trade agreements. For Canada it started with the Canada–U.S. Free Trade Agreement, which morphed into the North American Free Trade Agreement (NAFTA), and, more recently, the Canada–European Union Comprehensive Economic and Trade Agreement (CETA), but the beginnings can be traced back much earlier.

In 1989 John Williamson, an economist at the Institute for International Economics, came up with a list of principles that, he claimed, represented the common wisdom within institutions such as the World Bank, the World Trade Organization (WTO), and the International Monetary Fund (IMF). He called it the "Washington Consensus." This so-called consensus calls for deregulation in the financial and environmental spheres, privatization of state-owned assets, free trade in goods and services, reduction of taxes for corporations, and unfettered movement of capital. These objectives were aimed initially at Latin American nations in financial trouble and were applied with disastrous consequences in other parts of the developing world.

The recession of 1981–82, combined with an increase in interest rates engineered in Washington to curb runaway inflation, caused a worldwide trade slowdown that hit export-dependent developing countries, especially in Latin America. Governments in the Organisation for Economic Co-operation and Development (OECD) that were flush with petrodollars from the dramatic surge in oil prices were only too happy to invest their money in sovereign debt. However, these debts were short-term. When the recession hit, the creditor nations refused to renew the loans. They called in their debts and the shock waves reverberated throughout the region.

First Mexico and then other countries caught up in the crisis were forced to turn to the IMF and the World Bank to bail them out. The World Bank and IMF were supposedly set up to alleviate and reduce world poverty, but the remedies they offered only did further damage. As a condition of receiving bailout money, debtor nations had to agree to a set of measures referred to as a Structural Adjustment Program (SAP). The SAP looked a lot like the remedies described in Williamson's Washington Consensus. In practice, they amounted to little more than theft. Public assets were sold to foreign investors at fire-sale prices. Argentina's airline and railway systems were practically given away. The price of debt relief included not only privatization, but also deregulation and the erosion of workers' rights.

Bolivia's situation was similar, only worse. The country's indigenous population, having lived for years under a brutal dictatorship, was governed by a white ruling class of European descent based mostly in the cities. When the debt crisis erupted, the country's white rulers readily accepted the terms imposed by the IMF and World Bank, the harsh effects of which were felt mainly by the indigenous people. Public assets, including the railway, telephone, water, and sewage systems, were privatized, along with the airline industry and the provision of healthcare and education. Wages for public-sector workers were reduced, labour laws were eliminated, corporate taxes and tariffs were lowered, and subsidies for Bolivian industry ended. At the same time, the government agreed to expedite the extraction and export of raw materials, a measure benefiting foreign companies rather than local ones. But their biggest blunder was the privatization of the Cochabamba water system, given to the U.S. engineering giant Bechtel Corporation. Cochabamba erupted with riots on the street, and eventually the government was forced to cancel the contract. Evo Morales, a cocoa farmer and congressman, emerged from the "water wars" to become the president of Bolivia in 2006.

Bolivia and Argentina are just two examples of sovereign Latin American nations' economies the World Bank and the IMF took control over. The same policies set out in the Washington Consensus and SAP became the principles that found later expression in the free trade agreements negotiated by the United States with partners around the world. Especially after the collapse of the Soviet Union in 1989, the United States used the IMF, WTO, and World Bank to export its free-market ideology across continents. Globalization was becoming a reality.

NAFTA was signed early in 1994 despite resistance from unions and civil society. By the end of that year, at the First Summit of the Americas in Miami — at which all thirty-four countries of North and South America together with the Caribbean countries, with the sole exception of Cuba, were represented — the United States was floating the idea of a hemispheric free trade agreement. This became known as the Free Trade Area of the Americas (FTAA). Over the next seven years little or no public discussion of the proposal occurred, but behind the scenes about a dozen multinational committees met regularly to figure out how such an agreement would work. Then president George W. Bush announced that the FTAA would be the focus of discussion at the Summit of the Americas in Quebec City.

Early in 2001 I called together CUPE Ontario's International Solidarity Committee ("CUPE" being the Canadian Union of Public Employees) to develop a campaign to fight the FTAA. Edgar Godoy would coordinate the campaign and work closely with CUPE Ontario's executive director, Antoni Shelton. I appointed Stella Yeadon to head up the communications strategy.

The proposed FTAA agreement would bind all thirty-four signatory countries to terms modelled on those incorporated in NAFTA. During the run-up to the summit, word leaked that the terms included the Chapter 11 provisions of NAFTA, giving investors in one country the right to sue other governments that pass laws or regulations seen to restrict their ability to profit from their investments. Prime Minister Jean Chrétien had expressly denied that these provisions would be part of the deal and was chagrined when Maude Barlow of the Council of Canadians exposed his dirty little secret. She used the revelation to demand the full text of the FTAA document be placed before the Canadian public.

I travelled the province giving speeches to alert our members to the dangers embedded in the draft agreement. Antoni Shelton and Edgar Godoy attended weekly planning meetings in Quebec and Ontario. The International Solidarity Committee arranged for busloads of our members to take part in demonstrations at the summit. We reached out to other civil society organizations to make our protests as effective as possible. From the beginning, however, we heard rumblings that certain unions in Quebec and some of their civil-society organizations had a different vision of what our participation should look like.

The two main factions were loosely aligned under a couple of banners. The Quebec Federation of Labour (Fédération des travailleurs et travailleuses du Québec [FTQ]) and some non-governmental organizations

With Antoni Shelton at the Common Front anti-poverty assembly in 2012.

(NGOs), such as Oxfam, Common Frontiers, and others, worked together in a loose coalition under Réseau québécois sur l'intégration continentale (RQIC). Their approach was a moderate one. More radical organizations of students, anti-poverty activists, feminists, and anarchists worked with Convergence of Anti-Capitalist Struggles (CLAC) and CASA (Summit of the Americas Welcoming Committee). RQIC, representing the moderate faction, negotiated $300,000 from the Canadian government to hold an alternative Summit of the People. The alternative summit would allow civil society to make its concerns known and the final statement would be delivered to the hemispheric leaders. The more radical organizations looked upon this process as a sellout.

The People's Summit, to the extent that it provided workshops on free trade agreements and plenary sessions for debate and discussion, was a huge success. The panel of speakers included Maude Barlow and Naomi Klein, with their unique international experiences, as well as legal experts who explained the intricacies of the proposed trade deal. However, the organizers were somewhat embarrassed when the three thousand delegates in attendance voted overwhelmingly to reject the FTAA and its hemispheric aspirations. This wasn't what they had anticipated. At least some within the labour organizations and their

Medhi Kouhestani-Nejad, CUPE Ontario executive board member, and me, CUPE Ontario president, at the Quebec City protest against FTAA.

civil society allies intended the final statement to offer conditional support for the FTAA, with some "labour, environmental and social inclusion clauses" to be written into the text. They didn't want rejection. They wanted a seat at the table.

The next day, Friday, CLAC and CASA organized a protest march from Laval University into the Old City of Quebec, where the area around the conference centre had been cordoned off. A small contingent of CUPE members joined the march, including Antoni Shelton, Edgar Godoy, Brian O'Keefe, and me. A group of protesters managed to pull a section of the fence down, which led to a running battle between protesters and the heavily armed police. Eventually the police blanketed the area with tear gas and fired rubber bullets to disperse the crowd. The leaders or senior representatives of thirty-four states were hunkered down inside that fenced perimeter. Images of ordinary citizens being gassed, harassed, and chased through the streets on the outside conveyed the message the CLAC and CASA protesters had wanted. The message of violent repression was flashed around the world.

It was not, however, the message that RQIC and the organizers of the People's Summit wanted broadcast. Earlier in the week, organizations under the banner of RQIC had made plans to march sixty thousand protesters away from the fence during Saturday's main protest event. Instead of confronting the hemisphere's elite inside their fortified enclave, they proposed to lead their members to a parking lot in the suburbs. When I heard this, I issued a press release saying that CUPE Ontario would be marching *to* the fence with anyone who chose to accompany us. My announcement was greeted with consternation by CUPE National, the Canadian Labour Congress (CLC), and the Quebec Federation of Labour (FTQ). Judy Darcy, the CUPE National president, had already agreed to go along with the CLC's support for the non-confrontational RQIC plan. Clearly, some still thought a seat at the table was preferable to taking a stand in the streets.

Naomi Klein hugged me when I got to the People's Summit compound on Friday evening. She thanked me for the press release and the support it implied. Everywhere I went that night, I was greeted with high-fives from the leaders of the activist unions and civil-society organizations that wanted to march to the wall. Only when I entered a restaurant outside the compound, along with Antoni Shelton and Edgar Godoy, did I meet with a cooler reception.

Henri Massé, president of the FTQ, was at a table just inside the door. Massé was a past regional director for CUPE National in Quebec, so I knew him reasonably well. He spotted us as soon as we walked in and his expression was hostile. When I was about three feet away, he blurted in English: "What the fuck do you think you are doing in my province? We have made a decision not to go to the fence and you better live with that decision." Rather than respond immediately, I stuck out my hand and he instinctively took it. I squeezed his hand tightly and I said: "Brother, free trade is a pan-Canadian issue, not just a Quebec issue, so this Saturday I will be marching with my members to the fence." Massé pulled his hand away and muttered: "We'll see about that." Antoni, Edgar, and I ate at another table while Massé glared at us across the restaurant.

Saturday was a perfect, sunny day. The assembly area for the big march was jam-packed with sixty thousand protesters, their banners held high and flags flapping in the breeze. The crowd was a mix of young and old, representing civil society and trade unions, with causes ranging from the environment to health and human rights. The mood was festive but determined. My group of activist members from CUPE Ontario was about two thousand strong. Of course, the largest contingent, with several thousand people in the staging area, was from Quebec. They would form a bloc in front of us in the marching order.

Just before the march was to begin, about twenty tough-looking, French-speaking guys pushed through the crowd and positioned themselves at the tail end of the CUPE Quebec contingent, directly in front of us. I wondered what their game was. Antoni Shelton and Edgar Godoy noticed them, too. They remarked that their attitude seemed unfriendly, and we speculated that they had been planted in front of us for a reason. About twenty minutes into the march, that reason became clear as we approached an intersection where a turn to the left led to the perimeter fence, and a turn to the right led to the parking lot.

The CUPE Quebec delegation, led by CUPE Quebec president Claude Généreux and CUPE National president Judy Darcy, marched together and peeled off to the right. (Judy, Claude, and Wayne Lucas protested at the wall following the march to the parking lot.) The tough guys in front of our Ontario contingent then broke away from the other marchers. They ran ahead and formed a line blocking the turn to the left. I waved my arms from the front of our contingent, pointed the way, and shouted that there was no way we were following the Quebec lead. We were going to the fence! Antoni, Edgar, and I, with CUPE National secretary treasurer Geraldine McGuire, CUPE Ontario secretary treasurer Brian O'Keefe, and CUPE Alberta president Terry Mutton, marched up to the men blocking the road. One held a flagpole

The protest march to the wall in Quebec City, at the 2001 Summit of the Americas. Geraldine McGuire, CUPE National secretary treasurer, is behind the banner. To her left is Brian O'Keefe, CUPE Ontario secretary treasurer. To his left is Terry Mutton, president of CUPE Alberta. I am on the left, in a bandana and white shirt.

across his chest to stop us from passing. I grabbed the pole with both hands and pushed hard, and he stumbled backwards. Antoni and Edgar stepped into the opening with Geraldine, Brian, and Terry right beside them. Together we held open a gap wide enough for the rest of the three-thousand-strong Ontario delegation to pass through. The plan to weaken our protest was beaten. We would make our voices heard.

The toughs eventually regrouped. They managed to halt the rest of the march by sitting down on the roadway in front of the advancing protesters while the CUPE Ontario delegation and a few thousand enterprising others headed for the wall. Then they assumed the role of route marshals, directing traffic off to the right. Most of the demonstrators were unaware they were being pointed down a road to nowhere, and they were pissed when they realized how thoroughly they had been misled.

But thousands of demonstrators made it to the perimeter. Here the reality of corporate governance — a privileged elite on the inside, the great unwashed beyond the barrier — had physical expression. The wall, a combination of concrete blocks and chain-link fences, was some two-and-a-half miles long. It was guarded by more than six thousand police officers, backed up by soldiers of the Canadian Armed Forces. They were armed with five thousand canisters of tear gas, pepper spray, and, reportedly, a water cannon, at a total cost for security of roughly $100 million. This was the face of democracy in Canada in 2001.

The area outside the wall was divided into red, green, and orange zones. Those in the red zone had direct contact with the police. Some of the more militant activists made several futile attempts to pull down the fence using grappling hooks and rope but their efforts were met with volleys of tear gas, pepper spray, and rubber bullets. The gas quickly became thick enough that it was almost impossible to breathe. Geraldine, whom no one would ever have described as an anarchist, or even radical, was having a ball. Sufficiently infused with the crowd's energy, she tied a CUPE bandana onto the fence, shouting out her message: "We will never accept your secret trade deals, negotiated in secret, while civil society is locked out!"

Events played out as they had before and would again. Police provocateurs were caught on camera posing as protesters, provoking trouble with rocks in their hands, partly to justify the massive police presence and partly to undermine the demonstrators by representing them as vandals and thugs. Still, the mobilization in Quebec City was one of the largest and most important anti–free trade demonstrations on Canadian soil. It was an especially important milestone on the journey to defeating the FTAA, and I was immensely encouraged to see sixty thousand Canadians show up to say, "Not if we can help it."

Two groups, each with different goals and tactics, competed to control the protesters' message in Quebec City. At the time, our differences seemed insuperable, but with the passage of time it is clear that both played an important role. The CASA/CLAC group of activists and anarchists were right to challenge the capitalist underpinnings of free trade agreements that have the Washington Consensus principles at their heart. At the same time, the RQIC grouping of trade unions and NGOs was justified in its attempt to modify the FTAA by incorporating labour, environmental, and social standards into the text of any future agreements. Both radicals and moderates are needed in the ongoing struggle. Maude Barlow from the Council of Canadians said in the aftermath of the protests, "The alienation and disillusionment caused by government reaction to their concerns has pushed protesters and civil society down new paths … The grass roots is fusing and co-operating with established organizations to a greater and greater degree."*

It is important to emphasize that labour's goal is not ultimately to stand in the way of trade among sovereign nations. It's not about protectionism or limiting the standard of living in the developing world. In fact, the opposite is true. For example, the WTO talks failed in Seattle because, among other reasons, the developing nations wanted equal access and equal treatment for their goods and services. The greedy bastards of the developed nations were having none of it.

The Quebec summit ended with a statement titled "Declaration of Quebec City: Third Summit of the Americas," in which the participants committed to finalizing the FTAA negotiations no later than January 2005. Hugo Chávez of Venezuela was the lone dissenter among the hemispheric leaders. He insisted that any free trade agreement had to involve all citizens in the decision-making process. Meanwhile, the one leader excluded from the meeting was Cuba's Fidel Castro, an exception that would eventually come back to haunt the FTAA negotiations. The Cuban government was heartened by the massive protests in Quebec City and by the rejection of the FTAA by the People's Summit delegates. These actions allowed the Hemispheric Social Alliance (HSA), a transnational coalition of civil society, unions, and social, environmental, and indigenous movements, to change tactics and sharpen its message. Cuba decided to lend its support and host future meetings in Havana, sending a signal to the entire left in Latin America to get on board. The Quebec City protests had completely altered the dynamics within the left movements across the hemisphere.

---

*Allison Hanes, "After 5,148 tear-gas canisters, we're still trying to put events of Quebec into perspective," *Montreal Gazette*, May 22, 2001.

Chapter 1
GROWING UP IN IRELAND

My great-great-grandfather, Michael Kennedy, was born in Ireland in 1823. He married Mary O'Brien in 1847, the second year of the Great Famine. During the seven-year-long catastrophe during which the potato crop was lost to blight throughout much of the country, thousands of men and women, small landholders and farm workers, died from starvation while the British government looked on with cruel indifference. Michael and Mary Kennedy managed to eke out a modest life despite the hard times. They inhabited a neat little cottage in the village of Greenhills, now a suburb of Dublin, where they had ten children. My great-grandfather, John Kennedy, born in 1861, was one of their nine boys.

Settling into adult life, the Kennedys did not move far from the family nest. Six of the Kennedy brothers all lived within walking distance of one another, the three bachelor brothers sharing a house. Lucy, the only girl, married Nicolas Staunton. John Kennedy married Annie Staunton, a sister of Nicolas.

John and Annie set about building a life for themselves in the waning years of the nineteenth century. Their house was of simple

Francis Jameson, my grandfather, circa 1906.

construction, a rectangular bungalow with stone walls and a slate roof, six rooms, and eight front windows. Many houses at the time were constructed of wood, with little or no insulation and a thatched roof, but the solid and relatively spacious Kennedy cottage was rated a first-class private dwelling in the Dublin census of 1911. The couple had six children, two of whom died early in life. My grandmother Margaret Kennedy, born in Greenhills on January 12, 1891, was one who survived.

Margaret, like most children of the day, went to school and helped around the house. She had lots of cousins and a circle of friends from the nearby Ballymount and Tymon districts. In time, Margaret formed a special interest in a young man, Francis Jameson, a few years older than her. Francis had joined the British Army some fifteen years earlier, in 1904. He served in India in the early part of the century and was among the ranks of soldiers who celebrated the coronation of King George V at the Delhi Durbar in 1911. At the end of January the following year, he returned to England and was transferred to the Army Reserve. From there he was mobilized again and posted to the 2nd Battalion of the 5th Brigade at the outbreak of the First World War.

His battalion crossed over to France on August 14, 1914, as part of the British Expeditionary Force (BEF), embroiled within days in the Battle of Mons. I have often wondered whether he was part of the badly outnumbered British infantry division that decimated so many German troops in that bloody battle. By the time the BEF was forced to pull back, they had lost 1,600 troops in action while the Germans lost between 5,000 and 10,000. It is said that Francis's regiment, the Connaught Rangers, marched away from the battle singing their famous marching song, "It's a Long Way to Tipperary."

My grandfather fought in more than thirty major battles altogether — in India, on the Western front, and later in Mesopotamia, Egypt, Palestine, and Turkey. He retired, his wars finally over, on March 28, 1919. On his release from the British Army, Francis Jameson and Margaret Kennedy courted, married, and settled down.

While Francis had been away fighting for the Empire, the Irish back home had been rebelling against British rule. The Easter Rebellion of 1916 was violently suppressed and its leaders captured and executed. The brutality of the British actions provoked discontent among the Irish, worsened a few years later when the British government sent the murderous Black and Tans, mostly veterans of the First World War, to bolster the Royal Irish Constabulary (RIC) in its campaign to quash any further nationalistic endeavours. Those endeavours continued unabated, sometimes taking on a social, rather than a strictly political or military, form. The working class in Dublin's inner city, for example, began to organize themselves into a union under the leadership of Jim Larkin. In 1909 Larkin formed the Irish Transport and General

Workers' Union (ITGWU), giving a voice to the workers living in the slums. In August 1913 Larkin took twenty thousand labourers from the slums of Dublin out on strike for better wages and working conditions, including an eight-hour day and pensions. The strike dragged on for six months before it was brutally repressed by the state police and a coalition of four hundred employers. The poverty-stricken workers and their families were starved into submission.

Amid this tumultuous social and political background Francis and Margaret Jameson moved into a cottage on Rutland Avenue in Dolphin's Barn, about two miles from Dublin city centre. This is where my mother, Mary (Maureen), was born a few years later, on December 15, 1927. A younger brother, Patrick, died in infancy, and Mary was raised as an only child. Around this time, mostly due to the agitation initiated by the ITGWU, the slums of inner-city Dublin were being torn down. New housing estates were built in places like Crumlin,

The only photograph of the entire Ryan family, Crumlin, Dublin, 1986. Back row (left to right): Sid, Deirdre, Maureen (Mom), Michael, Danny (Dad), Sean, and Ken. Front row (left to right): Yvonne, Frank, Sharon, Noel, and Don.

Ballyfermot, and Drimnagh. Crumlin, at the time, was regarded as the wilds of the countryside by many city folk, and they strongly resisted being forced to move there. For my grandparents, however, it was an opportunity to move closer to their roots in Greenhills. In 1933, when my mother was six years old, they moved from Dolphin's Barn to a new house on Downpatrick Road in Crumlin.

The house they moved into, one of thousands built by the Dublin Corporation, was rather drab and dreary-looking, with its grey-pebble dashing and its anonymous street presence as one unit in row after row of identical terraces, but it served their needs. The design offered them privacy, practicality, and pride of ownership. The walls, concrete on the outside and plaster inside, provided good insulation and incredible soundproofing. Despite the houses' shared walls, they'd never hear their neighbours on either side. Each house had two bedrooms upstairs and two rooms downstairs — a living room and a scullery. The scullery was where the cooking was done, and it also featured a bathtub with a wooden lid, which served as a work surface when closed. A door off the scullery led onto a back porch, where the toilet was located.

Francis Jameson died in 1947 from chronic asthma more than likely brought about by the gassing and horrific conditions he had endured in the trenches during the First World War, during his years of service in the British Army. Maureen was a beautiful young woman of twenty when her father passed. She went to work in a sewing factory on Cork Street in Dublin and began to attend the local dances. Soon she was courted by Danny Ryan, from Roscrea in County Tipperary. She and Danny married in 1948, and he moved into her parents' home in Crumlin, where her mother still lived.

Within eight years, five children were born to Danny and Maureen Ryan: my brother Noel in December 1949, Daniel (Don) in April 1950, me in July 1952, Michael in March 1954, and Deirdre in 1957. There would be five more brothers and sisters — Frank, Yvonne, Ken, Sean, and Sharon — before the Ryan family was complete.

The Republic of Ireland was an economic basket case in the 1950s. Jobs were scarce, and for many young men the only option was to take the boat to England for work on the building sites or in the newly

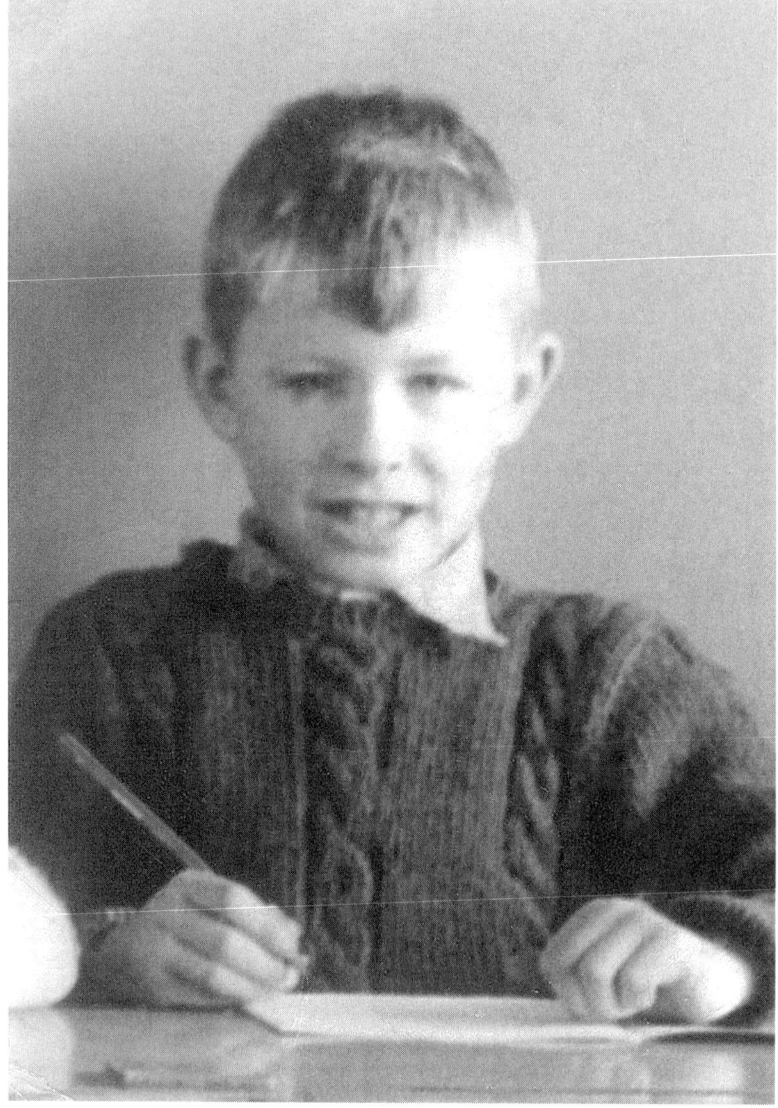

Me, in a 1962 school photo. Scoil Iosagain, Dolphin's Barn, Dublin.

invigorated auto sector. And so it was, in 1955, that Danny Ryan left Maureen in Dublin with four young children to care for and went off in search of work across the Irish Sea. He found a job as a labourer in a power station in Birmingham and was able to send money home to his family. He returned to Ireland in 1957 and took a job as an insurance

Danny, my father, and Maureen, my mother, circa 1980.

salesman, but the pay was poor and commission-based — the Irish were not terribly interested in insurance when life's big struggle was just to put food on the table. By 1959 he was back in Birmingham, but even at the best of times the money he sent home was not enough to cover the expenses of a growing family, and my mother was forced to rely upon my grandmother for help. My grandmother received a widow's pension after my grandfather died — sixteen pounds and sixteen shillings a month, thanks to his army service. Ironically, the Brits were keeping the young Ryan family afloat in the 1950s.

But life was difficult for my mother. Friday mornings were an anxious time as she waited for a money order from Birmingham that did not always come. My job was to keep an eye out for the telegram man on his motorcycle. When I heard the rumble in the distance, my heart would jump because I knew my mother would take us with her to the shops later in the day. On far too many Fridays, however, the telegram man never arrived and I would hear her crying to my grandmother, "What am I going to do? How on earth am I going to face the shopkeepers and feed the kids?"

Like a lot of Dubliners then, we got by on credit, or "tick." Some shopkeepers would advance the groceries, providing you paid the bill the following week. Not every store was so accommodating, but my mother had this arrangement with Ernie Watchorn's general store on Old County Road, where bread, cold cuts, milk, cereal, cigarettes, and so on were sold. It was an accepted practice to send the kids, once they turned eight or nine years old, to pick up groceries, or "messages," from the stores. My brothers and sisters hated the chore and we often argued about whose turn it was. The weeks when the money order failed to arrive were the worst. My mother would write a note for us to take to Ernie Watchorn. Invariably, he was understanding and gave us groceries for the coming week. Our biggest concern was that our mates might see us in Watchorn's getting our messages on the tick. The slagging that followed was merciless though a lot of families were in the same boat or worse off. At times, people in the working class can be very cruel to each other.

Margie Weir owned a tiny shop on Bangor Road that was squeezed in between the butcher shop and a barbershop. My mother had a good relationship with Margie, and she often dropped in to have a chat and buy us choc ices or to pick up a pack of cigarettes. Like Ernie Watchorn, Margie would give my mother tick when the telegram man failed to show up. As teenagers we discovered that Margie was a great

Me, circa 1955.

source of loose cigarettes. Many a time we purchased a single cigarette, such as a Major, or a five-pack of Woodbines — skinny cigarettes that left us hacking and coughing.

Other good friends also helped out. When times got really rough and there was no bread in the house, my mother would send one of us down the road with a handwritten note for Josie Conway and instructions to hand it over without opening it. Josie was a beautiful woman with a big smile and a mop of black curly hair. She always seemed genuinely delighted to see us and never failed to remark on how much I looked like my mother. "Yer the spit out of her mouth," she'd say. Of course, we figured out the note was asking for the loan of a few bob (shillings). If Josie could help out, the next stop was Watchorn's. If not, sometimes in desperation we knocked at Aunt Molly Kennedy's house next door and asked for the loan of a single shilling for the gas meter.

Molly was not really our aunt, but her father and my grandmother's father were brothers, and she played a huge role in our lives. Molly helped to deliver six of the Ryan clan in our back bedroom. She had learned a lot from her mother, who was a midwife, and in many ways Aunt Molly became our family nurse, doctor, and medical advisor. When I was very young I remember Molly telling me, "Your Mammy is very sick and the boys will have to be quiet." I saw her take towels and pots of boiled water upstairs to the bedroom. My mother was crying out in pain, and I was frightened that she was going to die. A few hours later, Molly announced that we had a new baby sister. I, too, was born in the back bedroom with Molly assisting. According to my mother, I almost died at birth because the umbilical cord was wrapped around my neck. I'm sure many employers in Canada wish that cord had been a little tighter.

Groceries weren't the only thing in short supply. Heating the house was another major task. Along with her pension, my grandmother was entitled to receive a couple of bags of turf (or peat) from the government each week. She was given a blue docket from the post office, which was exchanged for burlap sacks of peat from the depot on Windmill Road. Getting the turf from the depot to home was a challenge. My brother Noel had made a gig for the job: it was basically a soapbox with a set of ball bearings for wheels. We loaded it up with bags of turf, not just for ourselves, but also for Aunt Molly and neighbours who were pensioners. Sometimes, if the gig was broken, we'd take the baby out of the pram, remove the pram's false bottom, and use it instead. The slagging was fierce when we passed our mates on the way home from the depot with the pram in tow. "Jasus, Ryaner! That's fine-looking baby ye have there!" It was important not to take any guff or you'd never live it down, so a typical response would be, "Fuck off, or I'll give ya a kick in the bollocks." That usually put a halt to the slagging.

Once the turf was secured we had fuel for the fire, but turf alone burned too quickly, so we had to order in a half ton of coal every month or so. Normally, the coal was delivered by two or three burly dockworkers in a big lorry from Donnelly's coal yards down on the docks. To us kids, the "coal men" were a frightening sight, their faces blackened by coal dust. They lifted the sacks of coal onto their shoulders, manoeuvred their way into the house and around the furniture, and finally dumped the sacks into the space under the staircase. When the coal supply ran low and my mother or grandmother could not afford to buy another load, one of our jobs as kids was to listen out for the local coal man ringing his bell. My grandmother called this coal man "Oul Specky" because of the round, thick-lensed glasses he wore. He was a jolly fellow, his face also blackened by coal dust like the men from the docks. He sold his coal by the stone (fourteen pounds). On occasions when we couldn't even afford to buy coal from the coal man, Granny sent me out to the streets to look for cinders. It was common for people to toss out the cinders along with their rubbish from the previous day's fire. Granny always said, "nothing bates the bit o' coal with the turf … ye need the coal to give a base to the turf." My mother became very upset whenever she heard my granny ask me to look for cinders.

The fireplace was our only source of heat — there was no central heating in our house — and sometimes the only means by which we could cook a meal. Most homes in Dublin in those days were hooked up to coal gas from the Dublin Gas Company. Each house was equipped with a meter that took one shilling to operate and controlled the flow of gas to the stove. The meter was in the coal storage area under the stairs. When my mother had no money for the gas meter, she would improvise by cutting a piece of cardboard from one of the small boxes of Friendly-brand matches into the shape of a shilling. Sometimes the "cardboard shilling" got stuck in the gears of the gas meter and the flow of gas was cut off. This left us with no way of cooking until the gasman came to open up the meter and remove the cardboard, which often took several days. Until then, there was no alternative but to place the pots, pans, and kettle onto the burning embers of the turf-and-coal fire to cook a meal. It broke my mother's heart to have to go to these lengths. Once the gasman came and turned the gas back on, the work of cleaning up the pots and pans began. My mother always had packs of steel wool, and my brothers and sister and I would scrub away until all the pots and pans were shiny clean again.

Above the fireplace in the living room, a small door opened to reveal an oven containing two trays. And behind the fireplace was a hot water boiler. In theory, the heat from the fire warmed the water in the boiler and sent it to a storage tank above the bathtub in the scullery. The intention was laudable, but the system never worked well enough to provide hot water for one bath, let alone enough for our large family. Likewise, the oven was supposed to provide enough heat to bake bread. My mother used it to air baby nappies and the kids used it to harden chestnuts to play conkers. Occasionally, when we had a roaring fire going all day long, the oven would grow so hot that many a nappy that we had forgotten about went up in smoke.

The hearth was the focal point of family and social gatherings in our home. In the cold autumn and winter evenings, my mother sat in front of the fire with my grandmother and an old family friend, Mrs. Kavanagh, who came to visit a few times a week. The two upstairs bedrooms were freezing at that time of year, so everyone huddled together around the fireplace in the tiny living room. It was torture going to the toilet outside. Not only were we frightened by venturing into the darkness beyond the back door, but we also faced the absolute certainty of losing a fireside seat. Invariably one of my brothers jumped into the spot I'd vacated if it was warmer than the one they occupied.

We had no television, so we listened in on adult conversation for entertainment. We loved their stories about ghosts and haunted houses, stories that had been passed down through generations. The evenings in Crumlin crept up on us stealthily. We would never notice the light slipping away, giving over to the crimson glow of the turf and coal embers. Mrs. Kavanagh would tell the story of the coachman picking up my grandfather and others from Dolphin's Barn and taking them to Greenhills, as we sat in terrified silence. She made the story more real with details about what the men were wearing and how they spent their days. "They were heading up to Greenhills," she might say, "to finish the evening with a game of cards." We had heard the story several times, but we still got goosebumps, and the hair stood up on the back of my neck when she described the men's horror when they discovered their coachman had no head. They could only watch helplessly when, without waiting for payment, the headless driver took off down Ballymount Lane.

A few years later my parents took us to visit their friends who lived on Ballymount Lane. The last bus home left at 11:30 p.m., and it was pitch-black as we walked the mile down the winding lane to the main road. My mind was full of the events described by Mrs. Kavanagh in her story. My brother Don — who is eighteen months older than me — whispered into my ear, "Cyril, do ye hear the coachman coming to get ye? Listen! Ye can hear the horses' hooves." I pissed my pants on the spot and Don got a clatter across the back of his head from my mother for his trouble.

There were occasions when neither tick, my grandmother's pension, nor the generosity of neighbours was enough to cover essentials. During those times my mother resorted to businesses that provided loans to working people at exorbitant rates of interest. Every Friday evening at about 7:00 p.m., a man with greasy black hair, dressed in a dark suit, came to our door and asked cheerfully, "Is your mammy home?" This was the "cheque man," the representative of a loan company that preyed on Dublin's working class. These companies were especially busy around Christmas and special occasions such as first holy communion and confirmation days. It was tradition that every boy and girl was dressed to the nines for these milestone ceremonies, but at that time Dublin's working class rarely had spare cash for fancy clothes. Parents, like my mother, turned to the loan sharks. No sooner was one loan paid off when the next child's special event rolled around. It was impossible to escape the poverty trap.

When my mother didn't have the money to pay the cheque man she'd say, "Here's that oul fecker looking for his money. Tell him I'm not home and to come back next week." I'd go to the door as instructed and say, "Me mammy says she's not home and will ya come back next week." The look of disgust on his face was priceless as he turned on his heel and stomped away from the door.

The moneylender's cheque could be redeemed only in certain stores. One of these was Frawley's on Aungier Street, an old-fashioned store that didn't carry the latest styles and fashions. When it was my turn to be outfitted for first communion, I reluctantly settled for one of their suits with long trousers, which made me feel all grown up, but the shoes were another story. The shoe shops that accepted the moneylender's cheque didn't sell the pointy or chisel-toed shoes that were all the rage among my contemporaries. My mother insisted I wear Tuf shoes, which were as durable as the name implied. I capitulated, because I had just gotten rid of a pair of shoes that had holes in them, and I was wearing plastic sandals that made my feet and socks wet with sweat.

My mother had a difficult time keeping our growing family in shoes. I remember being in church one Sunday morning when the kids behind me were giggling at the newspaper inserts sticking out from the holes in my shoes. After that, I took the breadknife from the drawer and hacked off a chunk of linoleum from under the bed to use for inserts. That worked great until my mother moved the bed to dust and clean: she let out a roar when she discovered that somebody had been hacking away at the linoleum. When the time came, I had no choice but to settle for the big, chunky Tuf shoes.

Once the big events were behind us, the fancy clothes were sometimes put to another purpose. On occasion, when the money order failed to arrive from Birmingham, the brand-new suits, dresses, or overcoats might be taken to the pawnshop at Leonard's Corner and exchanged for cash, the amount depending on their condition. This was a useful source of income in an emergency. The pawnshop wouldn't sell the clothing, but would hold onto it until the following week, when it could be retrieved with an added cost to the customer. My mother, a proud and private woman, did not take this step lightly. Having to visit a pawnshop was just a horrible and belittling experience for her. My brother Don accompanied her on a few occasions, and he relayed that she wouldn't get off the bus at the Leonard's Corner because everyone knew that's where the pawnshop was. Instead, she waited until the next stop and walked back. On at least one occasion, according to Don, she was mortified to bump into a neighbour coming out of the shop as she was walking in.

Though we had few possessions and barely scraped by from week to week, there was always someone worse off than we were. One such group was the "travelling people," or "Gypsies." Most people shunned the travelling people, calling them horrible names, such as "knackers" or "cream crackers." Once every few months the travelling people came around the neighbourhood. They usually asked for old clothes or a few pennies to feed the children. Most people on the street would not open their doors, but I recall my grandmother once saying to my mother, "Let that poor divil in to warm herself up." The woman had a shock of flaming red hair that needed a good combing. Her face was heavily freckled and she had ruddy cheeks from the bitter cold wind outside. Around her shoulders she wore a green plaid shawl with a baby girl of maybe eight or nine months wrapped inside. My mother pulled up a chair for her beside the fire and asked her if she could "make a bottle for the baby." While my mother was in the scullery heating up some milk, my grandmother chatted to the woman, inquiring about her other children. My mother returned with a warm bottle of milk and some Farley's Rusks wrapped in greaseproof paper. Before the woman left, my mother rooted around upstairs and gave her a few pieces of baby clothing. When I recall those times I can see it was the spirit of giving and sharing among the working class that enabled them to survive the harshest of times. There was always room by the fireside or a seat at the table for one more.

I had a friend, Tony Joyce, who lived across the street. He had older sisters and his older brother John was in the Irish Army. Tony and I were friends from before we started school. On Tuesday afternoons Tony's mother always took him to the movies. I was often invited along, but most of the time my mother didn't have the sixpence it took to get in, so I would rely on Tony's description of what he had seen.

I'd pepper him with questions about the details. What were the "chap" (the hero) and the bad guys wearing? What did they look like? The movies I did get to see were a wonderful source of entertainment and an inspiration for months and years to come. After every movie we saw, we dressed up and acted out the parts in his backyard. After seeing the movie *Lancelot and Guinevere*, for example, I remember making newspaper hats, turning pieces of wood into makeshift swords, and making clucking noises as we rode imaginary horses.

There weren't many public swimming pools in Dublin in the 1960s. One of the few was located in the inner city, a short bus ride from where we lived in Crumlin. The Iveagh Public Baths were built into a social housing complex funded under a trust set up by the Guinness family. The magnificent Victorian red brick buildings are situated between Christ Church and St. Patrick's Cathedrals. My friends and I generally walked to the pool to save the bus fare we got from our parents, or in my case from my grandmother. We thought nothing of walking into the city centre as nine- or ten-year-olds, with our swimming shorts rolled up inside our towels. In the summer months the kids lined up by the hundreds to get into the swimming pool on Bride Street and were allowed into the pool in batches of about forty for one hour at a time. The stench of chlorine would be with you for days.

One day, following our dip at the Iveagh Baths, ten of us decided to visit Strongbow, in the thousand-year-old Christ Church Cathedral. The Norman lord who brought peace to Ireland in the twelfth century lay in effigy in the famed cathedral. Our heads had been filled with his feats by the Christian brothers. However, we had also been led to believe that we would go straight to hell if ever we entered a Protestant church. After some discussion, we decided that God would forgive us if we slapped Strongbow in the face as we passed his tomb. Six of the ten chickened out, and we remaining four charged into the cathedral looking for Strongbow's tomb. Once inside, we were shitting our pants because we hadn't expected it to be so dark. Joe Whitley whispered to me, "Jasus! This is like Dracula's Castle — I'm bleedin' getting outa here!" We scurried down one side of the nave, our hearts exploding with fear, found the tomb, slapped the face, and ran like blazes down the aisle and out into the sunlight. Seized by fits of laughter, we were giddy to have escaped alive. We ran around the corner down Fishamble Street, past the remains of the Music Hall where Handel's first performance of the *Messiah* took place, and out onto Wood Quay. We were kids full of life, with not a care in the world. We walked along the quays down into Fleet Street and hopped on the Number 50 bus to Crumlin. I went to sleep that night with the day's adventures dancing around in my child's mind: Vikings and Roundheads, Count Dracula's castle, and the everlasting fires of hell.

Monday nights were a special night for us. We had no phone at home, but on Monday night my mother usually made a long-distance call from a public phone booth to my father in Birmingham. She often took one or two of us along so we could say hello, too. I came to dislike the outing because, more often than not, when she stepped out of the phone booth saying, "Your daddy wants to talk with you," there were tears streaming down her face.

I looked forward to Christmas or summer holidays when I knew he would be coming home. The kids on the street and in school often jeered at us, saying, "You have no oul fella," meaning a father, so it was priceless to be able to boast about our "Da" bringing us new football boots or a rifle as a present. The new football boots never appeared, and it was usually the *Victor* or *Hotspur Annual* that we got instead. The disappointment soon faded, however, when he spent hours playing board games with us. My siblings and I played draughts, Chinese checkers, and Snakes and Ladders with him for hours on end. I hated when the time came for him go back to Birmingham. I hated the pain in my mother's face as she watched him packing his cases to leave. It still haunts me today to remember her pleading with him to stay: "Please, Danny, I can't do this on my own. Don't go!" But he always walked out the door, a suitcase in either hand, as my mother watched him turn the corner on his way to the train station to catch the boat to England. My grandmother didn't get along with my father and she would mutter under her breath about him being a "louser … going off like that and him with children to look after," but my mother would tell her, "Mind your own business. There is no work for him here."

When I look back at those years and think about the hardships my mother went through to raise her children, I marvel at her courage and the determination it must have taken to ensure we all had the best of opportunities with such limited resources. What she did, day in and day out, was extraordinary.

My grandmother had suffered a stroke around the time my grandfather died in 1947. This left her severely paralyzed down the left side of her body — especially in her arm and leg — although she was able to get around with the assistance of a cane. After school each day I would go upstairs to visit her in the front bedroom. She had a rubber ball she would try to squeeze to prevent her fingers from stiffening up, and I would help her manipulate her grip.

My grandmother was very religious. She always told me I was going to be a priest because I was forever finding and bringing home religious artifacts such as rosary beads, crosses, and religious medals. Because she was incapacitated, the priest came to our home once a month to say mass. My mother turned the sideboard into a makeshift altar for his visit, and I loved to help by fetching the candlestick holders and candles. When the priest arrived, we were all sent to play outside so he could hear my grandmother's confession.

In fall of 1962, my grandmother was confined to her bed after she slipped and broke her hip. It was a cold autumn and my mother lit the fire in the bedroom upstairs. This was startling — we rarely had enough coal and turf to feed the fire downstairs — and I knew my granny must be very sick. I overheard her more than once telling my mother that she would never go into St. James's Hospital. According to my mother, St. James's Hospital had a bad name with older people because "in years gone by that's where they took the paupers to die." I asked my mother what a pauper was. "Poor people with no family to look after them" was her reply. Eventually, Grandma Jameson was taken to the hospital.

On February 23, 1963, my mother came into the front bedroom that my four brothers had shared with my grandmother. She was crying. "Your nana is in heaven … she died this morning." She hugged each of us and left the bedroom. The funeral took place a few days later. My mother would not allow any of her children to attend the funeral. Presumably, she felt the graveside service and the lowering of my grandmother's coffin into the grave would be too traumatizing for us as young children. My grandmother was buried in a tiny graveyard in Bluebell, Inchicore, alongside my grandfather, Francis Jameson.

After my grandmother died, my father stayed on in Dublin. The Irish economy was coming out of recession and he found work as a car assembler in the Volkswagen factory on the Naas Road in Clondalkin. Life changed for the Ryan family.

Danny liked his drink on the weekend. Before leaving the house on a Saturday evening, he made sure a heaping of pigs' feet was on the stove to simmer. Later, when he came home from the pub, Danny and his mates (but not my mother, who found the idea of pigs' feet disgusting) would wolf down the delicacy and join in a singsong. We had been accustomed to a quiet house. My father, however, had a wide circle of friends, and they and their wives regularly filled our front room with their talking and laughter. We were allowed to stay up late and listen.

Danny had a million rebel songs in his repertoire, many of which he had learned from his Irish compatriots in Birmingham. He didn't have a great voice but he could carry a tune. His favourite party piece was "The Boston Burglar" and he was apt to sing it regardless of where he was. Once Danny had a drink in him he might burst into song without warning. He couldn't care less where he was or who was listening. Not all his friends were as gregarious as he was, but they too had their party pieces. Old Ned Bolger was a quiet man. He was tall and thin, with a craggy face lined from years of hard living. He had to be coaxed to sing. When he finally overcame his shyness (or had enough to drink), Ned would sing "Raglan Road," the haunting ballad of unrequited love. The tiny sitting room would fall silent as Ned, his eyes closed, sang with passionate intensity, and it was pure magic to hear the beautiful lyrics fall from his lips.

Often the next to sing was Jimmy Mooney. Jimmy was a big man with a round face, bald head, and ruddy complexion. He was my father's best friend, and the nicest, kindest man you could ever hope to meet. Jimmy and Danny were inseparable at times, which often meant they spent too much time down in the pub together, to my mother's chagrin. Jimmy loved to sing a traditional ditty, "The Old Bog Road." When he did, a hush fell upon the room once again.

When Danny wasn't singing, he was likely to rise to his feet, saying, "Come on, Maureen!" and sweep my mother up off her chair to dance with him. Maureen loved to dance, and her smile lit up her face as she took his outstretched hand in hers. They glided over the floor while their friends called out encouraging words: "Way to go, Maureen!" and "Jasus, she's a grand dancer!" My mother was in her prime and looked it. She was five feet, six inches tall and slim-figured, despite having seven children already. She had perfect skin, blue eyes, and her shoulder-length brown hair had a fullness to it that made her look like a movie star. I loved to watch my parents dance because I knew it made my mother happy. I had too many memories of her crying her eyes out and pleading with him not to leave, all those times he headed out the door for Birmingham. I have never been to Birmingham but I hate the place to this very day.

As I grew into my teenage years, I began to share my father's interests in politics and sport. He was an avid supporter of the Tipperary hurling team. Hurling is a team sport, not unlike field hockey, but faster, more exciting, and dangerous. It's Ireland's national sport. Dad was born in Moneygall, County Offaly, but was raised in Roscrea, County Tipperary. Tipperary has a fabled history in hurling, having won more All-Ireland Hurling Final trophies than any other team in the country. I began a scrapbook filled with photos of Tipperary hurlers clipped from the newspapers. My father and I developed a bond of sorts as a result of my interest in the game. On several occasions, he took me and my brothers to watch Tipperary play in Croke Park, the revered stadium of Irish Gaelic sports arenas. In those days, fans were allowed to lift their kids over the turnstiles without having to pay for them. The stadium held close to ninety thousand fans, and just to walk to the game from the city centre among the tens of thousands of supporters was exciting. Everyone was in good spirits. Opposing fans exchanged good-natured ribbing. I got to see my father in a different setting and admired his ability to mingle easily in a crowd. He could strike up a meaningful conversation with a total stranger, just by being interested and amiable, a useful gift.

My father didn't read the tabloid newspapers. He preferred the broadsheets, either the *Irish Times* or the *Irish Independent*. From time to time he pointed out an article for me to read. He was not a supporter of Prime Minister Seán Lemass, the Taoiseach, and his comments would often prompt me to read up on the politics of the day. On Sunday mornings, he bought three or four newspapers and read each one from front to back. I recall sitting up with him late one night in 1964, listening to the radio as the results rolled in from the British general election. He was delighted that Harold Wilson, the leader of the U.K. Labour Party, was winning and would form the next government. The following morning, I went to school feeling a little tired. The teacher, Brother McArdle, a Christian brother, asked me why I was yawning. He was horrified to hear that I'd been up late listening to the U.K. election results. This was almost heresy in Ireland in the 1960s. As far as the Christian brothers were concerned, the Brits were our mortal enemies, having colonized Ireland and in the process tried to stamp out Catholicism and Irish culture. I thought to myself, *Tis a good job Brother McArdle doesn't know about my grandfather fighting for the Brits in the First World War.*

In 1965 the Volkswagen factory where my father worked was shut down when the union went on strike. My father belonged to the ITGWU, the same union that Jim Larkin had organized nearly sixty years earlier to help lift Dublin's working class out of poverty. Our tiny home became something of a strike headquarters. My father was a member of the bargaining committee, so he and the other leaders would sit around our kitchen table arguing for hours on end before taking off to a meeting. My brothers and I listened in on these discussions. It was not that we were invited to listen: We paid attention because the house had only two downstairs rooms. There was nowhere else to go.

The strike went on for nearly six weeks and placed a tremendous strain on our family. I recall more than one occasion when my mother broke down and cried her eyes out because there was no money to put food on the table. She begged my father to end the strike and go back to work. But my father and his fellow committee members were determined to win job security protection, a critical issue because of Volkswagen's new strategy of importing fully assembled cars from Europe. The union ultimately settled for enhanced job security provisions together with severance packages for those who wanted early retirement. This was one of the first strikes in Ireland against a free trade–type policy that threatened workers' jobs. Almost forty years later, we see auto workers in Canada and the United States fighting the same battle.

It was during this strike that I first heard the expression "blackleg." I asked my father to explain what it meant. He said a blackleg was someone who had been ostracized by fellow workers for crossing a picket line during a strike. A couple of my father's friends, men who had been guests in our home for the Saturday night singsongs, crossed the picket lines. He never spoke to them again.

I found my first job in the summer of 1963 when I was eleven years old. My task was to deliver shoes from a shoe store on Aungier Street to other stores in the chain across the city. The store supplied me with a bicycle with a heavy metal basket in the front. The basket, which projected out over the front wheel, was large enough to hold several shoeboxes. The front wheel was about half the size of the rear wheel in order to accommodate its cargo. I received an awful lot of ribbing from my friends who laughed at me for having what they disparagingly called a "scabber's job." This was a throwback to the turn of the century, when American messenger boys rode en masse in a protest against the telecommunications companies for giving their jobs to scabs for lower wages. Somehow this style of a bicycle became known as a "scabber's bicycle." I was barely able to handle the cumbersome thing, and I was terrified of the double-decker buses that zoomed past me on the crowded streets. Eventually, my mother forced me to give up the job when I told her about a near collision with a bus. I dare say it was a good decision.

My next job was in Michael Hough's General Store on the Crumlin Road. Mr. Hough was a cranky old git, about five feet, five inches tall, who spoke with a heavy country accent. His abrupt manner of speech conveyed the false impression that he was always in a bad mood. Underneath the crusty exterior, however, was a man with a generous soul. My wage for a Saturday's work was ten shillings, half of which I gave my mother. Mr. Hough often paid me a little extra if we had a busy day.

Early in the morning, when business was slow, it was my job to make up the one- and two-pound bags of sugar. The sugar was kept in large burlap sacks at the back of the store, out of sight of the customers. It was not unusual to find a few mouse droppings on top of the sacks. Hygiene was not exactly a top priority back in the 1960s. I just scooped off the mouse droppings and filled up the brown-paper bags. Later in the morning, when business picked up, I worked the vegetable stand outside the store, helping the "ould wans" find a head of cabbage with a firm heart or sift through the potatoes until they found the ones they wanted, and then weighing the produce on the old-fashioned scales. Strips of sticky flypaper hung inside the front window and around the shop, and from the vegetable stand I could watch the lucky flies feast on the delicacy of the day, while the unfortunate ones got stuck on the flypaper. Toward midafternoon, I delivered the "messages" to the customers' homes on Hough's scabber's bicycle. The store sold everything from groceries and produce to meat, fish, and even peat briquettes. Briquettes were a popular fuel of shredded peat compressed into a brick-like shape and laced together in a bundle that weighed two stone (twenty-eight pounds). Usually I tried to take four bundles per trip, but on a windy day, when I had to get up off the saddle to pedal, the bicycle's back wheel would come off the ground because I was not heavy enough to counterbalance the weight of the briquettes at the front. This imbalance became dangerous on the main roads, but the alternative was to double my workload by making extra trips. Sometimes, after I had risked life and limb to deliver the briquettes, some *ould wan* would give me hell for not being there earlier. I was eleven years old and thought to myself, *Ye old shite, I hope ya freeze your arse off tonight!*

I left Hough's at the end of the summer and began working for the Alma House Hardware Store farther down the Crumlin Road, part-time on Saturdays and one or two days after school. My job was roughly the same as at Hough's, delivering everything from peat briquettes and chunks of carpet to paraffin oil for gas heaters. Delivering paraffin was unpleasant. A storage area built onto the side of the shop housed two large cylindrical tanks of paraffin oil. On the shelving sat several one- and two-gallon plastic containers. On the floor underneath the shelves were a dozen five-gallon metal cans. My job was to fill the containers and deliver the oil to customers. Once again, the mode of transportation was the scabber's bike, except this time the front wheel was the same size as the rear wheel, and the metal basket was even bigger.

I soon learned how to juggle cans on the bicycle. But no matter how cautious I was not to spill the paraffin oil when filling them up, some always splashed onto my clothing and skin. Over a period of weeks, the backs of my hands became raw from constant contact with the paraffin oil. The bitter cold of a biting easterly wind on rainy days made my hands ache even more. I recall one dark winter evening, while cycling around Clonmacnoise Road in Crumlin, looking for a house to make a delivery, when I began to cry. The gale-force wind, the driving rain, and the scurvy-like effects of the paraffin on my hands, combined with my frustration as I tried to find a house in the dark, were too much for me. I cried and cursed the owner of the store who had sent me out in such dire and miserable conditions. I was twelve years old, and I stuck it out for twelve months because the money was good. I was earning one pound and fifteen shillings a week, with tips on top of that. I gave my mother one pound a week to help out.

By the summer of 1965, however, as I was entering puberty, I grew conscious of the smell of paraffin oil that permeated my clothing and of the scurvy-like condition of my hands. I was ready to move on. I had heard from a few of my friends that the Gate Bar on the Crumlin Road was hiring lounge boys. I applied and, to my surprise, started that same evening. The barman gave me a float and explained to me how it worked: I was to take the customer's order and come to the bar to fetch it. I paid for the order from the float and then retrieved payment from the customer. If I was short at the end of the night, I had to make up the shortfall. My first evening on the job, I was petrified. I was a shy kid and having to talk to adult strangers was a challenge. To make matters worse I was assigned to the bar rather than the lounge. The bar was a dingy and smoky place. The customers were working-class men (you rarely saw a woman there) who dropped by for a pint before going home. Later, they might come back (in some cases, they never left) and stay until closing time. The orders in the bar were straightforward: typically, they asked for a pint of Guinness, Harp, or Smithwick's, a few occasionally ordered a Jameson or Redbreast whiskey.

I gradually became more confident and was able to joke around with the customers. I also got to know the crotchety *ould feckers* and stayed away from them as much as possible. None of the lounge boys liked working in the bar because the *ould feckers* never tipped and were always cranky. I learned to memorize the drinks and could take several orders at once without having to write them down. I gradually acquired a degree of assertiveness — essential if I was to catch the attention of the barman when the pub was packed. It was not uncommon for this shy thirteen-year-old to shout down the bar over top of all the other customers, "Peader, can ya give us three pints of Guinness, two pints of Harp, a bottle of Smithwick's, a pint of shandy, and a Jameson?" all the while fighting for space at the counter among the ould fellas.

Eventually, I was moved to the lounge and I found myself in a new world. This was the place the men brought their "mots" (girlfriends) at night. The float was bigger and the orders were far more complicated. Now I had to remember gin and tonics, vodka and cokes, Babychams, Singapore slings, and glasses of lager, as well as the more familiar pints of beer and Guinness. More often than not, I was taking orders for three or four tables at once. Everything had to be committed to memory and you dare not forget somebody's pint. I also discovered that a guy sitting alone never tipped, but if he was sitting with his wife or girlfriend, he would become more generous.

Over the next few years I worked in several different pubs: the Good Companions on Bangor Road, the Submarine Bar in Crumlin Village, and the Lower Deck beside the Grand Canal. Each had unique characteristics and clientele, and each in turn provided me with lessons and experiences I found to be valuable later in life.

I graduated from Scoil Iosagain Primary School in Dolphin's Barn in June 1966, when I was fourteen years old. At the time, students were streamed into secondary school, which prepared them for university, or technical school, which prepared them for the trades. Brother McArdle suggested to my mother that I be streamed into secondary school but she was adamant I was going to technical school, just like my two brothers before me. I argued strenuously that I wanted to go to secondary school, but the conversation ended when she said with great finality: "I will not make fish of some of my children and fowl of the others." She was basically telling McArdle — and me — that the Ryan family had limited means and all of her children would be treated equally. It's a lesson I still take to heart.

I entered Clogher Road Technical School like any fourteen-year-old, full of piss and vinegar, and relieved to get away from the oppressive rule of the Christian brothers. Technical schools were staffed by lay teachers and the environment was much more open than primary school. Students in mid-sixties Dublin tended to identify with hippies, mods, or rockers, each representing a different style and approach to life, but all more or less rebellious. Long hair was the norm, but in our home my father railed against it. As soon as my hair touched my ears, it was time for a haircut. Hipster pants with wide belts and flower-patterned shirts were common streetwear. We could not afford to shop in the fashionable city centre stores, so instead we went to the Tivoli Market on Francis Street, in an area called the Liberties, the oldest part of Dublin. The "Tivo" also sold the popular army surplus and reefer jackets.

Clogher Road Tech was a great place to spread our wings. We made new friends from different parts of Dublin and were bombarded by the explosion of folk and rock music: Bob Dylan, Bob Marley, the Troggs, Donovan, Manfred Mann, the Byrds, and the Beatles were everywhere in the air. We also were hugely influenced by the peace movement and the sexual revolution. Dublin was changing, but slowly in comparison to other cities, such as London. Similarly, Ireland was on the edge, rather than at the centre, of the music revolution. Irish folk music enjoyed a comeback and we also saw the emergence of

Celtic rock, led by groups such as Planxty and the Bothy Band. The Irish rock scene had yet to blossom; although Van Morrison, who was then the lead singer with Them, and blues guitarist Rory Gallagher were exceptions.

Nevertheless, a small but thriving club scene existed. As teenagers, we followed a local band, the Black Eagles. The lead singer, Philip Lynott, lived nearby on Leighlan Road, close to the park on Sundrive Road. Philip was a couple of years older than me and stood out from the crowd as the only black kid in Clogher Road Tech. He later went on to front Thin Lizzy, one of the greatest live rock bands in the world. He died tragically of a drug overdose in 1986.

My marks were not exactly stellar. The minimum requirement to get into a trade was the Group Certificate, basically a two-year diploma in general studies that incorporated practical skills in carpentry and the metal trades. I hated the skills-training classes and quickly began to resent the hours spent planing blocks of wood and filing metal blocks. At the same time, I loved the English classes and relished discussing T.S. Eliot's *Murder in the Cathedral* and the poetry of William Wordsworth. I became disillusioned with the system. No matter how well I did in English, history, and the languages, I felt I was on a treadmill that led inexorably away from what I loved most.

I was almost sixteen in June 1968 and I didn't have a clue what would happen next. I waited anxiously all summer long for my marks. A passing grade meant I would enter a trade; a failing grade meant I would end up in some low-paying, semi-skilled job. The results were released on a Monday in late August and, to my relief, I passed. I was the proud recipient of a Group Certificate. All the students were advised to talk with the guidance counsellor to settle on next steps. Because my grades weren't great, my options were limited to a handful of trades — glazier, plumber, sheet-metal worker, pipe lagger, and the likes. I knew nothing about any of them and hightailed it home to ask my father what he thought.

Eventually, I settled on plumbing. The apprenticeship board sent me to the Thermo Heating Company in Merrion Square, where I would begin my five-year apprenticeship. The address was impressive.

Merrion Square, one of the few remaining majestic squares in Dublin, was built by and for the aristocracy of the Georgian era. It is bounded on three sides by magnificent terraced townhouses, while the fourth side opens onto the garden of the Oireachtas — the Irish parliament building. The exterior of the townhouses is yellow brick, punctuated by splendid doorways topped with half-moon shaped fanlight windows and fronted by intricate wrought-iron railings. The interiors boast ornate plastered ceilings and handcrafted fireplace mantles and staircases.

On Monday, September 2, 1968, I hopped off the bus on O'Connell Street and walked around the back of Trinity College onto Nassau Street past the spot where James Joyce met his wife, Nora Barnacle. It was a balmy Dublin day and I was feeling pretty good. I was about to start my first real job as an apprentice plumber! I imagined myself working with small-bore stainless-steel piping, magically clicking it all together, just as it was depicted in the ads on television. I envisioned myself as a white-coated technician, installing the latest, most sophisticated and technologically advanced central-heating systems. I imagined myself entering a brave new world.

From my years of working as a lounge boy, I had acquired a taste for smart clothing. I was wearing a grey checked jacket and black pants. My shoes were polished to a fine sheen. A nervous energy built inside me as I crossed the street to the top of the stately square. I was early, so I circled the square to delay my arrival. I walked past the house where Oscar Wilde lived from 1855 to 1876. Farther along was the former home of Daniel O'Connell, the great Irish liberator and champion of Catholic emancipation. Across the square, I stopped to read the plaque outside number 82, where William Butler Yeats once lived. A few doors away was the home of Sheridan le Fanu, the author of Gothic tales and mysteries. Finally, my circuit complete, I came to the house occupied by Thermo Heating Company. I took a deep breath, bounded up the steps, and pushed open the heavy wooden door.

It wasn't quite what I expected. I recall remarking to myself, with a fair degree of disappointment, *this is a bit of a fucking dump!* The offices did not live up to the majesty of the square outside. The paint was peeling and there was a kind of emptiness about the place. I could hear a woman's footsteps upstairs echoing throughout the building. Off the main hallway was a huge white door, slightly ajar. I pushed it open. A woman stood behind a desk with a file in her hand. She looked startled. I said, "I'm here to see Mr. Rice." Almost before the words were out of my mouth, she sniffed and said, "Go back outside. Around the corner is a laneway. At the bottom of the laneway is the entrance you are looking for."

Jasus! I thought to myself. *She's a frosty one.*

I followed her instructions and ended up outside a huge storage area and beyond them, two massive wooden doors. I smelled smoke from a coal fire. I stepped inside the doors into a shed so gloomy I could see nothing but the glowing embers of a forge. Once my eyes became accustomed to the dark, I saw an old man dressed in coveralls with a bellows in his hand, pumping air into the coke fire. The old man said nothing.

"Hello," I said. "I'm Cyril Ryan. I'm supposed to start here today."

He looked me over and said in a broad Belfast accent, "Welcome, son. Why the hell would you want to work here?" My heart sank. The warehouse was filthy. Rusty pipes, heavy steel flanges, and pipe fittings were strewn all over the place. Through my deep disappointment, I could only mutter, "This is where ANCO sent me." ANCO was the government agency that had oversight of apprenticeships in Ireland.

Any notion of working in a white lab coat as a central-heating technician went out the window. As I stood there, mulling over my fate, Charlie Rice came bounding through the open doors. "What are ye standin' around for?" he bellowed. "Follow me into the office."

Charlie was your typical Dublin gaffer. He was rough and gruff and eternally impatient. He looked a bit like the actor Lloyd Bridges, with his grey-blond hair, beady eyes, bushy eyebrows, and a long hooked nose. He barked at me to grab the broom. I still had my lunch in my hand, six sandwiches wrapped in greaseproof paper. I placed them on the bench and he said matter-of-factly, "Ye better get yer sambos outta there, or the rats will have them." I felt like crying. I took off my coat and asked him where the coat rack was.

"Coat rack?" he yelled. "Are ye fuckin' jokin' me? Do ye see that fuckin' nail on back of that door? That's yer fuckin' coat rack."

He charged out of the office and I could hear him saying to Billy Barr, the old Belfast man, "What the fuck have they sent me now? Yer man in there is dressed up for a wedding." I heard his car door slam shut and he took off in his car like a maniac.

Later, after I had swept the floor, I approached Billy Barr, cautiously, because I was unsure how he felt about Charlie Rice. He was once again compressing the bellows to breathe fresh life into the fire. When he sat down, we struck up a halting conversation. Billy was in his sixties, with a ruddy face and a moist lower lip that protruded as if he was pouting. When he spoke, his accent was so thick that I found it difficult to understand him. Except for a few trips to visit cousins in County Tipperary, I had hardly ever ventured outside of Dublin. I wondered if his reticence had something to do with the sectarian tensions that were beginning to roil the North of Ireland. I thought to myself, given that his name was Billy, that he was most likely of Protestant descent and therefore disinclined to discuss politics.

Reticent or not, he was one of a very few craftsmen left in Ireland who fabricated high-pressure boilers by hand. He was employed by Thermo Heating to design and build one-of-a-kind boiler heating systems. The pipes he used were no longer available because the new boilers employed a different technology. The ones he needed had a much thicker wall and could be obtained only by salvaging pipes from old buildings. Billy Barr was a genius at what he did. He could take a twenty-foot length of high-pressure piping, heat a ten-inch section over the furnace until it glowed red, and then bend it precisely into a U-shape or ninety-degree angle. His equipment consisted of old-fashioned, handmade pipe-benders of various dimensions. The boilers he made were a maze of piping that formed a perfect four-foot cube that intertwined in a continuous loop. Whenever I was in the head office over the next couple of years, I'd spend my breaks with Billy.

I spent most of my first day cleaning up the warehouse. Charlie Rice stormed in and out several times. I was somewhat demoralized: this wasn't exactly the career I had envisioned. On my second day he decided to have some fun at my expense. I heard him talking to somebody on the telephone. He said, "Don't worry, I can't drive down there but I'll send the kid over." He turned to me and said, "Jimmy Kavanagh is working in the Cafolla Restaurant on O'Connell Street. I want you to bring him over a length of half-inch piping."

"You mean one of those pipes out on the rack?" I asked.

"Yes, what the fuck do ye think I mean?"

"But they're twenty feet long! How am I supposed to get it over there?"

"Ye can walk," he said.

The Cafolla Restaurant was at the north end of O'Connell Street near Parnell Square, about two miles from the warehouse. I had to walk there, through crowds of shoppers on some of Dublin's most crowded streets, with a twenty-foot length of steel piping balanced precariously on my shoulder. Abuse was heaped upon me practically every step of the way: "Whoa! What the fuck do ya think yer doing?" "Ya silly little bollocks, ye almost hit me with that feckin' pipe!" "Look at that eejit!" "Jasus, Mary, and Joseph! Why are ye carrying that feckin' thing down the street?" I thought it would never end.

I arrived at the restaurant drenched in sweat. Jimmy Kavanagh was a short, bowlegged man in a dark grey suit. He wore the kind of peaked cap that's hip among young people today but was worn only by older men back in the sixties. He had a tuft of hair sticking out from underneath it. I never saw Jimmy without his cap until one day, I was in Mass, and there was Jimmy sitting in front of me with his cap beside him. He was as bald as a billiard ball. I was surprised that Jimmy made no mention of how I got the length of pipe across the city except to say, "Charlie is an awful man," but then he was not one to criticize Charlie Rice.

I liked Jimmy. He didn't talk a lot, but he was a good tradesman, and he willingly passed along his skills to me as his apprentice. He was a Dubliner through and through. He was of the old school: working men of Jimmy's generation accepted a load of crap from employers without complaint. The humiliation heaped upon me by Charlie Rice, with all its pettiness and abuse of power, was typical of this mentality.

What I learned from Jimmy and Charlie Rice contained the seeds that would germinate years later, in the work I took on in the labour movement.

Late one September in 1968 Charlie Rice introduced me to Terry O'Brien. Terry was in his early twenties and had just become a journeyman. He was tall, with long, sandy-coloured hair and an easygoing manner. Charlie said the company wanted Terry and me to work on a job in Belfast. Thermo Heating was owned by a man in Belfast, Mr. Reid, and he wanted his employees to install a central-heating system in his home. The job was expected to take four to six weeks to complete. Charlie asked if I could travel to Belfast, and I jumped at the opportunity.

My mother was less enthusiastic. The Republic of Ireland had gained its independence from Britain in 1949. However, the six mainly Protestant counties of Northern Ireland remained under British rule. Tensions between the Protestant Unionists and the Catholic minority in Northern Ireland had erupted into violence. Recently, the Troubles — petrol bombings, murders, sometimes even running street battles — in the North were dominating the news. It was not surprising that my mother was concerned. My father, however, said, "Let him go. It will do him good to see a bit of the world outside Dublin." I was excited but a little worried, as well. I spent the weekend before we left reading whatever I could find about the more recent Troubles in the North and peppered my father for his views.

Civil rights was at the heart of the problem. Catholics were demanding to be treated fairly, insisting on the principle of one man, one vote; the repeal of repressive police powers; and an end to discrimination in housing and employment. The world's media had picked up on the protests and begun to report on the injustice and sectarian nature of Northern Ireland's governance model. The Protestant Unionists maintained power through a system of gerrymandering, meaning that constituency boundaries were drawn to give an advantage to Protestant communities. In Derry the situation was particularly bad: twenty thousand Catholic voters elected just eight municipal councillors, while ten thousand Protestant voters elected twelve. This system is used extensively in the U.S. by Republican-controlled State Houses to frustrate Democrats and, in many cases, disenfranchise black and minority voters. Recently, in Ontario the newly elected Conservative Ford government moved to gerrymander the boundaries of wards in the City of Toronto.

Mr. Reid met us at Belfast's Great Victoria Street Train Station. He wasn't talkative and I got the impression he couldn't be bothered to chat up the hired hands. He drove us past our digs, just off the Upper Newtownards Road, which I knew was a mainly Protestant area. I asked Terry if we would be safe, but he seemed oblivious to politics. We checked out the layout of the boss's house, so we could start thinking about how to go about installing the new heating system, then retraced our path to our digs. The owner welcomed us warmly and pointed out the dining room before showing us upstairs. Five men were already sitting at the dining-room tables. I found out later they were from out of town, working on contract in the Harland and Wolff shipyard.

As Terry and I came downstairs after cleaning up, we could hear chatter in the dining room, but when we entered, the place fell silent. We took a table by the window, away from the other workmen. I heard one of them say, "Sheesh," and a big, rough-looking guy facing him said loudly, "They shouldn't be here." He abruptly turned around and shouted across to us in a heavy Northern Irish accent, "Hey! Where're ye from?" Terry answered equably, "Dublin. We're here to install a heating system in our boss's house." The big guy said, "Ye shouldn't be here. We have lads here that can do that work." Then he turned to his companions and added, "They're Fenian bastards. They should fuck off back to Dublin, so they should." Terry and I finished our meal and left the dining room quickly. Luckily, the burly bigot and his friends were not staying there overnight.

Earlier in the week, the Northern Ireland Civil Rights Association (NICRA) had announced they would be holding a march in Derry to protest discrimination against Catholics in the allocation of housing and government jobs, and in support of the principle of one man, one vote. On October 1, 1968 — the day after we arrived in Belfast — the Apprentice Boys of Derry, a Protestant organization, announced they, too, would march along the same route that NICRA had selected. In essence, the Apprentice Boys were protesting the protest. On October 3, two days before the planned protests, the Stormont government banned all marches. The following day, the organizations backing NICRA met and decided to go ahead in spite of the ban. The scene was set for a major confrontation.

On Saturday, October 5, the NICRA march went ahead and the protesters were attacked by baton-wielding policemen. Ninety-six people were seriously injured. The international media were on hand and the Troubles went global. Four days later, on October 9, two thousand students from Queen's University Belfast marched on city hall in support of the civil rights movement. Once again, the protesters were blocked by the police. At the same time, Reverend Ian Paisley held a counter-demonstration with his Protestant supporters in front of city hall, unimpeded by the police. The march and the vicious police attack on NICRA radicalized the student movement and on October 9, at a mass meeting at the university, they formed a political organization called People's Democracy. Out of this organization came the fiery and eloquent activist, Bernadette Devlin, who eventually went on to become the youngest woman ever elected to the British Parliament at that time.

Our job was meant to last four weeks, but in the end it stretched to almost three months because the boss's neighbours asked to have heating systems installed in their homes, too. Meanwhile, Northern Ireland's sectarian conflict grew worse by the day. The newspapers were filled with reports of horrific crimes, brutal repression, and civil unrest that sometimes led to riots and the firebombing of Catholic homes. I felt fear every Monday morning when I had to take the train from Dublin to Belfast. On several occasions the train was delayed for hours because of bomb scares. What began in September as a pleasant two-hour train journey turned into a nightmare.

Religious hatred was new to me. I had never been exposed to it as a child in the Republic of Ireland — perhaps because roughly 95 percent of the population in Ireland was Catholic. We were educated by the Christian brothers in primary school. Most of them were fervent

Republicans who drummed into us the litany of atrocities committed by the Brits against the Irish through the ages. They especially hated Oliver Cromwell, whose army raped and pillaged its way through Ireland from 1649 to 1653 in a deliberate campaign to stamp out Catholic clergy and Catholicism from the countryside. The Irish were forced into the fields and mountains to hold secret Masses on "Mass Rocks" for fear of execution. But it wasn't just the ancient battles that riled the blood of the Christian brothers: a short four decades earlier the leaders of the 1916 Easter Rebellion had been executed by the British Army. The brothers told these stories with great relish, and as kids we were imbued with a sense of national pride that the Brits were unable to break the spirit of the Irish and force their "hedonistic culture" upon us. In the Republic of Ireland we had no quarrel with Protestants. It was the English we were taught to revile. However, the bitter battle wounds between Protestants and Catholics in Northern Ireland over civil rights burst into the open in 1968, undoubtedly influenced by the struggles of Martin Luther King in the United States.

I grew up a lot during my three months in Belfast. I discovered that the world could be a nasty place and that inequality and injustice existed, not only in the world at large, but also on my own doorstep. I had been shocked by the rough men where we had stayed, who made no distinction between a teenager and an adult when it came to their poisonous politics. To them, I was a Fenian bastard to be despised and looked down upon. I read more about the Troubles and I was astonished by the scale of the injustices stacked against the Catholic community. I found it hard to believe that the state was complicit in blatant acts of discrimination against an entire community based solely on their religion. I learned that might is not always right and that the majority can behave as tyrants. These lessons stayed with me.

The year following my stint in Belfast, Mr. Reid sold Thermo Heating, and ANCO placed me with a new employer, Leo Lynch in Crumlin. In 1971 I was fired for the first and only time in my life. I was a third-year apprentice working on the construction site of a new shopping centre. The foreman, Vincent Massey, was a tall guy with a shock of sandy hair and a snotty sense of his own superiority. He was a know-it-all who, when he found himself on the losing side of a discussion, could be difficult. He smoked a pipe, which added to his self-satisfied air. He had a habit of pausing in mid-sentence to puff away at it. Following one of his lunchtime discussions, Massey reached into his inside pocket, took out his pipe, and fetched around inside his side pockets for matches. When he realized he didn't have any, he scanned the trailer that served as our lunchroom and stopped when he came to me.

"Hey!" he said. "Run down to the shops and buy me a box of matches."

I was furious. This was not a work-related chore; he wanted to use me as his personal errand boy. I said, "Look, I'm here to learn a trade, not to be your personal slave."

He got up from his bench, picked up the telephone and made a call while glaring at me. I heard him say I had refused to buy matches to light the welding torch. He put the telephone down and said, "You have two choices: go buy me matches or go back to head office."

I knew going back to the office meant I would be fired. I said, "Fuck you. Go buy your own matches."

I walked out of the trailer and took the bus back to the office. Sure enough, I was fired that afternoon. I was out of work for about two months when I decided to go back to technical school for another year.

By then I was almost nineteen and it was tough, after three years of working, to adjust to the routine of classes and study. My interest in school work waned even more as I became increasingly preoccupied with girls. I made a bunch of new friends who were exciting and fun to be around. Most of them had cars and money to spend in Dublin's pubs and nightclubs. I had a part-time job working at the Lower Deck pub in Ranelagh, but I wasn't making enough to keep up my new-found lifestyle.

One of my new friends, Eddie Crilly, was twenty-two and a bit of a crazy bastard. He was wiry, about five feet, nine inches tall, 150 pounds soaking wet, and always dressed to the nines. He wore John

Lennon–style granny glasses that in a certain light had a pinkish hue. He was fun to be around and full of life, but trouble followed him everywhere.

Eddie worked as head waiter and maître d' in some of the city's best restaurants. He knew everybody, so we could get into practically any nightclub, no matter how long the line. He also had enemies: as teenagers, he and his brothers had gotten into trouble with local gangs. Eddie and I became inseparable. Together we partied and fought our way through the pubs and clubs of Dublin. Life was grand, except I had no money and was still in technical college. I decided that when my school year was complete, I would go back and finish my apprenticeship as a plumber.

One night in the spring of 1971 I was in the Carlisle nightclub in the suburbs of Dublin. The place was packed. In the middle of the dance floor, I spotted a girl who looked cute. I was with Fergus, a classmate, and I elbowed him, pointed to the girl, and said, "I'm going to ask her to dance."

"Ah, no!" he said. "So was I."

I pulled a half-crown out of my pocket and said to Fergus, "I'll toss you for it, heads I win, harps you lose." (On the flip side of an Irish half-crown is a harp.) He agreed and he lost. I made my way into the middle of the crowd and asked the cute girl to dance before Fergus realized what had happened.

Sheila was wearing hot pants with a silk top. Her blonde hair was shoulder-length and turned under in pageboy style. She asked me my name and I said, "Don't laugh, it's Cyril." She laughed out loud and said, "I dated not one but two guys named Cyril." I thought to myself, *That's very weird, I have never met anyone in my life named Cyril!* We danced several more times through the evening. I continued to see her for several months before we broke up.

Meanwhile, Eddie talked constantly about a woman he was in love with. Her name was Marie, and he had been dating her since she was a teenager. They had split up over some silly disagreement. It was obvious he was still crazy about her, but he was too stubborn to phone and fix the relationship. All summer long he pined for Marie. One day toward the end of the summer, he phoned me at work, said they had finally gotten back together, and asked if I would like to come to her parents' home to meet her. He gave me Marie's address and as I walked down the street to her house, counting down the house numbers, 397, 395, 393, it suddenly struck me. *Holy shit! 387 is where Sheila Kenny lives.* I walked up to the door and rang the doorbell. Sheila answered. She welcomed me with a big smile and a look on her face that told me she knew I was Eddie's friend. I was floored. Marie, the love of Eddie's life, was Sheila's sister. That night we all headed to the pub together. Eddie and Marie decided to get married. Sheila and I began dating again.

The Troubles in Northern Ireland continued to escalate. In 1971 the British government brought in the policy of internment, meaning imprisonment without trial, aimed at the Nationalist community. Hundreds of suspected IRA activists and sympathizers were arrested in the middle of the night and imprisoned. No members of the Protestant paramilitary organizations were arrested. Internment inspired widespread fear and loathing within the Catholic community. Stories of torture and beatings began to appear in the media.

At 3:00 p.m. on Sunday, January 30, 1972, several thousand peaceful protesters set out to march on Guildhall in Derry to protest the government's harsh tactics. The British Army blocked William Street to divert the march from its goal. While most of the marchers turned as intended by the blockade, a small group kept walking toward the barricade. Several youths began throwing stones at the soldiers and the fracas escalated into a riot. The soldiers — members of the elite Parachute Regiment — responded by firing tear gas canisters at the crowd, but at 4:00 p.m. the army commander gave the order to open fire with live ammunition. The paratroopers chased the last of the protesters as they ran away. Within minutes, twenty-seven people had been shot. Thirteen of the marchers lay dead on the streets of Derry. Another died the next day.

Riots broke out across the North. In Dublin, thirty thousand demonstrators burned down the British embassy in Merrion Square. The embassy was kitty-corner from where I had worked in Thermos Heating. The events of Bloody Sunday and the riots the next day in

Dublin had a profound effect on me. The Troubles I had witnessed in Belfast now were on my doorstep. The NICRA, which I had seen march in Belfast, had been turned into an enemy of the State, its members shot like dogs in the street.

Bloody Sunday was a seminal moment in Irish history. It marked the second or third time in the struggle that Irish Catholics had been murdered in cold blood, not by paramilitary organizations, but by British soldiers. It effectively transformed the Northern Ireland Civil Rights Association from a social movement into a counter-insurgency against British rule. And finally, it marked the emergence of the IRA as the de facto protectors of the Nationalist (Catholic) communities in Northern Ireland's six counties. Violence began to spiral out of control. In the three years prior to Bloody Sunday, 210 recorded deaths were attributed to the Troubles. In the eleven months that followed, there were 435 deaths.

I spent most of the year after I left technical college (for the second time) working around the country on various building sites. My apprenticeship was nearly complete and my assignments more complex. My first major solo job was to install a heating and plumbing system in a new two-storey pub in Walkinstown, on the south side of Dublin. I had to figure out how best to work with the engineer's drawings. It was a fairly large work assignment, but if everything went to plan, it would lead to much greater responsibility. I was thrilled by the challenge, but something was nagging away inside of me. I was not happy at my work. I felt unfulfilled, as if life were passing me by.

With this not-yet-fully-formed idea that I needed to be doing something different with my life, I filled out an application for the Irish police force: the Garda Síochána. In the months that followed, I took several exams and survived a couple of interviews. In late spring 1972, I received a letter informing me that out of over seven thousand applicants, I was one of the lucky one hundred recruits to be accepted into the police training academy in Templemore, County Tipperary. My parents were delighted. Sheila, however, did not like the idea at all. She couldn't see me as a cop. What was worse, she said, "You will have to get your hair cut. You will look like a geek!" Which was true enough.

This was 1972 and I had shoulder-length hair. In late May, after I got the letter, Sheila and I took a bus into the city centre. She went shopping while I went to a barbershop for a short back and sides. When I met up with her again, she took one look at me and jokingly refused to walk beside me. When we did finally set off together to meet up with Eddie, the slagging from people I met along the way was merciless. Eddie took one look, rolled his eyes, tossed his head back, and uttered a long, drawn-out, "Muther of Jayus, Ryan … what have ye done to yer fuckin' hair?" Both Sheila and Eddie spent the afternoon looking at my head and then bursting out laughing. The following Monday, I gave my employer my quitting notice. He called me into the office and wished me all the best.

At the end of May, I found myself standing in the large Assembly Hall in Templemore, County Tipperary. The hall was packed with about three hundred recruits who were about to graduate, plus the group of one hundred new recruits that I belonged to. Several local dignitaries welcomed us before the superintendent stood up to speak. He was a tall, grey-haired man with a no-nonsense military bearing. I found his speech unsettling; he referred constantly to "us" and "them," as if the public we were sworn to protect had become our enemy. He finished by reminding us that we have "no friends on the outside" and that "the people we can rely upon are in this room. These are your friends. This is the family you can count on from here onwards." I looked around the room, and I felt lonely. In my estimation, this was not a friendly-looking bunch, but an exclusive club to which only a select few were admitted. I left the hall feeling a little disillusioned about my new career.

We were quartered in what looked like a military barracks, large rooms containing rows of bunk beds. On the second morning, we were awakened at 5:00 a.m. and told to be out on the square by 5:30. Just before we left the dorm, the heavens opened and rain danced off the square in drops as big as tupenny bits. We were lined up in rows of ten men across and ten deep. Within minutes we were soaked to the skin. Nonetheless, we were marched in formation around the square for a solid hour. We spent the rest of the day in the classroom and in workouts in the gym. This was to be our daily routine.

By the third week I felt it was time to have a heart-to-heart with the centre's chief administrator. I wanted to know what my long-term prospects looked like. He rattled off a load of statistics about wages, benefits, and housing allowances, but very little about career opportunities. When I pressed him, he admitted that the current crop of recruits would most likely be assigned to communities on the border between the Republic and Northern Ireland. This, he explained, was in response to the political situation. He said it would be several years before I could work my way back to Dublin. This contrasted sharply with what I had been told during my earlier interviews, where I had been assured there would not be a problem getting a posting in Dublin. I left his office reeling: several years spent in a small border town was not something I had planned for, nor was it something I was willing to accept.

That night I mulled over the consequences — including my parents' inevitable disappointment — if I were to resign. The next day, I told the chief administrator I was prepared to stay in the Garda Síochána only if I were guaranteed a posting to Dublin. He could not make that promise and a day later I was on a train back to Dublin.

I had walked away from one of the most sought-after jobs in the Irish civil service. Unemployment was running about 15 percent and higher in the construction industry. My mother was broken-hearted. Years later when she came to visit me in Canada, however, she said it was the best decision I ever made.

Within a week of leaving Templemore, I was back working as a fourth-year apprentice plumber. By this time I was following politics keenly. My brother Noel was an avid reader and I dove into the stack of books he kept under the bed and sometimes under the mattress. The books under the mattress were the raunchier ones, such as Lee Dunne's *Goodbye to the Hill*, a story about the steamy side of life in Dublin. Like the work of all good Irish authors, Dunne's book was originally banned by the Church and immediately became a bestseller.

I was fascinated by the writings of Leon Uris, particularly his book *Mila 18*, with its depiction of the horrors inflicted upon the Jewish community in Warsaw during the Second World War. I spent hours reading his other works, including *Exodus*, *Topaz*, *Armageddon*, and *QB VII*. Later, after I had moved to Canada, I read *Trinity*, about the Troubles in Northern Ireland. I worked my way through much of Noel's stash before he brought in more.

Among his new acquisitions was Tolstoy's *War and Peace*. It took me an eternity to read but provided me relief from the reality around me. The reality, of course, was that I was twenty years old and still living at home in cramped quarters with several of my brothers and sisters, all of us wanting our own space and privacy. I had one year left in my apprenticeship.

Unfortunately, while the works of Uris and Tolstoy were powerful, they weren't enough to eclipse the irritations and distractions of my everyday life. The three months I spent working in O'Keefe's, one of Dublin's abattoirs, were especially irksome: the smell, indescribably horrid, permeated my clothes and body throughout the entire assignment. The dreariness of Ireland's climate also started to get to me. The constant drizzle of rain in summer was deeply depressing. I recall sitting on the bed one evening, the rain lashing against the bedroom window, and dreaming of escape. Perhaps I could go to Canada. For the first time, I contemplated a life away from Dublin. My only trip overseas to that time had been a week's vacation in London with Sheila.

The Irish economy was in crisis by the summer of 1973. The OPEC nations had jacked up the price of oil to the West, which wrought havoc with Western economies that were wholly dependent on oil from the Middle East. Almost overnight, long queues sprang up at petrol stations across Ireland. Meanwhile, the Conservative government in the United Kingdom went to war with its trade unions. Inflation was rampant and wages lagged behind. These were hard times for ordinary workers.

In January 1973 Ireland became part of the European Economic Community (EEC), an international free-market zone designed to bring about the economic integration of European nations. The country's entry into the EEC provoked widespread debate. Much of the discussion on the building sites as we ate our sandwiches at lunch was about how foreigners from Europe could now live in Ireland without a passport and take away our jobs. In a tight economy with massive unemployment, the threat was not unfounded. The discussions reinforced my notion of emigrating. (Of course, the free flow of labour within the EEC cut both ways. Two of my brothers, Don and Frank, took jobs in Denmark.)

The transition from isolated sovereignty on the island of Ireland to European membership posed serious challenges for the Irish economy and workers alike. Irish farmers now had to compete against the modern factory farms of Europe. Construction companies found themselves bidding against multinational giants for contracts they had been guaranteed in the past. Massive transport trucks from Europe began clogging tiny Irish roads. Wealthy Germans and other rich Europeans snapped up land and holiday homes at bargain prices along the Irish coast. Irish laws on abortion and marriage were challenged in the European courts. Throughout the 1970s Ireland was in a state of flux. And always compounding the problem were the Troubles.

In December 1973, with the British coal miners on strike and fuel supplies running low, the U.K. government announced a three-day workweek. It was intended as a conservation measure, but it had an immediate impact on the Irish economy. Irish farmers depended heavily on exports of produce and cattle to the United Kingdom. The shortened workweek made it difficult to get livestock and produce to U.K. markets. In addition, supplies and parts for the small Irish manufacturing sector began to dwindle. Before long, most sectors of the Irish economy were forced to adopt a three-day workweek, too.

On top of these already convulsive events, in early 1973, the British government issued a White Paper aimed at resolving the conflict in Northern Ireland. The paper proposed the creation of a national assembly in which Nationalists and Loyalists would enter into a power-sharing partnership. Powers were to be devolved from Westminster to Stormont — Northern Ireland's traditional seat of government. Elections for the new assembly took place in June. The election was based on a system of proportional representation (PR) that prevented the gerrymandering that had distorted municipal elections in Northern Ireland for so long. Thanks to PR, and despite Protestant opposition to power-sharing, a coalition of pro-assembly politicians won the day.

One of the thorny issues not dealt with in the White Paper was the role to be played by the Irish government in the Republic. The U.K. government in Sunningdale convened a meeting in December to discuss the issue. Eventually, agreement was reached on a Council of Ireland, with representation from both Stormont and the Republic. Unionists were incensed that the Irish Republican government was to be given a say in Northern Ireland's affairs. To assuage their concerns, it was agreed that the executive powers of the council would be confined to "tourism, conservation and aspects of animal health." This did nothing to relieve Unionist fears. The day after the Sunningdale Agreement was released, a group of Loyalist paramilitaries, including the Ulster Volunteer Force (UVF) and the Ulster Defence Association (UDA), formed the Ulster Army Council. Northern Ireland was sliding into civil war.

On May 14, 1974, a motion condemning power-sharing was soundly defeated in the new Northern Ireland Assembly. The next day, a group calling itself the Ulster Workers' Council (UWC) called for a general strike. The strike was overseen and enforced by the Ulster Army Council and the Ulster Workers' Council, both of which included the paramilitary organizations of the UVF and UDA. The strike started off slowly in the morning as most workers ignored the call. But by midafternoon following shop-floor meetings, factories began to close. A key component of the strike was the shutting down of the Ballylumford power station, which supplied most of the electricity for the north. Once the power supply was cut, more factories began to close and the workers were sent home. The UWC and their paramilitary allies were now running Northern Ireland. They issued communiqués about which essential services they would allow to operate. They ordered pubs to close their doors. They threatened postal workers who attempted to deliver mail.

More than eight hundred barricades were set up across Northern Ireland, all manned by UVF and UDA paramilitaries, some wearing balaclavas. The British Army stood by and allowed civilians to be intimidated. Members of the Northern Ireland police force, the Royal Ulster Constabulary (RUC), chatted amiably with the thugs manning the barricades. Incredibly, the British Army Engineers said they were unable to step in and run a mid-sized power-generating station. In effect, the British Army, the RUC, the UDA and UVF, together with Loyalist politicians such as the Reverend Ian Paisley, were all colluding to bring down the democratically elected power-sharing government of Northern Ireland.

Petrol stations were forced to either close or ration fuel. Small business owners were threatened and forced to close their businesses. The electricity supply to industry and residential areas was shut off and public transportation ground to a halt. At night, sectarian fighting broke out between Catholics and Protestants. The North was aflame, insurrection was hanging thick in the air, and the fate of the Northern Ireland Assembly was hanging in the balance. Those elected politicians who had not joined with the paramilitary thugs were rendered impotent.

Three days after the strike began, on May 17, at 5:28 p.m., a bomb exploded without warning on Parnell Street, Dublin. Within minutes, two more bombs exploded, one on Talbot, the other on South Leinster Street. At 6:58 p.m., a fourth bomb exploded in the town of Monaghan. In all, thirty-four innocent civilians, including nineteen women and two baby girls, were killed. The death toll was the highest in one episode since the Troubles began. Nobody claimed responsibility for the explosions at the time; although twenty years later, in 1993, the UVF admitted to the crimes. Many believe that the British Army assisted the UVF and point to the sophistication of the explosives as proof. Other theories abound, all more or less based on the assumption that the Wilson government was so unpopular with the British military that it was willing to sabotage the power-sharing arrangement by abetting Unionist violence.

The strike lasted for fourteen days. Over that period, after the bombings on May 17, six more civilians were murdered. On May 28 the Ulster Workers' Council achieved its goal when Merlyn Rees, the secretary of state for Northern Ireland, refused to meet with its representatives. Brian Faulkner, chief executive of the new Northern Ireland Assembly, resigned along with his colleagues, in a move that effectively killed self-government in Northern Ireland. The administration of the six Northern counties reverted to Westminster.

Journalist Robert Fisk later wrote:

> The fifteen unprecedented, historic days in which a million British citizens, the Protestants of Northern Ireland, staged what amounted to a rebellion against the Crown and won …
>
> During those fifteen days … for the first time in over 50 years … a section of the realm became totally ungovernable. A self-elected provisional government of Protestant power workers, well-armed private armies and extreme politicians organised a strike that almost broke up the fabric of civilised life in Ulster. They deprived most of the population for much of the time of food, water, gas, electricity, transport, money and any form of livelihood.*

The Sunningdale Agreement was an attempt to compel the Unionists to share power with the Catholics. It would take another twenty-four years of bitterness and bloodshed before the Unionist community would finally agree to treat Catholics as their equals.

I was twenty-two years old in July 1974. Sheila and I were talking about getting married and looking at houses that we could not afford to buy. I was desperately worried about my employment prospects. The high rate of joblessness, Ireland's entry into the EEC, the imposition of the three-day workweek, the bombings and subsequent unrest across Ireland hardly combined to inspire confidence in the

* Robert Fisk, *The Point of No Return: The Strike Which Broke the British in Ulster* (London: Times Books/André Deutsch, 1975).

future. I began to look seriously at my options. I had become friendly with Kay Byrne, a young woman who worked on the reception desk in St. James's Hospital, when I had been assigned there on a construction project. She had just spent three months with her family in Canada and had recently acquired a visa to live in Canada before summer's end. She offered to help me settle in if I decided to take the plunge. My brother Noel and a few of his friends had also looked into the idea of emigrating to Canada, which further piqued my interest. It sounded like an exciting place.

In the fall of 1974, I made my application at the Canadian Embassy in Dublin. Within weeks I was called for an interview and filled out the requisite paperwork. In February 1975 I was notified that my application had been accepted. The visa was good for six months from the date of issue: I had until August to make up my mind whether to seek landed immigrant status in Canada or let the visa expire. In spring of 1975, Sheila and one of her friends had an opportunity to work in a holiday resort in Wales for the summer months. We decided she would spend the summer in Wales and I would go to Canada and see what I thought.

By now, things were easier for my mother. She was no longer totally reliant upon my father's wages to pay the bills. My brothers Noel, Don, Michael, and Frank, and my sister Deirdre were working, and each of us contributed to the household bills. Nevertheless, when I broke the news that I had made up my mind to emigrate, my mother was heartbroken. The night I told her, she cried her eyes out. "Why is it," she wanted to know, "that the people I love always leave me?" I knew exactly what she meant: I had seen my father walk out the door with a suitcase in either hand far too many times. And now I would be the one who was leaving.

Chapter 2
A NEW LIFE IN CANADA

I arrived in Toronto on April 5, 1975 — a Saturday evening — to a freak storm. I'd never seen so much snow. It was a foot deep on the roads outside the airport. Everywhere I looked was white.

I had $500 in my pocket and two suitcases of clothing and other belongings. I spent a few weeks on a sofa in Kay Byrne's basement apartment on Parkside Drive, directly across from High Park. Kay and another girlfriend of hers from Mullingar were sharing the small apartment. On the Monday morning after I arrived, I was on the Bloor subway line heading to the Canada Manpower agency on Dundas. The snow had begun to melt and leave grey mounds of crystallized ice and rivers of dirty slush. It was like nothing I had ever seen.

On Yonge Street I found myself swept along in a sea of humans from the four corners of the world. Here were people from Sri Lanka, Jamaica, Guyana, Italy, the Philippines, and a host of other nations. I was struck by the seeming cohesion among them: I was used to the stifling class-consciousness of Ireland, where your position in life began and ended with your postal code. I was from Dublin 12 in Ireland, an address that pigeonholed me irrevocably as working class, with limited opportunities to succeed in life. Here my address meant nothing. I understood instinctively that I would succeed or fail based on my personal drive and skills. It was liberating.

I soon came to understand, however, that my white skin enabled me to blend into the Canadian mainstream more easily than if I were a person of colour. It also helped to have come from the "old country." The phrase served almost as a code that implied common ground. In 1975 Canada was just opening up to immigration from countries other than Europe. Pierre Trudeau's Liberal government announced an amnesty that allowed many illegal immigrants to obtain legal status and, in turn, to apply to sponsor family members to join them. Toronto was a magnet for the new arrivals. While in the past, immigrants to Canada had come mainly from Europe and were more or less easily assimilated, it would take some time before these newcomers were widely accepted. Many Canadians weren't comfortable around them. In the Canada of the seventies and eighties, immigrants from the Caribbean nations were the outsiders looked upon differently than the "old stock" white Europeans. Today, it is Muslims who receive the brunt of the racist commentary in the media and generally in society. Only when I became deeply immersed in union politics did I begin to get a full appreciation for the level of discrimination felt by people of colour and by Muslims. However, I am still impressed and, indeed, proud of the fact that Toronto is one of the greatest multicultural cities in the world. Sadly, the Conservative parties in Canada both federally and provincially seem to be stoking the fires of intolerance against asylum seekers in their pursuit of votes. It is a dangerous can of worms to open.

I arrived at Manpower, filled in the requisite forms, and met with a counsellor; and then my problems began. I was a plumber and steamfitter, but tradesmen's jobs came through the union hiring halls, not the government agency. I had no clue what a union hiring hall was all about, so I naively decided to take matters into my own hands. On my way back to the subway, I saw a massive building under construction — it was the new Eaton Centre. *Perfect!* I thought, and walked onto the site. Within seconds somebody yelled, "Hey buddy! Where's your hard hat and safety boots?"

"I'm looking for a job," I replied. "Where's the gaffer?"

"The what?"

"The foreman," I said. "I'm looking for a job."

"What kind of job? Are you an engineer?"

"No, I'm a plumber."

"Well, you'd better go to the hiring hall on Eglinton," he said. And then he added, "You don't look like a fucking plumber to me." Apparently I was wearing the wrong clothes, once again.

I felt embarrassed and wondered if I was going about things the right way. Within seconds another man appeared beside me. "Can I help you?" he asked.

I told him I was looking for work as a plumber, but he didn't understand my Dublin accent and asked me to repeat myself. I did, but he still couldn't make sense of what I was saying. Meanwhile, from up above, the first guy yelled down again. "Hey! I told you, you cannot be on this site without your safety equipment!"

Jasus! I thought to myself. *No need for an international incident over my looking for a bleedin' job.* I looked at the guy who couldn't understand me and then at the guy who was fuming about my hatless condition. What could I do? I mumbled a thank you and walked back onto Yonge Street. This wasn't going to be easy.

The next day I returned to the Manpower agency. The counsellor explained that I needed to write an exam to show that my Irish qualifications matched their Canadian equivalent. So, I went to the union hall on Eglinton Avenue and got pretty much the same answer, except the union rep didn't offer much hope that I would find a job. A lot of their members had been laid off. But before I could do anything, I needed to take the exam, which could take months. Meanwhile, my savings were dwindling.

I concluded that my best course of action was to look at the maintenance side and forget about construction. I saw an ad in the *Toronto Star* for a maintenance plumber in the Royal York Hotel. I phoned and was told to come for an interview.

I arrived early and took in the surroundings. I was intimidated by the opulence as I entered the foyer. The magnificent chandeliers hanging from the ceiling only added to my insecurity. I checked with the bellman and he told me to wait downstairs until someone came to get me. After a while, a thin, scraggly looking man came up and told me to follow him. When we got to his office, he talked about practically everything except the job I was interviewing for. When he finally got around to it, he startled me by saying how glad he was that I wasn't one of "those blacks." I bristled. He opened a drawer and said, "See all those files? Well, those are my interview notes from all the black guys that come in here looking for a job. I make sure I keep those notes and the results of their tests because they usually complain to Human Rights when they don't get the job. In your case," he said, "I don't need to test you because you come from the old country and you know your stuff."

I was stunned and elated at the same time. On the one hand, I had just landed my first job in Canada. On the other hand, I was sickened by his blatant bigotry and racism. I had the same feeling in the pit of my stomach I'd had in Belfast at sixteen when I was called a Fenian bastard. I needed the work and agreed to start the following week, but I left the Royal York determined to find something else.

Over the next few days I travelled by bus and subway all over the city in pursuit of work. The closing refrain at most interviews was that I needed some Canadian experience. I felt like a dog chasing its tail. Everyone required Canadian experience, but nobody was willing to take a chance and hire me so I could acquire that experience.

At the end of the first week, I saw an ad at the Manpower office for a steamfitter at the Kendall Company factory in the east end of the city. The factory was a subsidiary of Colgate-Palmolive and employed more than seven hundred people making products such as diapers, gauze, and medical bandages for hospitals. It also had a large plastic-extrusion mill. When I arrived for the interview, the hallway was full of job seekers. Many were people of colour from Jamaica, Guyana, and the Philippines. To my delight, practically all were applying for jobs in the mill and the warehouse sections rather than the maintenance department.

I filled out the requisite paperwork and waited in the mechanical engineer's office for him to interview me. When he arrived, he caught me completely off guard by saying, "*Conas ta tu, a chara?*" (How are you, my friend?) in a broad Belfast accent. *"Taim go mhat, buiochas du"* (I'm good, thank you), I replied. He asked how long I had been in Canada and talked about his family before going into some detail about the job, which involved the steam and heat recovery program they wanted to implement. He explained that hundreds of steam traps were attached to the plant equipment and he suspected that most of them were inoperable, so the steam was escaping straight into the drain. He asked if I could handle the job and told me, if I was up for it, my starting rate of pay would be $5 per hour, with modest benefits.

I was over the moon. In my darker moments, I had imagined having to get on a plane and go back home, a failure. Now that nightmarish possibility was gone.

With my immediate future secure, I began to enjoy my newly adopted country. The freak snowstorm soon gave way to the beauty and warmth of a Canadian spring. I was fascinated by the speed with which the seasons changed. Trees began to bud and daffodils poked their heads through the earth. My part of Dublin was largely paved over. The few trees along the boulevards there were regularly vandalized and rarely lasted more than a couple of years. It was a treat to see mature trees everywhere.

I spent the remainder of my second week in Canada looking for an apartment. Most of the places I could afford were dumps and almost all were empty — but I needed a furnished apartment. Then one evening, I came across an ad for a room in a shared apartment. I phoned and a jovial guy identifying himself as Fred Haroun answered the phone. He said, "You sound perfect and you have an English accent." I was a little ticked off and corrected him, but he laughed and said, "Oh! England, Ireland, Scotland! You are all the same, you all have funny British accents." I was about to hang up, but I badly needed an apartment, so I swallowed my pride and set up an appointment to go see his place.

Ninety-one Browning Avenue was a three-storey brick house in the Broadview-Danforth area. I knocked on the door and Fred Haroun greeted me as if he had known me all my life. As he showed me around the house, he explained that he was a real estate agent. He bought homes in need of repair, fixed them up, and sold them at a profit. This was one of three he owned in partnership with a couple of friends. He was having trouble with one of the partners and had decided to live in the house himself and rent out a few of the rooms until the problems were resolved.

The floor was covered in white shag. The ceilings had huge oak beams and the walls had been sandblasted to reveal the brick underneath. The staircase had been stripped of paint and sanded down to reveal the original oak underneath. It was a beautiful restoration. The second floor, where I would live, had two bedrooms, a bathroom, and a den with a magnificent fireplace. The third floor was rented out to a Scottish woman named Avril who, I found out later, had a veto in the choice of second-floor tenant. Fred asked if I would mind going upstairs to chat with her and we got along just great. He phoned me later, asked how much I would be earning in my new job, and said, "Okay, the apartment is yours for $28 a week," but he wanted me to find a friend to rent the other bedroom on the second floor. I moved in two days later. I was twenty-two years old and for the first time in my life I had a place I could call my own. I felt wonderful. A week later, out of the blue, I bumped into Fabian Smith, an old classmate from Clogher Road Tech. He was looking for a place to live, and he moved into the apartment the following week.

The Kendall Company's plant was just off O'Connor Drive in East York. On my first day, I was met by the maintenance shop supervisor, George Carefoote, a tall man who was the perfect stereotype of a shop-floor supervisor: neatly groomed black hair, a touch of gel to keep it in place, black-rimmed glasses, perfectly pressed pants, and shiny black shoes. He showed me around the maintenance shop and introduced me to Phil Frick, the maintenance foreman. Phil was in his early fifties, sturdily built and fit, with a receding grey hairline. He spoke English perfectly with a trace of a German accent. He was the brains of the operation.

The maintenance shop was conventionally laid out, with lathes down one side and workbenches on the other. Phil introduced me to all the millwrights and electricians. I was the only steamfitter in the department. My workbench was between two workers from Jamaica. Ossie was a quiet man in his midfifties who was never idle, always pottering around with some part or other. David Brown was Ossie's opposite in many ways. He was tall and lean, in his mid- to late thirties, outgoing and friendly. David was interested in my Irish background and joked about the Irish being rebels.

Later that day I made my way around the rest of the plant, trying to get a handle on the task ahead of me, going down to the mill and shipping areas where the rotating drums used to dry the rolls of gauze were located. The drums were enormous, about twenty feet long and three feet in circumference. They were heated by steam piped into the centre of the drums, which rotated at high speed. It would be my job to repair them. The heat in this part of the plant was unbearable at times and even more so when there was a leak. Because the machines usually had to be shut down to have work done, I would have supervisors and engineers breathing down my neck to get the line back up and running. The work would be hot, both physically and mentally.

I was feeling pretty good after my first day at the Kendall plant. When I opened the door to the splendid house on Browning Avenue, I almost had to pinch myself. I had access to a sundeck and a barbecue on the third floor beside Avril's apartment. There I could bask in the late afternoon sunshine — yet another treat for one who had so recently escaped from the damp and dreary Irish summers. As I relaxed on the sundeck, I could see the CN Tower — still under construction at the time — with a helicopter buzzing around bearing components for its completion. It was as if everything around me was being made new.

I was doing so well that I decided to buy my first car: a brand-new sporty-looking Camaro for $6,700, which I bought without even having a driver's licence. My good friend Robert Cruise, a fellow Dubliner, took me out several times for lessons in his car. After a month, he concluded that I was the worst driver he'd ever seen. He was right; I failed my test the first time and barely got it on the second try. I have not improved very much since then, and Sheila, to this day, hates getting into a car with me.

Late in the summer of 1975, Sheila and I decided to get married and I started the process of sponsoring her to come to Canada. While Sheila had worked at the resort in Wales all summer, we spoke on the phone

Left to right: My brother Don (deceased), my brother Noel (deceased), me, and Eddie Crilly — my best friend, best man, and brother-in-law.

Sheila and me on our wedding day.

several times a week. I was excited about living in Canada, but was not sure I wanted to stay permanently. Like many immigrants, we talked about giving it a try for a couple of years, and if nothing came of it, we would leave with a decent deposit for a house back in Dublin. We set December 26 as our wedding day, which is an unusual choice in Canada, but quite common in Ireland. I was the first of my siblings to get married, so it was a big deal in our family.

I arrived home several days before Christmas on what turned out to be a cold, miserable, and rainy day. Sheila, a gifted seamstress, had already designed and made her own wedding dress and the dresses for the bridesmaids and flower girls. After many telephone discussions, Sheila had also selected the suits for me and the groomsmen. We settled on navy blue crushed-velvet suits with flared pants and platform shoes. This was the 1970s, after all! The wedding service took place in St. Agnes's Church in Crumlin village. My father showed up with a Band-Aid over his eyebrow. The night before he had scoffed down a good portion of the forty ouncer of Crown Royal I had brought from Canada and hit his head on the fireplace mantle when he tripped. My mother rolled her eyes when she saw the look on my face. The service went off without a hitch. Sheila looked radiant in her wedding dress. The reception was held in the Cill Dara Hotel on the Naas Road, and we partied all afternoon and into the wee hours of the morning. It was wonderful to see my brothers and sisters with Sheila's family, all having a great time.

Sheila and I had to be up early to catch a flight to Toronto, so we left the party while it was still in full swing. Somehow, we'd been given the wrong room — apart from everything else, it came with two single beds — but we were there with all our belongings and suitcases and couldn't be bothered with the hassle of moving at such a late hour. I set about dragging the night table out from between the beds and then pushing them together.

Ten minutes after I had rearranged the beds there was a loud knock on our door. I yelled out, "Hello, who's there?" The answer came back, "Cyril, it's Nuala. Ritchie and I left our coats in the room. They're in the closet." I opened the closet and to my astonishment there must have been twenty overcoats hanging there. We had been mistakenly put in the room set aside for family and friends to freshen up following the church service. I spent the next two hours answering the door and handing out overcoats.

Despite all the diversions, at 8:00 a.m. on December 27, 1975, Sheila and I boarded a plane for Toronto and embarked on a new life together, arriving to a foot of snow on a bitterly cold day. We celebrated New Year's Eve in a restaurant atop the Harbour Castle Hotel.

By the middle of the summer of 1976, I understood what was expected of me and, because my job took me to the four corners of the plant, I got to know many of the other employees. I became aware of the great dissatisfaction among the mill-area workers and among the women in the packing and sewing divisions. Their main beefs centred around wages and the absence of opportunities for people of colour. The plant employed about seven hundred people, but very few leadership positions, if any, were held by people of colour. All promotions went to Caucasians.

One day as I was working in the mill area Herman Stewart approached me. Herman was a friendly, talkative guy from Jamaica, a few years older than I was. He filled me in on the issues and wondered how I felt about forming a union, remarking that I was in a unique position to help because I got to visit all sections in the plant. I didn't hesitate for a second — joining forces with our fellow workers was clearly the right way to go — and immediately set to work. Herman and a few others had already contacted the United Steelworkers of America (USWA, which later became the USW), and over the next few weeks I talked to scores of workers and persuaded them to sign union cards. Several meetings with representatives of USWA were held on Sunday afternoons in a hall on O'Connor Drive not far from the bowling alley.

Not everyone was happy about the idea. Some of our co-workers came from Soviet bloc countries, such as Poland, Hungary, and Czechoslovakia (as it was then), where unions were tied to the Communist Party and existed to enforce the party line, rather than to represent workers. I was in the change room early one morning — work began at 7:00 a.m. — putting on my work clothes and chatting with one of my co-workers, trying to get him to sign a union card. Beside me was a stocky, red-headed guy who worked with me in the maintenance department. He usually kept to himself, but when he spoke, he had a heavy Hungarian accent. I was focused on my conversation, not paying much attention to anyone else, when the red-headed

Hungarian let fly with a string of expletives directed at me. His tirade was, in essence, that all trade unions were nothing but a bunch of communists and that he had lived under Soviet rule for long enough. I turned around to reply, but he didn't wait to hear what I had to say. Instead, he threw a punch that caught me on the side of the head and knocked me back against a row of steel lockers. The hit took me by surprise, and I knew instinctively that he wasn't finished. He stepped forward to grab me by the collar. I turned my body and at the same time shoved him hard. He lost his footing and fell into an open locker on the other side. Others stepped in before either of us could take the fight to the next stage. Neither of us was hurt but word spread throughout the plant that the Irish guy had been in a fight. I signed up more cards that day than on any other day in the course of the union drive. It wasn't the message I had meant to send, but the rest of the workers in the plant were impressed. I had shown I was prepared to stand my ground for the principles I believed in.

That same summer, even as I was drumming up support for the union, I began to search for a new job. The novelty of my work at the Kendall plant had worn off, and I felt I needed something more challenging with a better wage. Eventually, I obtained an interview with Ontario Hydro. The advertised job was for a stationary engineer, for which I wasn't qualified. Although in Ireland, as part of my steamfitter's job, I had worked on the installation of steam boilers, I didn't have the relevant certificate to do the same work in Canada. However, one of the panel of interviewers, Neil Donnelly, told me after the interview that he believed there might be a place for me in the nuclear division. He told me he would see to it that my application was forwarded to the appropriate official, and Donnelly was as good as his word. In August 1976 I was called for an interview. Within weeks I got word that I had been successful. I was to report to Ontario Hydro's Nuclear Training Centre (NTC) in Rolphton, a small village close to Deep River, in the heart of the Ottawa Valley. I gave my employer notice that I would be leaving in mid-October.

Meanwhile, as the campaign to sign up workers at the Kendall plant gained momentum, the company began to circulate propaganda designed to undermine it. They warned, for example, that unionization could cause the plant to close. Then one day, out of the blue, everybody received a fifty-cent across-the-board hourly wage increase. The implication was that the workforce didn't need a union to negotiate a fair wage, and that they could rely instead on the goodwill of management. We told the employees that if the company was willing to pony up a fifty-cent raise before we even started bargaining, there was a lot more to be had when we got to the table. Besides, the fifty cents did nothing to address the underlying issues of favouritism and discrimination. We signed more than enough cards for the union drive to be successful. The workers had their union, and I became a shop steward for my remaining few months with the company. Nothing enhances a worker's sense of self-worth more than the knowledge that he or she no longer has to go on bended knee to the employer. It was a great day at Kendall and an epiphany for me.

Soon the workers at Kendall had the opportunity to feel like part of a powerful movement. Prime Minister Pierre Trudeau had declared war on Canadian workers by imposing wage and price controls. The move was a crude response to spiralling inflation, high interest rates, and a troubled economy. As is always the case with this type of legislation, workers' wages were frozen, but the business community was permitted to keep jacking up prices. The Canadian Labour Congress, under the leadership of Dennis McDermott, called for a nationwide one-day strike to protest the move.

The day of protest was set for October 14 — as it happened, my last day on the job with the Kendall Company. I spent that day on the picket line marching with my co-workers while company executives went ballistic inside the gates, demanding that we go back to work. Herman Stewart, a small group of union executives, and I stepped inside the gate to explain the situation to the bosses. We were part of the labour movement now. We no longer had to be afraid to speak out about injustices. Management had to sit across the table from worker-elected representatives and negotiate working conditions, wages, and benefits. It was a watershed moment. I had mixed feelings about leaving. I was going to work for one of the best companies in Ontario, with my wages almost doubling, but the success of the union drive gave me a powerful sense of accomplishment. I left with a heavy heart but knew I had found my calling.

Sheila and I arrived in Deep River in October 1976. All our worldly belongings were in the back of our 1975 Camaro. We had purchased furniture in Toronto a few weeks earlier and were promised that it would be delivered on the day we got to Deep River. It wasn't. Meanwhile, for a whole week until our furniture finally arrived, our only chair was a beer cooler. Fortunately, we bumped into Frank Howie and his wife, May, a wonderful couple from Fife, Scotland. Frank was an electrician also studying at the NTC. They graciously offered us the loan of a spare mattress and a few chairs. It was a sparse beginning.

The first day in the NTC was spent in orientation sessions. One of the presenters, Gary Huff, was in his late fifties, a gruff man with a gravelly voice and a no-nonsense attitude. His job was to brief us on the hazards we would face and to instruct us in protecting ourselves from various levels of radiation. He was very clear that if you did not get a passing grade, which at NTC meant a minimum of 70 percent — higher in some courses — you were out of a job. This put the fear of God into every student. Most of us had been out of school for several years and some for even a decade or two. We were out of practice and sometimes out of our depth when it came to studying and taking exams.

In the spring of 1977, word spread that the instructors might be going on strike over contract issues. The spokesperson for the union was Gary Huff, and I had some great conversations with him about union affairs over the remaining months I spent at the school. In the summer I was transferred to the Bruce Nuclear Power Development (BNPD) on the shores of Lake Huron. Housing was cheap there, so Sheila and I decided to buy a tiny bungalow rather than live in an apartment. We paid $39,500 for a newly constructed bungalow on a fifty-foot lot. The house, wood-framed and clad in siding, was 980 square feet on the main floor and had an unfinished basement. Two years earlier I had been living with my nine siblings in my parents' two-bedroom house in Crumlin; now I owned my own modest home. I was twenty-four years old and on top of the world.

I was assigned to work in the Bruce Heavy Water Plant (BHWP), which has since been torn down. At the time, it employed about five hundred workers. Heavy water is used in the CANDU nuclear reactors to slow the neutrons as they pass through the reactor, in order to provide an enhanced fission rate. (The slower the neutrons pass through the reactor core the more efficient the chain reaction.)

In heavy water the hydrogen atoms are replaced with deuterium atoms, so heavy water is denoted by the chemical sign D_2O, as opposed to natural water, which is denoted as H_2O. D_2O is found naturally in H_2O in quantities of about one part in every five thousand parts. A cascading distillation process, involving eight massive towers, was used to extract that one part. Each tower was about 450 feet high and forty feet in circumference. Hydrogen sulphide, a deadly gas, is used as an agent to extract the naturally occurring D_2O from the H_2O. It takes about 350,000 pounds of intake water to produce one pound of D_2O.

As part of a mechanical maintainer team, my job was to ensure the plant kept running 24/7. Health and safety were always major concerns. Because of the hydrogen sulphide gas, we worked in a buddy system. One sniff would be enough to knock a person unconscious and kill them, so we never entered the tower pad area alone or without wearing a Scott Air-Pak. Our system was to have the first of a pair walk ten feet ahead of his or her partner. If the lead person dropped, it was up to the person following to sound the alarm and assist. Each worker received mandatory CPR training. Facial hair was prohibited because it could keep the Scott Air-Pak mask from making a perfect seal.

The job was most challenging in the dead of winter when gale-force winds whipped the snow in off Lake Huron and the temperature dropped to minus twenty degrees Celsius — or colder. If a report came in that a leak had occurred on top of one of the 450-foot towers, I'd have to put on my winter clothing, don an Air-Pak, and climb the side of the tower hauling a bag of heavy tools. Very often, the repair would require scaffolding to be suspended over the edge of the tower. Scaffolding crews were mostly drawn from the local community of hobby farmers and handymen. I had enormous respect for those men and women, who knew our lives depended on them. In all my years as a tradesman, I have never seen more professional or dedicated workers and I cannot count the number of times I found myself, along with a co-worker, hanging several hundred feet in the air out on a platform. At the time, the scaffolding crew's expertise was not appreciated by Ontario Hydro as it should have been. Later in my career as a union rep I worked with my counterparts across the Hydro system to win these workers a significant wage increase. They deserved every penny.

Between 1976 and early 1980 I became heavily involved in the union. The Canadian Union of Public Employees (CUPE) was the bargaining agent for the Hydro workers, but the local union preferred to call itself the Ontario Hydro Employees' Union (OHEU). The name reflected the sour relationship between the local and the national office of CUPE, antagonism that had been simmering for decades. The OHEU had an excellent record of negotiating really good contracts for its members. They had one of the best pension plans in the country, a top-of-the-line benefits plan, and one of the best shop steward training programs. Some misunderstood the OHEU's insular mode of operation as a form of elitism. Others complained that the local was out of step with the rest of the labour movement on key policy issues. Later in my career I discovered just how out of step. However, the representatives I worked with in my early days as a shop steward were excellent educators and leaders in their own right. My chief steward was a Scotsman, Jim Leslie. He was hard-nosed when he needed to be, but he also understood the art of compromise. He was sharp and well versed in the language of collective agreements. Jim and I became good friends through the years. I learned a lot from him.

Some of the problems facing the membership stemmed from workers having been promoted from the mechanical maintainer pool into supervisory roles. Once they had moved up to become lead hands or foremen, it seemed that some became hungry to enter the middle ranks of the management team. These were the supervisors who pushed to get the job done at all costs, turned a blind eye to health-and-safety issues, and cut corners. It was mainly mid-ranking supervisors who abused their powers so they could get ahead at someone else's expense. Not all of them were like this, of course, but in dealing with the issues raised by abusive supervisors, I cut my eye teeth in the labour movement.

The Occupational Health and Safety Act (OHSA) was passed by the Ontario government in 1978. This historic legislation is not used nearly as often as it should be. It gives almost every worker in the province the right to refuse an assignment they believe might be a danger to themselves or their fellow workers. The first occasion when I prevailed on management at Hydro to take the law seriously was a formative event in my career.

I had asked for a transfer to the Pickering Nuclear Generating Station in March 1980. The plant was hiring workers to bring new units online. My orientation session was led by the foreman, Steve Krezanowski, a mechanical maintainer from my class at NTC. As he showed the group of new arrivals around, he pointed to a massive rectangular concrete structure overhead and said, "This is the vacuum duct that connects all the reactors to the vacuum building. You wouldn't want to be in there if an accident happened." I asked why and he explained that if the vacuum system somehow became operational while you were in there, you could be sucked through the giant valves into the vacuum building at about fifteen hundred miles per hour. There was no chance that you would survive.

The vacuum building is actually one of the key safety features of the CANDU system. In theory, if there is a nuclear accident, rather than releasing radioactive steam and particles into the atmosphere — as happened at Three Mile Island and Chernobyl — the steam and radioactive particles would be sucked down through the concrete ducts into the vacuum building, where the radioactive steam would be doused with several million gallons of stored water. The hazard would be safely contained within a concrete structure. No meltdown. No disaster. But maintaining the system posed challenges.

I had arrived at Pickering with a reputation as a rabble-rouser. I was vocal with my opinions and in my support for the union, and I was quickly voted in as a shop steward, working closely with Frank Harris, the chief steward for the mechanical maintainers. I was working shifts rotating between days, afternoons, and nights. One evening, about two months after arriving in Pickering, I was told to enter the vacuum duct to repair rips in the tinfoil vapour barrier that separated the reactor from the vacuum building — the same vacuum duct that Krezanowski had pointed out. My immediate supervisor was Bill Net, a hobby pig farmer who was well liked and came across as a genuine soul. I said, "Bill, I'm refusing to go into that duct because I believe it could be a danger to my health, safety, and well-being."

Bill was flabbergasted. "Are you telling me you're refusing to work?" he asked.

"Yes, I am, Bill. Trust me on this. I know what I'm talking about."

Bill scratched his head and then his arse, as he always did when he was flummoxed. Then he took off to talk to Ross Mahadeo, the shift maintenance supervisor. They put their heads together for a few minutes before Ross came over to see me. Ross had a way of presenting himself as your best buddy, with a demeanour that suggested whatever he wanted was really in your best interest. He tried to explain how serious my refusal was and urged me to reconsider before things got out of hand. I stuck to my guns. If anybody was going to be in trouble, it would be the managers who ignored the provisions of the Occupational Health and Safety Act of 1978. It was his responsibility to provide me with alternative safe work until my complaint could be investigated by the Ministry of Labour, and I told him so. When Ross realized that I was not about to change my mind, he took the matter up with the shift supervisor, Bob Langdon.

Langdon called me to his office in the control room. The shift supervisor was god at the plant: he was controlling authority over the nuclear reactors on his shift and had the sole power to make decisions that could override even the plant manager's opposition. By the time I had reached his office, the story of my work refusal had spread across the plant. When I entered the control room, I found Langdon talking to Gerry Broder, the union health-and-safety rep and a shop steward for the nuclear operators. Langdon motioned me into his office.

First, I felt he tried to intimidate me. He said I had refused a direct order to perform an important task. He asked me to "do as I was told" and go into the vacuum duct to perform the work that had been assigned. He reminded me that the procedure laid out in the collective agreement was to do the work and grieve it later. I pointed out that the OHSA superseded any procedures described in the collective agreement. I told him I would not be going into the vacuum duct, and, what was more, he had an obligation under the law to inform other workers that I had refused the work on the grounds that it was unsafe. I'd be prepared to go into the duct only if the reactors were shut down or if I could be guaranteed that nothing would happen with the reactors that could trigger a differential in pressure in the duct that could lead to the vacuum valves opening and sucking me into the vacuum building.

Langdon wasn't used to being opposed. His eyes turned to beads and his mouth twitched as he tried to compose himself. A long silence filled the room until, finally, he told me to report back to my supervisor. And that is how the matter stood for the remainder of the shift.

The next morning, I phoned the CUPE union office in Toronto and spoke with staff reps John Sarginson and Jim Bolan about my work refusal. Both were supportive, but Bolan let out a long whistle as if to say, "Oh boy!" This part of the OHSA had never been tested at Ontario Hydro. They weren't certain the work refusal provisions of the OHSA had ever been tested anywhere in the province. I was in uncharted waters.

Later that day, I received a phone call requesting that I come into work a few hours early because the plant manager wanted to talk to me. When I walked into Jim Ryder's office, I was met by a phalanx of senior executives and engineers in a tension-filled room. Bill Net, the foreman, was seated at a little desk with a writing pad in front of him. He seemed nervous as hell, and the flimsy desk he leaned on collapsed under his weight, spilling his writing pad and pen onto the floor and providing a bit of levity. The plant manager, a gregarious Irishman, was an intimidating figure with a reputation for taking no nonsense from his staff. He opened the meeting by acknowledging that I had refused to perform an assigned task on the basis it was unsafe. His goal was to prove to me that it was safe and that we should get on with the business of generating electricity. He called on the handful of engineers in the room to support his position, and they rhymed off statistics about the infinitesimal likelihood of an accident that could lead to an increase in pressure in the vacuum duct and trigger the valves to open.

I asked about the likelihood of a steam pipe bursting. They all agreed it was highly unlikely and the risk extremely low. I told them that as a steamfitter I had seen many a burst steam pipe, and asked them to explain how an event they considered extremely unlikely could have happened so often in my relatively short career. They had no satisfactory answer, so I informed them that my work refusal was still in effect unless they dropped their demand for me to enter the vacuum duct. They were left with no choice but to call the Ministry of Labour. I subsequently met with the ministry inspector and gave my reasons for the work refusal. He met with management and investigated the on-site conditions.

A week later a meeting was convened in the plant boardroom. The ministry officials' investigation concluded that I had a number of grounds on which to refuse the task that had been assigned: I had not received any formal training in how to respond in the event that the pressure in the vacuum duct began to rise. A person sent into the duct had no means by which to ascertain whether or not the pressure in the duct was, in fact, rising. The duct lacked proper lighting and therefore maintenance staff had to rely on flashlights. It contained no railings on which to hook a safety harness. No procedure existed to let the operators of the other seven nuclear reactors know that a maintenance person was inside the vacuum duct, so other operators had no way of knowing that they should do nothing to alter the power levels in their reactors while the maintenance person was inside. The total estimated cost to the corporation to fix the problems identified by the ministry was said to be around $13 million.

Following my work refusal, the number of incidents that caused supervisors to send workers into the vacuum duct dropped dramatically. Procedures were established to keep the reactors in quiet mode while work was carried out. Suddenly the safety of maintenance staff was being considered. The success of my action led to an avalanche of work refusals all over the plant. Workers emboldened by my successful use of the OHSA refused to work with asbestos and other hazardous materials unless all proper precautionary procedures were followed to the letter of the law. Workers became far more aware of the potential damage to their health caused by ionizing radiation, and we pushed hard to lower the amounts of radiation workers were exposed to on an annual basis. The Pickering plant became a safer place to work.

Following this incident, and because I played a role in pursuing a number of high-profile grievances, I began to receive requests from across the province to sit on grievance panels from other sectors within Ontario Hydro. I meticulously researched the facts underlying each grievance. I also liked to find out what I could about the supervisor involved — sometimes knowing who you were up against was as important as understanding the nature of the complaint. In March 1984 I ran for chief steward against Frank Harris. I won the election, much to the chagrin of the right-wing leadership entrenched at the OHEU head office in Toronto. Pickering had a membership base of 2,500 and I was now the chief steward for more than nine hundred of them. Over the next year, I built a strong membership based on two fundamental principles: first, that workers' rights would be protected; and second, that the members would co-operate with management when treated fairly. I had an amazing group of shop stewards who were not afraid to stand up to the employer, people like Gerry Doherty, Ian Lilburn, Vance Morrison, Colin Rae, Dan Tutkoluk, Eddie Beck, and two dozen more who were fearless leaders.

Wildcat strikes in the Bruce and Pickering nuclear power plants in 1985, and a legal strike four weeks later, marked the beginning of my emergence as a union leader. These actions also opened my eyes to the cutthroat politics that exist in all spheres of public life, whether it's the union, a political party, or your local hockey league.

The year 1985 was tumultuous in the history of OHEU (CUPE 1000). In April management and the union were at the bargaining table trying to hammer out a new collective agreement. Relations between the parties had been in the dumper for quite some time. A backlog of more than seven hundred grievances had accumulated without any serious attempt by management to resolve them. At Pickering, management had attempted to introduce an "attendance management" program that penalized everybody who was off sick — even pregnant women. In addition, Hydro was claiming for itself a $600 million surplus in the pension plan. The mood of the membership was not good. The widespread perception was that Hydro was spoiling for a confrontation.

Both parties understood the situation was volatile. We had expected a new contract offer before us when the old collective agreement expired at the end of March. We were past that deadline and the Easter weekend in April was approaching. The parties were still at the table when the management bargaining committee informed the union that they were unilaterally suspending negotiations so they could enjoy the long weekend. When word of this leaked out, I was inundated by phone calls from members in the Pickering plant calling for a wildcat strike. Dan Heffernan, the divisional chairperson for the Bruce Nuclear Power Development, called to tell me that workers in Bruce were going to walk off the job. Heffernan left me with the impression that the job action had been given the green light by the president of CUPE 1000, Jack MacDonald. I later received a phone call from John Murphy, divisional chairperson for the Pickering nuclear power plant where we both worked, and he left me with the same impression.

I was on the day shift that weekend, and I went to work as usual. When I walked into the cafeteria, however, I was greeted by about a hundred angry workers banging on the tables and calling for job action. More were arriving for work as those finishing the night shift lingered, so the number was increasing. All were furious. Just about everyone believed that the suspension of negotiations was an attempt by management to gain some sort of advantage. Besides, everyone knew that management had been preparing for an extended job action.

Supervisory staff had brought in sleeping bags and had freezers delivered, presumably to demonstrate that managers were willing and ready to eat, sleep, and work in the plant if necessary to survive a long strike. Many workers saw this as an attempt to intimidate them.

Two hundred workers packed the cafeteria by the time I got up to speak. I explained that it was not legally possible to walk out of a nuclear power facility because of the danger the action might pose to the public. It was possible, if management agreed to begin the shutdown process in a controlled way, and if we agreed to provide the minimum number of personnel required by law to assist, to proceed with a shutdown. I said I would talk to the plant manager, Eric Dewar, and request that he begin taking the steps for a controlled shutdown. Somebody yelled from the back of the crowd that the Bruce nuclear plants were shutting down already. The cafeteria erupted in a roar of approval. I asked for thirty minutes to talk to management.

I walked to the active nuclear side of the plant and into the office of my immediate supervisor, Eric Rippen. Eric came from the shop floor and he knew full well the mood of the workers in the cafeteria. We talked about the seriousness of the situation and what the law required. I informed Eric that I was personally prepared to stay behind and fulfill any legal and safety requirements to comply with the procedure for a safe shutdown. Eric thanked me and said that the decision to stop operations had not yet been made. I left Eric's office and headed straight for the corporate suite. Eric Dewar was grim-faced behind his desk. I had always found him to be reasonable but inclined to be indecisive at times. I said, "I'm sure you have heard the news from the Bruce about the plant shutting down and that the cafeteria downstairs is full of workers refusing to come to work until the management bargaining committee goes back to the table."

"I have," he said, "and I have no control over what happens at the bargaining table but I do know I have a nuclear power plant to run here."

I asked him if he intended to shut down the Pickering plant and he responded, "I have no choice but to begin the shutdown. We do not have sufficient staff to safely run the system." I thanked him and headed back down to the cafeteria.

A hush fell on the crowd when I re-entered the room. I stood on a chair so everyone could hear me. The cafeteria erupted once again when I told them the plant would be shut down. Whatever advantage the management bargaining committee had sought by leaving the table had backfired. Two of the world's largest nuclear power plants, involving at least twelve nuclear reactors, were in the process of shutting down. The disruption in the supply of electricity to the province would be considerable. And for Hydro, it would be a monumental headache.

The next day, Easter Sunday, we had about one thousand workers on the picket line outside the gates of the Pickering plant. John Murphy, the union's divisional chair for Pickering, joined us on the line with his dog, an Irish wolfhound. He left after about thirty minutes, following a phone call he said he received from Noel McIntosh, CUPE 1000's vice-president for the nuclear division. McIntosh, in my opinion, was never one to push the edges of the envelope. I found he was generally the first to cave whenever there was any sign of trouble with management, and I knew the phone call Murphy received from McIntosh spelled trouble. Later that evening, Murphy phoned me to say that the wildcat strike had to end, and that I had no right taking the workers out in the first place. I almost dropped the telephone. I reminded Murphy that he was the one at the bargaining table, and he was the one who phoned me and left me with the impression that MacDonald had given the green light for job actions, and finally, that he (Murphy) was also the one walking the picket line with me earlier in afternoon. The workers had set two conditions for going back to work: the first was that management go back to the bargaining table, and the second was that there be no reprisals taken against any of the striking workers.

On Sunday evening, Murphy phoned me again to say that McIntosh was coming to the picket line the next morning to insist the workers go back to work. It was possible that Hydro would sue the union for damages caused by the illegal walkout. Clearly, McIntosh's planned intervention was a tactic worked out in consultation with MacDonald and Murphy to protect union assets. When I arrived at the picket line, around 7:30 a.m., McIntosh was already there. Our eyes locked, but we never spoke. McIntosh got up onto the back of a pickup truck that had a public address system installed and told the workers they had to go back to work or the union and workers would face heavy fines. He offered no assurances about protection from reprisals and said nothing concrete about compelling management to return to the bargaining table. The crowd was as disillusioned as I was. I could hear the chatter and sense the disappointment beginning to build. And then the heckling began.

As soon as McIntosh finished, I jumped onto the truck and told the crowd — and McIntosh — that we were going nowhere until our demands were met. The workers roared their approval. McIntosh and Murphy hopped into a car and drove away.

Later that morning, word came from the union office that management had agreed to go back to the bargaining table that afternoon. I spoke to local management by telephone and was given assurances that there would be no reprisals for any worker who had not shown up for work, provided that they pulled down the picket lines. The wildcat ended and we all walked back into the Pickering power plant together.

Two days later, I received a call requesting I meet with local 1000 president Jack MacDonald. MacDonald, John Murphy, and executive vice-president Lou Urban were waiting for me in the boardroom. MacDonald wasted no time in getting to the point: he wanted me to resign as chief steward, presumably to protect the assets of the union in the event that Ontario Hydro laid a lawsuit against the union.

I told him, more or less, to go fuck himself. I reminded him that he had put the word out through Heffernan and Murphy that job actions had the green light in order to put pressure on management. Murphy not only denied phoning to give me that message on Good Friday, he also denied being on the picket line with his dog on the Sunday afternoon. He pulled out a memo I had written weeks earlier, in which I had threatened to resign over some issue or other, and claimed that it constituted my de facto resignation as chief steward. Then MacDonald got involved again, saying that as president he had the authority to rescind my chief stewardship, and that he was notifying the membership at Pickering of his decision. I was shocked. They made me the fall guy for a decision the union's senior executive regretted making. I told them they were, in fact, setting me up to be fired. Under a little heat from the employer, they were folding like a cheap tent. The only honourable gesture in this whole disgraceful debacle came from Lou Urban who, in front of MacDonald and Murphy, promised, "Sid, I am the chair of the union bargaining committee and I will not sign a collective agreement with Ontario Hydro unless your job is secure." I shook Lou's hand and said, "Thank you, brother Lou. You are an honest man." I left the meeting and went back to Pickering and broke the news to my membership and shop stewards.

One month later, talks broke down and CUPE 1000 entered into a legal strike for the first time in more than twenty years. It was a bitter confrontation. Supervisors were bused across picket lines waving their big overtime paycheques in the faces of the workers. (Those supervisors have since joined a union, because senior management eventually screwed them, too.) Hydro announced during the strike that the wildcat action had cost the company $10 million in replacement power costs and that they were going after the union to recover the money.

Eight days into the strike, the picket line was a disaster. Even though there were more than two thousand picketers, cars and buses were being allowed to roll freely across the line. Management was barely inconvenienced. My replacement as chief steward was asked to resign at a meeting of the membership, which he did, and a vote was commenced to reinstate me as the chief steward. We left the meeting and headed straight for the picket line, where I advised the police liaison officer that I was instituting a new protocol: "We either agree to a set of rules that sets strict time limits on cars and buses crossing our lines or we will implement a nobody-in-nobody-out rule that will make life difficult for all of us." We agreed on a protocol that delayed each car for ten minutes and each bus for thirty minutes. These delays had their intended result. We began to hear stories from inside the plant about how angry and frustrated the managers were becoming because of the delays outside. It took up to two hours for some buses to get in and out of the plant.

Toward the end of the second week of the strike, I got a phone call from Dave Shier, the divisional chairperson at the Lakeview Generating Station in Mississauga. Dave wanted to know if I could send some of my members over to his plant the following day because he had heard rumours that management were going to send busloads of scabs through his lines. We scrambled to rent as many buses as we could and supplemented capacity by carpooling. The next day several hundred Pickering members showed up on the picket line in Mississauga.

The only entrance to the Mississauga plant was down a fairly narrow street. We jammed the street with a mass of men and women that stretched back thirty or forty yards. We reckoned nothing was going to move in or out as long as we were there. And then, around midmorning, we heard the chopping noise that only a helicopter makes. At first glance, we thought it was a security detail taking photographs, but then we realized the helicopter was ferrying managers in and out of the plant. By noon, at least three helicopters were in operation. A remarkable scene was thus created, made up of striking workers, whirling choppers, and the Peel regional police clad in riot gear and advancing toward the picket line. We made a split-second decision to adopt the tactics of passive resistance and called on everyone to sit down. The police ordered us to clear the street. Nobody budged. The police then began removing people physically from the line. The result was pandemonium.

That night on national television, viewers were treated to a graphic visual representation of management-labour relations gone disastrously wrong. Police in riot gear were shown manhandling the protesting men and women, who put up no fight but shouting, while helicopters throbbed in the air above it all. A spokesperson for Hydro tried to put a good face on the mayhem, but the company had overplayed its hand. The public's impression was that Mother Hydro was at war with its employees. Hydro's image had taken a beating and they knew it. The next day Hydro announced that a tentative collective agreement had been reached between the parties and the union announced the strike was over. A totally unnecessary strike had cost Hydro millions of dollars in extra costs in security, overtime, and replacement power — the latter alone totalling $10 million.

Hydro dropped their lawsuit against the union but demanded that Dan Heffernan and I be fired as the alleged architects of the wildcat strike. Lou Urban kept his promise to me and stuck to his guns. Hydro eventually relented and signed the agreement. And so ended the toughest round of negotiations in the long history of Ontario Hydro and CUPE 1000.

In 1988, women won the right to work on the radiological side of Canada's nuclear power plants. Prior to this, the Atomic Energy Control Board (AECB) had prohibited women from working in radiation fields for fear of damage to the fetus of a woman in the first trimester of pregnancy. Women argued that this practice shut them out of the more highly paid jobs in the plant and that it effectively amounted to gender-based discrimination. The union won that battle by coming up with a simple rule: any woman working in the plant could simply inform her supervisor that she required non-radiological work for a specified period of time. That victory was achieved with relative ease.

However, the real battle for gender equality became vicious when women began to show up in parts of the workplace that previously had been staffed entirely by men. Most men welcomed the decision that allowed women to work alongside them in these higher-paid jobs, but for a sizeable minority it was controversial. Overnight, disgusting pornographic pictures of women cut from magazines began to show up. Coffee shops set aside for the workers were plastered with these images from ceiling to floor. Women who complained were bullied and victimized. The struggle to assert the rights of all employees to be treated with respect and dignity had to be fought all over again on the shop floor.

One of the shop stewards for the clerical staff in the non-radiological administrative side of the plant found herself at the heart of the dispute. When she complained to her chief steward about the proliferation of pornographic pictures, nothing happened. She went over his head, taking her complaint to the union office on Eglinton Avenue. The union president, Jack MacDonald, regarded the issue as a local one and decided not to interfere. Meanwhile, at the plant, shouting matches broke out when workers tore down the offensive pictures.

The shop steward took the issue to Ontario Hydro's head office, where she met with one of the few women vice-presidents in the corporate suite. I wrote an open letter to all 2,500 employees in the plant, urging them to consider how they would feel if members of their family — a mother, wife, daughter, or sister — were subjected to this harassment and abuse in their work environment. The letter prompted debate among the membership. Some of the men argued that women in the administrative offices had pictures of Sunshine Boys pinned to their office walls, as if somehow this justified what was happening in the plant. It was irrelevant.

The turning point came quickly. One day after work the shop steward discovered a dead rat on the roof of her car. The news spread fast. I was already angry that she had been isolated and ostracized for her legitimate issue, but now she was being terrorized by some misogynist. Finally, the plant's management intervened, demanding that all pornographic pictures be removed from the plant and warning that anyone posting new images would face dismissal. It had taken almost two months of open warfare for women to be treated with respect in the workplace.

I was surprised and shocked by the bullying to which the shop steward was subjected. The events gave me some insight into the functioning of the mob mentality and into the deep-seated animosity some men direct toward women in the workplace. Later, as a provincial union leader, I came to understand how some of these prejudices played out in other public-sector workplaces.

The incident in the Pickering nuclear power plant also made me think about my three daughters, Lisa, Susie, and Amanda, who would be entering this type of work environment in the years to come. I never want anyone's children to have to overcome obstacles like the ones faced by women exercising their legitimate desire for equal treatment and respect in the workplace.

Chapter 3
PRESIDENT OF CUPE ONTARIO

A collision between the left- and the right-leaning membership of CUPE Ontario turned the 1988 convention in Thunder Bay into a tempestuous affair. The left was represented — initially — by Judy Darcy; the right, by Lucie Nicholson and her intended successor, Les Kovasci, president of CUPE local 43 for Toronto outside workers. But the action on the floor never followed either side's script.

Nicholson had just announced her retirement after twelve years as CUPE Ontario president. She and Darcy had engaged in innumerable battles on the floors of prior conventions. Darcy had challenged Nicholson in an election for CUPE Ontario president in 1986. Judy was a firebrand, and she felt Nicholson had failed to demonstrate strong leadership, especially during a wildcat strike by hospital workers in 1981. In fact, both Nicholson and Grace Hartman, then the CUPE National president, had served three months in prison for defying a back-to-work order during that strike. Darcy argued that Nicholson's incarceration in particular was the result of legal technicalities, but their actions had made them heroes in the eyes of the CUPE membership.

Judy later became good friends with Hartman, who had blazed trails for women in Canada from the day she won election as the president of her municipal local in North York in the 1960s.

The expectation of CUPE Ontario's left-wing membership going into Thunder Bay was that Darcy would once again run for the CUPE Ontario presidency. Consequently, members on the left were stunned to discover that she had agreed to a deal allegedly cooked up by the CUPE National president, Jeff Rose. The deal would turn her existing volunteer position as CUPE Ontario first vice-president into a full-time, paid position, in return for her supporting Rose's candidate for president, Les Kovasci, the president of CUPE local 43 in Toronto, at the time an unpopular local within the CUPE family.

Darcy's supporters on the left wing were furious, as her manoeuvre looked like betrayal. In their eyes, she'd sold out to the right wing within the union when that group had gone into the convention thinking it was their turn to lead CUPE Ontario in a new direction. Rose was obviously both aware of this presumption and greatly concerned by it: he viewed Darcy's base of support as a threat to his presidency.

Toronto Labour Day Parade. Left to right: Me, Judy Darcy (president of CUPE National), and Toronto mayor Barbara Hall.

Rose was a brainy guy. He had an encyclopedic memory for names and faces. He'd also had been a roommate of Bob Rae and Michael Ignatieff at the University of Toronto back in the 1960s. His greatest failing as CUPE National president was, in my opinion, that he trusted nobody and therefore failed to develop new talent to whom he could pass the torch. It's an age-old problem within most unions, and CUPE National was no exception. Rose's deal with Darcy was about having a friendly face — Les Kovasci — installed as president of CUPE Ontario.

Instead of following Darcy's lead with Kovasci, however, the left wing went looking for an alternative. They settled on Mike Stokes, the unassuming president of a small municipal local in the Niagara Falls region, who had the support of Lucie Nicholson. Stokes was not well known outside his base in Niagara Falls. His appearance, however, was memorable: he was a burly, broad-shouldered man with long, curly hair and an assortment of gold jewellery. The somewhat menacing effect was reinforced by two friends and really nice guys who pretended to be his bodyguards. The stage was set for a raucous convention.

The constitutional amendment calling for the change of the first vice-president volunteer position to a full-time, paid position was promptly defeated, and with that the deal Darcy had allegedly cut with Rose fell apart. Kovasci, too, went down in flames and the unlikely Mike Stokes won the presidency of CUPE Ontario. Darcy, realizing she was in danger of being defeated as first vice-president, made a plea for forgiveness and was re-elected, but the job remained unpaid. Most of the executive board members who had supported the Rose-Darcy deal were defeated. John Murphy, from CUPE 1000, was one of the few exceptions. He survived, mainly because he had aligned himself with Darcy's erstwhile friends on the left and was consequently not seen as part of the backroom deal-making even though he was more right wing than left.

Stokes proved a thoughtful and sensitive leader, and far more popular with the membership than he gave himself credit for. He had very little, if any, experience running a large executive board, and he was forever fretting about the left being out to get him. His worst nightmare came to pass the following year, when Judy Darcy rose from the ashes of her Thunder Bay debacle to become the secretary treasurer of CUPE National. Ironically, she was challenged by John Murphy, who had managed to keep most of Darcy's former left-wing friends in his camp. Murphy was a chameleon-type figure who projected left-wing policies on his rise through the CUPE 1000 ranks but quickly rejected them once he became president. He eventually quit the union to join the senior human resources ranks of the employer. Judy now controlled the purse strings, so in many ways she controlled the lifeblood of CUPE Ontario. Stokes seemed to me increasingly paranoid, spending hours poring over a letter to the membership to ensure it was politically correct in every possible detail and would provide no opportunity for criticism from his left flank. This paranoia led to paralysis within the union. It also gave ammunition to critics who complained, with some justification, that CUPE Ontario was not politically active enough. His fears fed the growth of what he feared most.

In May 1990, CUPE Ontario held its annual convention in Sudbury. I was elected to the executive board. Bob Rae was the keynote speaker at the banquet that followed the end of the convention. He was both eloquent and funny, speaking without notes for a full thirty-five minutes. He was fulsome in his praise of the work we did in the public sector while simultaneously — to the delight of his listeners — excoriating the record of the Liberal government of David Peterson. He was dismissive of the inexperienced Conservative leader, Mike Harris.

In July, Peterson called an election even though a full two years remained in his mandate. In September Bob Rae's New Democrats stunned the country by winning the election and forming the country's first NDP government east of Manitoba. Labour was ecstatic. Finally, we had a friendly government at Queen's Park!

In mid-1991, the executive board of CUPE Ontario met Rae and his senior staff in the premier's boardroom on the main floor of the Queen's Park legislature. Our board consisted of about twenty elected leaders from the five key sectors we represented (healthcare, education, municipalities, social services, and universities). Rae entered the room and stuffed his left hand into his pocket as he made his way around the table. I found him wooden and uncomfortable during

Left to right: Mike Stokes, president of CUPE Ontario; me; and John Murphy, CUPE Ontario's first vice-president, at the CUPE National convention in Winnipeg, 1991.

these introductions, but he came into his own once seated and talking about government policy. During the meeting, he complained that the Conrad Blacks of the world were on a capital-investment strike aimed at undermining his government. Indeed, Black had made no bones about his dislike of the "socialist" government in Ontario and vowed publicly not to invest in the province until the NDP was gone. We had heard that the government might be planning to use pension fund surpluses to invest in high-risk venture capital projects so the meeting was testy. CUPE members in Ontario belonged to several large public-sector pension plans and the idea that the government might interfere with their members' retirement income was anathema. Another rumour, to the effect that the government was about to abandon its election promise to introduce public auto insurance, further blighted the mood.

Later that fall, in the run-up to the CUPE National biennial convention in Manitoba, Jeff Rose unexpectedly stepped down as CUPE National president to become the deputy minister of intergovernmental affairs in the Rae government. Judy Darcy ran unopposed to become CUPE National president. Mike Stokes now found the left's champion ensconced as the national president. It didn't help that he had aligned over the years with Darcy's mortal enemy, Lucie Nicholson, who also hailed from Ontario's Niagara region. Stokes made a trip to Ottawa early in 1992 to appeal for Darcy's support in his bid for re-election, but to no avail. According to Stokes, Darcy told him not to bother running. He was devastated when he told me she "was throwing her weight behind Brian O'Keefe." O'Keefe had managed her successful campaigns for national secretary treasurer and national president. On May 3, 1992, Stokes announced he would be stepping down as president of CUPE Ontario.

O'Keefe was a strong candidate to replace him. A fellow Irishman from County Wexford, he was an executive board member of CUPE local 79, our largest local union, with almost twenty thousand members from the City of Toronto inside workers. He was the president of the Metro Toronto council of CUPE locals. He held a degree in economics from the London School of Economics and he had the backing of CUPE's national president. He was also a principled and likeable man — and had been in campaign mode for several months. At the time, I had no notion that I would challenge him.

Nineteen ninety-two had been full of promise as far as I was concerned. I was thirty-nine years old and committed to becoming more heavily involved in labour politics. I had been working full-time as a union chief steward and divisional chairperson in the Pickering nuclear power plant for five years, and I figured it was time to spread my wings. I felt I had accomplished all I could inside CUPE 1000. The opportunities for moving ahead within the organization were limited: several executive board members were eyeing the top leadership roles. John Murphy, for one, was clearly gearing up for a run for president of CUPE 1000. I made up my mind to run for third vice-president of CUPE Ontario. My plan was to spend two years in that position and build the support required to run for president in 1994. I made an announcement to this effect in April, three weeks before Mike Stokes declared his intention to resign.

His resignation wasn't a complete surprise. A rumour going around that Stokes would be taking over as the director of the Workers Health and Safety Centre turned out to be only partly true: Stokes became the executive assistant to the director of the centre. Nonetheless, the news came as something of a bombshell, breaking three weeks before the CUPE Ontario convention.

It was still the main topic of conversation when the CUPE National Health and Safety Conference opened in Ottawa the following weekend. Who would run against Brian O'Keefe? Cindy Henderson from the social services sector approached me and said it had to be me. I turned her down flat, reminding her that I had just mailed the letter offering my candidacy for third vice-president. Cindy, however, wouldn't take no for an answer. Over the weekend, she lined up leaders from locals big and small to approach me and pledge their support. Cindy is an impressive woman who commands attention with her shining personality. She had an amazing network of people in all five sectors of CUPE. Toward the end of the conference she offered to run my campaign if I agreed to take on Brian.

I wasn't sure what to do. If I said no, it would be at least ten years before the opportunity came around again. I had a young family to take care of and a steady job with Ontario Hydro. Any elected position was insecure: there was no guarantee that I'd continue to be re-elected if I won the presidency at the convention in Windsor. I had been elected to the executive less than two years earlier and I worried that the delegates would think I was trying to move up too quickly. Besides, O'Keefe had the support of the national president and all that entailed. All things considered, the cons appeared to outweigh the pros.

I knew from experience that the support of CUPE staff is important. Though members of staff are supposed to remain neutral, some clearly don't, and they can tip the balance in a tight race. The staff report to a director and through the director to the national president. Given that Judy Darcy was openly supporting Brian, staff influence could be a major problem. I was also concerned about my home local, CUPE 1000. It had a reputation for boozy parties that did not always sit well with other delegates. The president of the local, Jack MacDonald, was a big, gregarious man who was hostile toward me. When he had a few drinks, he was wont to look at me and mutter under his breath, "Fuckin' Sid Ryan." We didn't agree on any issue, especially after the wildcat strike in Pickering. To top it off, I had only three weeks to contact seven hundred CUPE locals in Ontario, many of which would have committed themselves to O'Keefe already. All this went through my mind as I considered Cindy's proposition.

On the plus side, I believed I had a lot to offer. I felt CUPE Ontario was missing a great opportunity to educate our membership and the broader labour movement on issues involving class politics. Most, if not all, of our educational materials lacked political perspective and class analysis. Indeed, some of the local union leadership was actually opposed to political engagement, even though our rights as workers were completely dependent upon decisions made at Queen's Park. I had considerable political experience. I was active within the NDP and had worked on the 1990 campaign that saw the NDP form a majority government. My political connections were an obvious asset. I also was deeply interested in and supportive of equity issues within the labour movement. I had a great love and affinity for immigrants, and I truly believed I could make a difference in how our union treated people of colour.

My public-speaking skills had greatly improved. I now was comfortable speaking without notes. I had a huge interest in health-and-safety issues stemming from my time in Ontario's nuclear industry. And, finally, I knew I could raise the profile of CUPE Ontario both within the labour movement and within the broader public domain. It bothered me that even though CUPE Ontario was by far the largest union in the province, and the largest component of CUPE National with 40 percent of the membership, our profile was practically non-existent. I knew I could change this.

After two days of intensive lobbying by Cindy and others — still at the Ottawa conference — I retreated to my hotel room to mull over my options. Through the window, I could see the Canadian flag fluttering over the Parliament buildings. I wondered how much my life would change if I won the election. I left Ottawa with my mind nearly made up, but I still wanted to talk it over with Sheila and a few people whose views could be decisive. Sheila was very supportive and said, "Go for it, we will deal with the situation if you ever lose."

Among others, I phoned Jim Anderson, the Ontario director of staff. Anderson was a no-nonsense-type guy with heavy jowls and an abrupt manner. He ruled the roost in Ontario: no staff member would dare cross him. When he spoke, people listened, and when he came to a decision, they paid attention. I told him I was thinking about running for president. I wanted to give him the courtesy of letting him know and I asked whether he had any advice. There was a long pause. This was typical of the man: he took his time pondering a question before answering. Finally, after what seemed like an eternity, he said, "O'Keefe called me also and I will tell you what I told him, and that is that I think either one of you would make a good president. But," he added, "not right now. Maybe two years down the road." With that, he wished me the best and hung up. I smiled and thought to myself, *What a cheeky bastard!* But at least he wasn't hostile, so there was a good possibility that he would keep the staff neutral. That pretty well clinched the decision for me.

Over the next couple of weeks Cindy had me attend every CUPE event in the province, regardless of where it was taking place. I worked with CUPE 1000's communications staff rep, Bob Menard, to pull together campaign materials. I managed to get my hands on a list of CUPE locals, including phone numbers, which was worth its weight in gold. I began working my way through the list and the response was encouraging. Most people thanked me for taking the time to phone and ask for their support.

Cindy phoned me on the way down to Windsor to go over last-minute details. I was nervous as hell but tried not to let her know. Normally, each candidate hosts a hospitality suite where free drinks and snacks are served. It's an opportunity to schmooze with the delegates prior to the vote. Cindy suggested that we break with tradition and instead host a "Breakfast with Sid" event on the morning of the election. Because of CUPE 1000's reputation for boozy and boisterous hospitality suites, she thought I could leave the delegates with a better image just before they voted on Friday. I reluctantly agreed. Later she told me she already had the invitations printed before she spoke to me. "That's what good campaign managers do," she said with a smile and a wink.

Windsor in 1992 was a sorry-looking city, especially downtown, where storefronts everywhere were boarded up. The world recession, which was ravaging the entire country, was hitting Windsor especially hard. As I drove through the city, I began to feel the enormity of the challenge that would face me if I were to win. How do we protect public services and jobs in these dire economic conditions? When I walked into the hotel lobby, I was met by a phalanx of O'Keefe supporters handing out buttons and campaign materials. My heart sank, concerned his team would overwhelm us; their several-months-long head start was going to be almost insurmountable. I took the flyer from one of the volunteers and it only added to my anxiety. It was good, professionally put together and addressed all the issues my team had identified.

I checked into my room and within minutes Cindy was on the phone telling me to get my ass down to the registration area. I asked her if she had seen CUPE 1000's vice-president John Murphy, as he had promised to help out on my campaign. She hesitated and then said, "Sid, let's not worry about John or CUPE 1000 right now. He is in the bar, and he is aware the campaign is on." Years later, I found out from Brian O'Keefe that just days before the election in Windsor, Murphy phoned Brian to say that CUPE 1000 was going to support him provided Brian would assure Murphy that he would support me over Mary Catherine McCarthy who was running for third vice-president. I wasn't surprised. Brian told him he couldn't do that to Mary Catherine.

I made my way down to the registration area, where I was pleased to see my volunteers handing out my literature and buttons. Out of the corner of my eye, I spotted a brightly dressed woman greeting every delegate and introducing them to O'Keefe. It was Judy Darcy. I was floored. It was very unusual to see a CUPE National leader so openly involved in a provincial election campaign.

After greeting delegates for an hour or so, I retreated to my room with Cindy and a few advisors. I was furious about Darcy's intervention. I decided the best response was to make it an issue. Adapting a phrase taken from a familiar Loblaws brand pitch, I told my team to ask delegates whether we were electing the President's Choice or the People's Choice. It worked. Delegates began to talk about how the national president wanted to hand-pick the Ontario leader.

The next morning, a choked-up Mike Stokes gave an emotional speech about his four years in office. He was an accomplished public speaker who knew how to inject both humour and humility into his speeches, and he got a huge standing ovation when he was finished. (Sadly, Mike passed away in 2016.) O'Keefe and I got our opportunities to address the convention that afternoon. O'Keefe went first and, to my surprise, the heart of his speech took a strange turn. He did his best to portray me as the representative of a big, bad local who could not be expected to understand the issues facing smaller locals. The irony and contradiction in Brian's logic was that he came from a local union that was larger than my home local. He had given me an opening to address the one issue that Cindy and others had warned me was of concern to the delegates: Namely, would I take care only of the big locals? Or would I be receptive to them all? We had each been given ten minutes, and I used my first seven to talk about the larger issues facing the union, taking care to touch on the concerns of all five key sectors in CUPE Ontario. I devoted my remaining three minutes to the makeup of my home local. I emphasized that, while indeed we had fifteen thousand members, the local was structured so that each unit across the province was fairly autonomous and made its own independent decisions. I spoke slowly and deliberately, only building the crescendo as I neared the end. I finished by offering a guarantee that "CUPE locals in Moosonee and Timmins will receive exactly the same representation as big locals from Toronto. There will be no favouritism given to any local, council, sector, or individuals under my leadership." My supporters erupted into applause and were standing on their feet cheering. They started to chant: "Sid! Sid! Sid!" For the first time since I had arrived in Windsor, I could feel the momentum swinging in my favour.

That evening there was a boat cruise for delegates along the Detroit River. Most of my supporters had gathered on the upper deck, where the music was pumping. I went down below and found that Brian's supporters were more subdued. The campaign, however, was far from over. O'Keefe had a great team, experienced at working the floor and hospitality suites. I regretted that we had not booked a hospitality suite ourselves when I overheard people talking about heading back to enjoy O'Keefe's hospitality. As the boat headed for the dock, I found an empty seat and was having a quiet moment by myself when Judy Darcy walked by. She stopped and said, "We need to talk. I may not be around for the election tomorrow morning. Call me." And with that she turned and left. Judy's comments were a signal to me — intended or not. She sensed there was a good chance I was going to win the following day.

I was never quite sure why there was friction between Judy and me. I tended to put it down to the hotly contested election between John Murphy and Judy for the position of CUPE National secretary treasurer back in 1989. I had spent a lot of time with Murphy during the convention in Vancouver. Murphy gave Darcy a serious run for her money in that election — she barely eked out a victory on the third ballot. She had also had some run-ins with the leadership of CUPE 1000 over the years, which were probably exacerbated by her left-wing progressive politics and the clearly right-wing politics of the CUPE 1000 leadership. Perhaps she assumed I was cut from the same cloth as others in my home local. Otherwise, as far as I could see, Judy and I were on the same page on most political issues. I supported employment equity. I had waged a huge fight within the Pickering nuclear plant for the rights of women. I was a strong opponent of privatization and public-private partnerships. I was active on international solidarity files and a fierce champion of workers' health-and-safety issues. Finally, I had no time for any of the old boy networks that permeated so many trade unions. In short, though I came out of CUPE 1000, I was much further to the left in my politics than many of Judy's inner circle of advisors. Judy went on to prove herself as an incredibly successful and progressive union leader. Today, she is still blazing trails as an elected MLA and cabinet minister in the B.C. NDP government.

Cindy's breakfast idea turned out to be a stroke of genius. The morning after the boat cruise, a lot of the delegates were feeling the effects of the partying the night before. They woke to find the invitation to join me for coffee and muffins slipped under their hotel room doors. It was easy for them to find us, strategically located at the foot of the escalator leading into the convention hall. The lineups were huge, and I managed to go up and down each line, shaking hands and chatting with every delegate. Meanwhile, Cindy had organized our crew of volunteers to work the crowd and hand out buttons. By the time the "Breakfast with Sid" event was over, my buttons and campaign flyers were everywhere.

Inside the convention hall, the atmosphere was electric.

The campaign had been clean and there was no animosity between Brian and me. He was a dedicated trade unionist and a bright and hard-working guy.

The election process followed the normal union procedure. The elections chairperson called for the doors to be "tiled," meaning that all the doors were closed so that nobody could either leave or enter the hall while the votes were cast. Staff guarded the doors to enforce the rule. Brenda Hartford, the popular and respected president of a nursing home local in Durham Region, nominated me to tumultuous applause. Muriel Collins, the similarly admired co-chair of CUPE Ontario's women's committee, nominated O'Keefe. The ballots were passed out, marked, and collected, the entire process taking about thirty minutes. My stomach was churning when the committee left the room with the ballot boxes in hand. I was relieved to know that the campaigning was over, but nervous energy still gripped me. CUPE staff rep Helen O'Regan, an Irish expatriate, pulled me aside and gave me a big hug. She told me how proud she was to have two Irishmen run for leader and then, as she let go, she looked me in the eye and said, "If you win, promise me you will never forget your roots." I made that promise and meant it.

Gerry Adams's first trip to Canada, 1994. Left to right: Me, Helen O'Regan, John Murphy, Terry O'Connor, and Gerry Adams.

At approximately 10:30 a.m., Mike Stokes announced that he had the results. The room fell silent. Every pair of eyes in the hall was focused on the podium. Stokes announced the total number of ballots cast and the number that were spoiled. Then he said, "The results of the election are, Brian O'Keefe ..."

My heart sank. Because Brian's name was mentioned first, I immediately thought that he must be the winner.

"... 318 votes." Stokes paused for a few seconds and then said, "Sid Ryan, 336 votes."

I was floored. I heard Stokes, as if from a great distance, say, "Congratulations, Sid! We have a new president!" A roar went up from my supporters and I was mobbed by Cindy and the entire campaign team. Everyone was on their feet, clapping and cheering, when a chant began from the back that quickly filled the hall: "Sid! Sid! Sid!" I stood on a chair to wave to my supporters. Some of my campaign team were crying with joy and relief. I made my way through the crowd to Brian O'Keefe. We hugged and chatted briefly; he was gracious and a true gentleman, offering me his full support. I made my way, finally, to a microphone on the floor to thank the delegates, my supporters, and

Brian O'Keefe, CUPE Ontario secretary treasurer, and me, CUPE Ontario president, in the CUPE Ontario office in 2000.

my campaign team. Just before I was about to step up onto the platform, I saw Jim Anderson, the CUPE director of staff, bounding down the aisle. He gave me a huge hug and held my arm up in the air and whispered into my ear, "Well done, Sid, you will make a great president." The significance of that gesture was important. He was telling both the national president and CUPE staff in Ontario, *Don't mess with Ryan! We're on the same team.* From that moment on, Anderson had my back, and I was always respectful of his jurisdiction.

After the pandemonium died down, I went to my room and phoned Sheila to give her the news. She was thrilled that I had won, but there was also a trace of trepidation in her voice. We had spoken often about the insecurity that goes with an elected position. Now we would have to live with it. Next I phoned my mother in Dublin. She was alone now, as my father had died a few years earlier, in 1988. She had been to Canada a dozen times and knew how involved I had become in labour politics. I could tell that she was delighted and

Left to right: Terry O'Connor, CUPE Ontario secretary treasurer; me; and Percy Huggett, past president CUPE Ontario (1967–1972), following my election as CUPE Ontario president in 1992.

proud. She sighed and said, "I wish your father was alive to share this with you." Then she broke down and sobbed about how much she missed him. We both cried for a while and reminisced about Danny. After the phone call, I lay on the bed and thought about my dad, sitting at the kitchen table with his workmates, trying to hammer out a deal that would end a bitter six-week-long strike. My mother was beside herself, sick with worry because there was no money to put food on the table for her six young children. For some reason, I thought about all the times I knelt down in church, embarrassed because the holes in my shoes were exposed to the kids behind me. Perhaps I was thinking that my new role was to ensure that no kids ever had to leave home with the bare soles of their feet scraping against the concrete sidewalks. I left my hotel room and returned to the convention hall with Helen O'Regan's words still ringing in my ears. I could never forget my roots, even if I tried.

Five past presidents and me on the day I was elected president of CUPE Ontario in May 1992. Left to right: Fred Taylor (1962–1963), me (1992–2009), Lucie Nicholson (1976–1988), Grace Hartman (1963–1967), Percy Huggett (1967–1972), and Mike Stokes (1988–1992).

On May 23, 1992, I drove out of Windsor in my six-year-old, second-hand Buick Regal, my head full of doubts. I was now president of the largest union in Ontario, representing more than 140,000 public-sector workers, covering five major sectors of the public service. A week or so later, I found myself in Vancouver at the Canadian Labour Congress convention. I went for a walk around Stanley Park with John Murphy and he asked me to let him take my position on the executive board of the Ontario Federation of Labour (OFL). I told him I would think about it. Gord Wilson, OFL president, got wind of Murphy's request, cornered me a week later and insisted that I not give up my seat. He said it would weaken his board to have somebody other than the president of CUPE Ontario at his table. I understood and agreed with Wilson's position and informed Murphy I would be taking the seat myself.

That Canadian Labour Congress convention came at a time of great change in the labour movement. Bob White, the legendary leader of the Canadian Auto Workers union (CAW), was about to take over from Shirley Carr as the new CLC leader. The outcome of the election was a foregone conclusion: nobody was about to challenge the iconic Bob White, with his stellar credentials and proven track record as a tough and intelligent leader. There was a battle, however, for the position of executive vice-president, where Jean-Claude Parrot from the Canadian Union of Postal Workers (CUPW) ran against the establishment's hand-picked choice, a relatively unknown CUPE staff rep from Montreal. Parrot was a working-class hero to many within the movement, stemming from his epic battles with Canada Post, and his eventual imprisonment for failing to obey a government back-to-work order. He won the VP spot, much to the delight of the hard left in the labour movement. With Bob White moving on to the CLC, his replacement as CAW president was Buzz Hargrove, a long-time assistant to White.

Things were changing in the Canadian labour movement. I was excited to help shape that change.

Chapter 4
BOB RAE AND THE SOCIAL CONTRACT

Some people say the greatest mistake made by Bob Rae's government was to turn against its labour allies in the Social Contract debacle, but I've always contended that the damage was done earlier, when it backed away from its promise to deliver public auto insurance.

Six months before David Peterson called the election in 1990, Peter Kormos, the NDP MPP for Welland, broke the Queen's Park record for filibustering when he single-handedly held up a weak industry-driven auto insurance bill introduced by the Liberals. The bill was a response, albeit an inadequate one, to the NDP's wildly popular public auto insurance plan. Its introduction by the Liberals was meant to rob the NDP of a powerful issue in the coming election campaign. Kormos's determined opposition to the bill's passage made him a hero both within and outside the party.

In the campaign that followed, I knocked on hundreds of doors for Drummond White in Durham Centre. We had a skeletal team of four or five unpaid workers, mostly senior citizens, and a few part-time volunteers. Besides the campaign manager, Brad Zubrick, I was one of two full-time union reps booked off by Public Service Alliance of Canada (PSAC) and my union to work full-time on the campaign. We had, at best, two people operating the telephones, one person looking up phone numbers, and a few volunteers. Incredibly, we won in a landslide, defeating the incumbent Allan Furlong, and beating Jim Flaherty into third place in his first attempt to win elected office at Queen's Park. We won primarily on the strength of one issue, and that was public auto insurance; it came up at every doorstep. The common refrain was "if you guys stick to your promises and bring in public auto insurance, you have my vote." When Rae buckled under insurance industry pressure and abandoned that promise, I thought to myself, *You fool! Now you will be subjected to blackmail by every two-bit right-wing lobby group in the province.*

Rae later dropped Kormos from the cabinet, allegedly for posing fully clothed as the Sunshine Boy in the *Toronto Sun*. It seems to me that the demotion was motivated not so much by Kormos's prank — which was harmless — but rather by the desire to remove a critic from the cabinet table. Others have said that Rae was concerned that this charismatic upstart had bigger political ambitions. I had my own reason for being angry: Kormos was the only sitting member of the NDP to help out in Durham Centre in the dying days of the campaign. Rae's action seemed vindictive and petty and driven by a caucus that was taking political correctness to a whole new level.

Of course, other factors chipped away at the Rae government's credibility. He had trouble wrestling with the then controversial proposal to permit Sunday shopping, which placed the government on a collision course with various religious groups and unions representing workers in the retail industry. This and other controversies were exacerbated by a mischievous opposition party smarting at its loss of power after a mere three years, and by an opportunistic neo-conservative third party led by Mike Harris. No matter what Rae turned his hand to, it seemed to lead to conflict.

The NDP government was already suffering in the polls when they introduced the Labour Law Reform Bill into the House. In 1991 the OFL submitted a modest proposal to the NDP to amend the Ontario

Labour Relations Act (OLRA) to make it easier for workers to join a union. This was exactly what the labour movement needed to maintain union density as the workforce expanded. Unfortunately, the government responded by entering into a convoluted consultation process that involved lawyers — three from the business community and three from the labour movement. The original idea was to have the lawyers draft the legislation and have the bill introduced and passed by the legislature before the Christmas break.

But the bill wasn't ready before the Christmas deadline, and the OFL leadership began to worry that the business community would mobilize its lobbying machinery to defeat the bill in the New Year. Labour was also concerned that if the NDP got pushback from business on this modest legislation, the government would give up entirely on the introduction of additional, much-needed labour law reforms. This fear prompted the OFL leadership to change tactics and ask the government to expand the original OLRA bill, transforming it into a much more comprehensive package of labour law reforms. The resulting list of demands that made its way into a government discussion paper was leaked to the media before a communications strategy was put in place. The backlash from the business community and their allies in the media was ferocious.

The heart of the discussion paper centred on banning the employment of replacement workers — scabs — during legal strikes and lockouts, and on preventing workers on strike from crossing their own picket lines. The paper raised several other important issues, such as making it easier for workers to join a union and granting newly organized workplaces access to a first collective agreement when employers were deemed to be stalling. These changes were relatively minor in the grander scheme of things, but the business community and newspaper owners saw it as a declaration of war: they went nuclear in their attacks on the proposed bill and on the NDP government. The fact that 98 percent of all contract negotiations end in a settlement without resorting to strikes or lockouts meant nothing to this group. Neither did the fact that making it easier for workers to join a union is a proven path out of poverty for low-paid workers. They acted, as they do so often, out of paranoid self-interest.

The first salvo in the war of misinformation was fired by an industry lobby group calling itself the Council of Ontario Construction Associations. It paid Ernst & Young to conduct a poll of 301 CEOs from a variety of economic sectors. The CEOs were asked how nine key components of proposed changes in a discussion paper would impact jobs in their corporation. The answers were no big surprise: 183 said it would result in severe job losses. Some even claimed they would have to lay off their entire workforce. This unscientific survey, drawing on a narrow and clearly biased body of business leaders, was extrapolated to represent all corporations in Ontario, arriving at the unbelievable conclusion that 295,000 jobs would be lost if this phantom legislation — which had yet to be written — was passed into law.

On July 8, 1992, the *Toronto Star* ran a story in the business section with the jarring headline "Study says new labour law could cost 295,000 jobs." Earlier in February they had reported on the same survey but made reference to its unscientific methodology. When Mike Harris, leader of the Conservative Party, began quoting the job-loss figures in July, most newspapers ran his quote without informing their readers that the poll was bogus, and that several of the provisions that the poll had drawn attention to had, by then, either been removed from the bill or drastically altered.

The mythical lost jobs now entered into the labour law reform debate, as if they constituted an indisputable fact. The number was quoted in every major debate and practically every time the issue came up in the Ontario legislature. On June 4, the NDP government released its discussion paper, and in July and August it held public hearings. The vast majority of presentations were overwhelmingly in favour of the reforms, but you'd never know it from the media coverage, which was overwhelmingly negative. In September, several umbrella organizations representing business interests stepped up their attacks. One such group, calling itself the Keep Ontario Working Coalition, was made up of nineteen organizations representing most sectors of Ontario's economy, ranging from manufacturers and retailers to stockbrokers and building contractors. On September 24, 1992, the popular mayor of Mississauga, Hazel McCallion, introduced the coalition to the public at a downtown Toronto press conference, where she claimed the proposed legislation would have "disastrous consequences for my municipality as well as the whole of Ontario." Later the president of the Retail Council of Canada and coalition spokesperson Alasdair McKichan said in a press release that their "new group would take a different approach than other coalitions, in that they would not be talking to politicians — as their minds were already made up — but rather, they will speak directly to the public." He went on to roll out an extraordinarily expensive campaign that included delivering flyers to three million households, and running TV, radio, and newspaper advertisements, all with the same message: "Kill the bill before it kills your job!" And, of course, it added the usual egregious statements about how the NDP "has a debt to pay to union bosses. It's paying for it with your job."

The campaign mounted by the Keep Ontario Working coalition was vicious. More shocking was the support lent to the coalition by the owners and publishers of Ontario's daily and weekly newspapers. In mid-September, as Bill 40 was in the final stages of review, the Canadian Daily Newspaper Association (CDNA) and Ontario Community Newspaper Association (OCNA) entered the fray, taking out six full-page advertisements in the coalition's thirty-eight daily newspapers and 276 weekly newspapers. These full-page ads by the newspaper owners were a shocking abuse of power and the public trust. Some ads depicted factory gates padlocked with the word "closed" emblazoned across the ad, while others conjured violence, splashing the word "conflict" across the page. Among the misleading factoids included in their ad campaign was the discredited Ernst & Young survey. A particularly galling abuse of power was the *Toronto Star*, which ran anti-NDP advertisements free of charge. The *Star*'s management knew perfectly well that the Ernst & Young survey was biased. The *Toronto Star* had used scabs to break a strike by their own employees only six months before. The conflict between the principles they supposedly espoused in the editorial pages of their newspaper and their private aggrandizement was particularly blatant. But the mainstream media, in this instance, was without shame. The publishers of Ontario's newspapers put their corporate interests ahead of editorial integrity.

Bill 40 passed third and final reading in November 1992 and became law on January 1, 1993. Following its passage, the OFL asked Professor James Winter of the University of Windsor to review the media coverage of the legislation and of the discussion and public hearings that accompanied it. Winter found that "two-thirds of the coverage was unfavourable." This bias, he said, "applied about equally to headlines, lead paragraphs and the overall stories, all of which were separately measured." There was also a bias, he reported, "in terms of sources used. Business sources averaged more than four mentions per story. This compared with about one and one-half Labour sources, and about two NDP government sources per story." Winter's findings confirmed what we already knew.

Bill 40 cost the NDP a lot of political capital for very little return. In my opinion, the labour movement was essentially MIA for the bulk of the debate. It had been lulled into believing that the NDP would carry the ball and that there was no need for labour to get involved by mobilizing its membership. In the heat of the battle, a modest media campaign was mounted by the OFL. The complexity of the issues played into the hands of the business lobby, which bombarded workers with deceptive and scaremongering propaganda. NDP MPPs reported that union members, swayed by what they read and heard in the media, were phoning their offices to complain about the bill. In hindsight, the labour movement overreached by asking for so much change all at once. If the OFL had stuck to its position of incremental change over four years as originally submitted in early 1991 — calling for OLRA changes to make it easier to join a union — I believe the furor would have been less apocalyptic, and the legislation would have passed and survived to this day. Instead, Bill 40 became a prime target for the Tories under Mike Harris. Following his election as premier in 1995, one of his first orders of business was its repeal.

The Rae government was already battered and bruised in the spring of 1992 when I was elected president of CUPE Ontario. On the Monday following my election, I received a phone call from David

Leadership of the Public Services Coalition. Left to right: Vanessa Kelly (CUEW), me, Liz Barkley (OSSTF), Fred Upshaw (OPSEU), and Ted Roscoe (SEIU).

Agnew, Premier Rae's chief of staff, inviting me to join the Premier's Labour/Management Advisory Council (PLMAC). Mike Stokes had told me to expect the call and indicated that the meetings were to be kept more or less confidential. The first meeting took place late in the summer of 1992, in the same boardroom where the CUPE Ontario executive board had met with Premier Rae earlier in the year. Nothing much had changed. Rae walked in, stuffed his left hand into his pocket and made his way around the boardroom table, shaking hands. In attendance for labour were Gord Wilson, president of OFL; Fred Pomeroy, president of Public Service Alliance of Canada; Tom Kukovica, Ontario director UFCW; Leo Gerard, Canadian director of USW; Fred Upshaw, president of the Ontario Public Service Employees Union (OPSEU); Buzz Hargrove, president of CAW; and me. Buzz Hargrove was, like me, also attending his first advisory council meeting. In attendance for the employer groups were the GM president Canada, the Inco president, and leaders in the hotel and public sector.

The meetings were fascinating. Buzz Hargrove and Bob Rae got into a major blow-up one day over the government's introduction of a "gas-guzzler tax" on large automobiles. Hargrove argued that the tax was going to hurt the auto industry. In my opinion, the Rae government showed some guts on an important environmental issue. If the industry had heeded the government's advice, its collective creative mind may have turned to manufacturing smaller, more fuel-efficient vehicles and avoided losing market share to foreign imports. The NDP government, meanwhile, was in the process of saving Algoma Steel in Sault Ste. Marie and the pulp and paper company in Kapuskasing, and lending support for Bombardier's purchase of de Havilland Aircraft of Canada. Rae's interventions to save these companies were generally dismissed by the business community and their allies in the press as meddlesome at best, and an attempt to please union bosses by saving union jobs at worst. Reference to "union bosses" was a recurrent motif in all the campaigns waged by the business lobby.

Over time, Rae increasingly used the PLMAC meetings to talk about the government's finances. He reiterated that his government faced a capital-investment strike by the business community. Indeed, many of the business leaders around the table were, behind the scenes, threatening to stop investing in Ontario unless the NDP withdrew its labour reform legislation. This left Rae in a quandary. The government had hiked welfare rates and increased the minimum wage. It had invested in social housing, dramatically opening up the co-op housing industry, and literally thousands of new and affordable homes got built. It had put thousands of unemployed workers back to work by giving subsidies to employers that hired workers off the welfare rolls. It had bailed out failing corporations and invested heavily in new roads and transit. All this investment resulted in the deficit ballooning, from $2.5 billion left over from the Liberal government of David Peterson, to a record high of $9.7 billion. Inevitably, the Tories and the official Liberal opposition pounced on this spending as irresponsible. Today, it is hailed as a wise investment in infrastructure programs that put people back to work.

There are severe limitations on the powers of any provincial government to solve macroeconomic problems. Eighty percent of all goods manufactured in Ontario head across the border to the United

States, which in the early 1990s was in a deep recession. There was nothing Rae could do about the U.S. economy, but that didn't stop the Opposition from blaming him for the decline in trade. Rae was feeling the heat. He started talking about the wealth-creating private sector as opposed to the wealth-consuming public sector. I was incensed by this notion that the public sector was sucking up dollars that might somehow have been made available for private-sector investment. It was inaccurate and divisive. I reminded the people around the table at the PLMAC meetings that public-sector investment creates the environment for the private sector to flourish. Every penny spent on roads, healthcare, childcare, and our educational system helps to establish the conditions from which the private sector benefits. It has been estimated, for example, that the auto sector saves $6 an hour for every worker in Canada because of our universal healthcare system.* I didn't realize that all this talk about wealth creators and wealth consumers was setting the stage for the next act, when the government would squeeze public-sector workers for $2 billion in wage concessions.

Meanwhile, the financial situation in Ontario grew worse with every passing week. The welfare rolls were exploding and unemployment was moving into double-digit territory. The premier went on television in January 1992 to lay the groundwork for a period of severe belt-tightening. He talked about the deficit rising to unsustainable levels. This, like the talk about wealth creation and consumption, was all part of the public relations campaign meant to soften up the public and public-sector unions for the cuts to programs, services, and wages that were yet to come.

In August 1992 I went to Ottawa to visit Judy Darcy and talk about the need to build the political capacity of CUPE Ontario. After two months on the job, I could see that the organization was in desperate need of staff resources. We had no internal or external communications capability. We had no research capacity. No one was responsible for campaigns or dedicated to health-and-safety or workers' compensation issues. In addition to these glaring deficits, CUPE Ontario was headquartered in a

* CAW/TCA Canada, "Frequently Asked Questions."

rinky-dink office at the back of an industrial strip mall in Scarborough. Meanwhile, CUPE National's communications, research, and servicing staff were housed in a modern office tower a half-mile away. Something was seriously wrong with this picture. The same CUPE membership was paying the freight for CUPE National and CUPE Ontario. In my mind, the political work, the lobbying for legislation, the mobilization of the membership, the conferences, and the educational opportunities organized by CUPE Ontario were all crucial contributors to the favourable climate in which CUPE National bargained collective agreements with employers and organized new members.

I expected Judy to be sympathetic. After all, she had been the first vice-president of CUPE Ontario for many years and had first-hand knowledge of our situation. Alas, my trip was a complete waste of time. I came away with nothing. There would be no research or communications assistance, no financial help, and no possibility of our moving into the main offices of CUPE National, where we could at least share some of their staff and expertise. I had to report back to my executive board that we were on our own. Nevertheless, I promised that we would build a political machine in Ontario using our own meagre resources and that we would take our case for a fair share of CUPE resources to the floor at the next and subsequent conventions. Around this time Jim Anderson asked me to come over to his office to talk about the assignment of one CUPE National staff rep that had been temporarily assigned to work at CUPE Ontario prior to my election. He suggested to me that he felt Jim Woodward would be a good fit for this assignment. How right he was. Over the next seven years Jim and I developed an amazing working relationship as he became my trusted and loyal friend and right-hand person. He was loved by the CUPE membership and staff and so was able to remove many of the political obstacles and assuage the fears of those within the organization who viewed my style of leadership as being too militant. CUPE Ontario created a tsunami of political actions both internally and externally that made the old guard very nervous.

In November CUPE and other public-sector unions heard rumours that the NDP government was about to renege on its commitment to increase transfer payments to the MUSH (municipalities, universities, schools, and hospitals) sectors by 2 percent. The unions were incensed. The top public-sector union leaders asked for a meeting with the premier and his senior cabinet ministers. The meeting was held in the premier's boardroom with his planning and priority committee members in attendance. After much debate, it was agreed that a one-time 1 percent increase in transfer payments would be made to cover collective agreements negotiated on the basis of the already announced 2 percent. It was not an outcome to celebrate.

The fact that the government could so cavalierly renege on a serious policy commitment, without consultation or any regard for negotiated agreements, was a clear signal that the relationship between the NDP and organized labour in the public sector was in trouble. In the ensuing weeks, the amount of work that CUPE Ontario had to keep on top of exploded. Every day brought a new crisis that had to be communicated to the membership. Because CUPE National refused to provide any communications help, I had to write the newsletters myself, along with all the correspondence pertaining to the Rae government's actions. I was on a steep learning curve, trying to get my head around the key sectors — healthcare, education, social services — whose issues were new to me. CUPE Ontario was a shell of an organization, and if I fell flat on my face that would be just dandy as far as the CUPE National office was concerned. I was determined to make sure that didn't happen.

In February 1993 word leaked out of Queen's Park that Premier Rae had been taken aback by an episode on CTV's weekly program *W5* about the financial crisis that had ravaged New Zealand following the election of a left-wing government. The documentary discussed the so-called debt wall that made it impossible for the government to borrow money on international markets to service its debt and deficits. This debt wall and its consequences supposedly led to massive layoffs and drastic cuts in healthcare, education, and social services. Naturally, the program provoked opportunistic commentators in Ontario to talk about the likelihood of a similar crisis striking here. They speculated that Ontario's deficit could grow to a staggering $17 billion if drastic measures were not taken. Supposedly, we would hit our own debt wall in fiscal year 1993–94. The province's public-sector unions were not buying it.

Once again, Premier Rae summoned his planning and priorities committee, and this time he asked to meet with the entire top leadership of the labour movement. Rae brought along cabinet members Tony Silipo, Frances Lankin, Dave Cooke, and Floyd Laughren. Attending on the union side were Bob White, Gord Wilson, Julie Davis, Judy Darcy, Buzz Hargrove, Leo Gerard, Fred Upshaw, and a number of leaders from mid-sized unions. Rae opened by outlining the financial situation and went on to say that he expected the labour movement — and especially public-sector unions — to play their part in helping to wrestle the deficit to the ground. The meeting got heated when Buzz Hargrove lectured Rae about not having raised taxes on corporations and the wealthy. Disappointingly, the finance minister, "Pink Floyd" Laughren, failed miserably to live up to his nickname and defended the government's position. Judy Darcy and I observed that the British Columbia NDP government had won praise for negotiating a "social accord" with the Hospital Employees' Union (HEU) who were part of the CUPE organization. The accord led to the workers accepting a wage and hiring freeze in exchange for job security and improved language to stop contracting-out during the recession, among other gains.

Suddenly Rae became animated. He sat upright in his chair and said something to the effect of "Now you're talking my language!" He went on to talk about shared responsibilities and the principle of power-sharing in the workplace. I emphasized that we were talking about a negotiated accord between labour and government. When the meeting was wrapping up, Rae undertook to put on paper his vision of what a social accord would look like. We were pleased by what appeared to be minor progress. Still, there was no mistaking that the Floyd Laughren at the meeting was not the same man who once stood up in the legislature and proclaimed loudly — while presenting his first budget in 1991 — that he was proud not to be fighting the deficit, but instead to be fighting the recession. Both he and the premier, along with their senior cabinet colleagues, had been converted on the fiscally conservative road to Damascus. We could see trouble on the horizon.

I held a CUPE Ontario executive board meeting on March 19 and 20. It was also a heated affair. Michael Hurley, president of the Ontario

Council of Hospital Unions (OCHU), pounded the table over hospital cutbacks, closures, and amalgamations. John Murphy, from the Power Workers' Union (formally CUPE 1000/OHEU), was equally upset about layoffs in Ontario Hydro under the new chairman, Maurice Strong. Rae, who had appointed Strong, had recently referred to him as a "man of courage" when he came under attack from the union for major layoffs. The fact that an NDP premier could offer praise in such circumstances showed how deep the rift had become between labour and the government. There was worse to come. Queen's Park sources were warning that as many as forty thousand public-sector layoffs were imminent. This was simply too much for my board to take. A motion calling on me to denounce the rumours and to urge Bob Rae to return to the party's socialist roots was passed unanimously.

A press conference was held on Saturday afternoon immediately following the board meeting, and the next day I was front-page news with the line about "socialist roots." In truth, I never believed that Rae's beliefs were rooted in social democracy. His ready abandonment of socialist principles was clear evidence that they meant little to him.

On Sunday evening, March 21, Rae and his senior cabinet ministers met with union leaders in the Sutton Place Hotel. In attendance for labour were Gord Wilson, Julie Davis, Judy Darcy, Buzz Hargrove, Harry Hynd, Leo Gerard, Fred Upshaw, and I. Just before the government entourage arrived, I got into a heated exchange with a few of the private-sector union leaders over my comments about Rae in the Sunday papers. We were still going at it when Rae walked in and ended the discussion, but not before I reminded the few complainants that I would not presume to lecture them about how they conducted their political affairs with their employers.

The meeting got underway with Rae reiterating the mantra he had delivered at our last encounter. By the time he handed proceedings over to Laughren, the tension in the room was palpable. The union leaders wanted to get down to discussing the government's intentions and next steps, but Laughren was avoiding anything of the sort. Instead, he droned on discursively in a monotone that might have been deliberately designed to grate on people's nerves. He trotted out the tired metaphor of a $6-billion, three-legged stool that somehow supported our continued prosperity. He proposed to find $2 billion in increased taxes on everyone — except corporations — $2 billion in program and service cuts, and $2 billion from wage concessions from public-sector workers. Take away any of the three legs, he warned, and the provincial economy would collapse.

Politicians of all stripes are experts at eating up the clock. Laughren finally reached the end of his presentation, after going on about the shortfall in revenue and increases in the number of people on welfare and how all this would lead to a projected deficit of $17 billion if nothing was done about it. When at last it appeared that there might be an opportunity to challenge his assumptions, he announced that he wanted us all to watch the program about the debt wall in New Zealand. He actually picked up the video cassette and made a move toward the video recorder when Buzz Hargrove bellowed, "I don't want to see your fucking videotape of New Zealand," and demanded we get on with the meeting.

Laughren sat back down and by now the tension was almost suffocating. Leo Gerard asked Rae if there was no way the deficit could be dealt with without going after public-sector workers. Rae skirted the question, insisting that everyone had to do their bit. But strangely absent from those being called upon to pony up was the business community — or maybe not so strangely. At the previous meeting, Rae had promised to draft a one-page document outlining his thoughts on what a social accord would look like. Judy Darcy again raised the issue, but Rae was evasive. Some of the union leaders expressed doubt that a social accord or contract could work in the context of Ontario, whose public sector with its 950,000 employees was much greater than British Columbia's. The meeting ended without agreement on any of the issues that had been raised — wage concessions, the social accord, or tax increases on corporations. Rae said he had a cabinet retreat the next day and a caucus retreat the following week, and we would be hearing from him.

It was evident to us that the government had lost its way. We had just received a lecture on fiscal conservatism from a supposedly social democratic premier and his senior cabinet ministers. I felt betrayed.

I knew in my heart and soul that this government was about to turn against the base that had helped to elect it. My executive board's reaction the previous day had told me they were getting the same vibes. Rae was still smarting from the thrashing administered by the business community in the debate over labour law reform. Now he was trying to appease his persecutors. Why he couldn't see that these bandits would never be appeased until he was run out of office baffled me.

Rae came from a privileged background, and I don't think he ever got it. He was the son of a career diplomat, educated in the best schools that money and privilege can buy. I don't think he ever watched his mother boil potatoes over a coal fire because the gas bill had not been paid, or witnessed the despair of a parent having to choose between putting food on the table and paying the bills. To listen to Rae, we were all a bunch of ingrates, the great unwashed who declined to kowtow to their enlightened leader. Rae was not cut from the same cloth as his labour minister, Bob Mackenzie, who saw the fight over Bill 40 as part of his duty to his class. Mackenzie was a worker, proud to be a worker, and he never forgot his roots. He looked upon his rise from the working class to the corridors of power as a privilege bestowed on him by the working men and women who put him there.

Just how far the NDP government had strayed from its base of support and its socialist principles became evident in the months that followed. Both Rae and Laughren were fixated on the deficit and the worrying gap between the revenue coming in and the expenditures going out. Their fixation was somewhat appropriate but completely overblown; their refusal to consider sharing the pain equitably was wrong. Corporate, wealth, and inheritance taxes were all off the table. This so-called social democratic government had decided its base was going to carry the burden of paying down the deficit. It had chosen to make cuts that hurt the most vulnerable. Tax increases were going to be borne not by the rich, but by the middle class and low-income workers. Rae had turned the world upside down.

The corporate honchos and their lobbyists must have been splitting their sides laughing. Not only had they kicked the crap out of the NDP's public auto insurance policy, thrashed the NDP over labour law reform, and ridiculed the NDP's intervention to save bankrupt companies. Now they were watching the socialist party go to war with its own base. To top it off, some private-sector union leaders were attacking the public-sector union leaders for criticizing this egregious attack on workers by their own party. Ironies abounded.

A week after our meeting, Rae held his cabinet retreat near Kingston, and the media, which were onto the rift between the government and its labour allies, set up camp outside the resort. When the retreat ended on March 24, the premier issued a statement about the need to get the government's finances under control. "This will mean everybody has to pitch in and make some sacrifices," he said. Everybody, that is, except the corporate sector or the wealthy. He told the media to stand by for more announcements. On March 30, he met with his caucus in Niagara-on-the-Lake. Global TV was covering the event, and they asked me to be in the studio to comment following the premier's announcement. Rae stepped up to the microphones in midafternoon and told the assembled reporters that he was summoning all public-sector unions and employers to begin negotiating a social contract at a meeting scheduled for April 5. This accord, he said, "would involve wage rollbacks, mandatory days off without pay, early retirements, and any other ideas that the unions and employers may have." Failure to reach agreement, he warned, would result in thousands of layoffs. He further announced the unilateral suspension of all public-sector collective agreement negotiations until a social contract was in place.

Robert Fisher, the Global TV host, turned to me for my response. I was stunned. It was difficult to take it all in. I couldn't believe an NDP premier could do this to his allies, and I said so. I talked about the implications for labour and the party going forward, but I could not wait to get out of the studio to talk to my executive board. We needed time to formulate an appropriate response.

Judy Darcy summed it up in one word: "unbelievable." Rae's stated intention, to unilaterally suspend free collective bargaining for the public sector, was unprecedented. Never, in the history of labour relations in Canada, had a government suspended the right of workers to freely negotiate their wages, benefits, and working conditions. Everyone was furious: the CLC, OFL, teachers, university professors, police, firefighters, doctors, private- and public-sector unions — everyone. Rae had just walked into another crisis entirely of his own making. We weren't about to let him get away with it.

We announced that we would not meet April 5 unless he rescinded his ridiculous edict, which had absolutely no basis in law. If Rae wanted to suspend free collective bargaining, he would have to introduce legislation to achieve it. Two days later, he admitted he had made a mistake and that collective bargaining could continue while the Social Contract talks were underway.

The damage was done. Not only had Rae attempted to suspend the hard-won rights of his supporters, but he had also set us up for a public confrontation by demanding we attend an open forum with our adversaries. Everything employers had been trying to take away from the unions for the better part of two decades was on the table. We had a choice: either cave in to the government's demands and destroy our unions in the process, or fight the government and save the labour movement to fight another day. The decision was a no-brainer.

If Rae had truly been interested in a social accord, such as the one Judy Darcy and I had proposed at earlier meetings, he would have called us and explored the possibilities long before issuing his risible ultimatum.

The government had been shocked by the sustained ferocity of the business community's attacks, and Rae was determined to show the world that he was not in the pocket of organized labour. Hence the public circus called for on April 5. I'm sure he was desperately worried about the deficit and all its implications for the economic well-being of the province, but in politics choices always exist. Rae had decided to demonstrate his strength and independence by forcing his base to cough up $2 billion in wage concessions while corporations and the wealthy got off scot-free. In so doing, he committed himself to pursuing precisely the same solutions that Tories and Liberals alike had been imposing on public-sector workers for fifty years. The ramifications of the "invitation" he issued at Niagara-on-the-Lake were evident to anyone with a cursory knowledge of politics.

I had been president of CUPE Ontario for less than a year at that point. However, I knew enough to know that CUPE Ontario could not fight the government alone. The media were clamouring for labour's response, so I told them I would call on all public-sector unions in the province to form a coalition to fight Rae's so-called Social Contract. I didn't have a clue at the time whether the other public-sector unions would be interested. The next day, I received a call from Liz Barkley, president of the fifty-thousand-strong Ontario Secondary School Teachers' Federation (OSSTF), who had read my remarks and wanted to meet. She volunteered to phone the teachers' unions, and I agreed to phone the unions affiliated to the OFL. (OSSTF was not affiliated to the OFL at that time.) My first call was to Gord Wilson, president of the OFL, who was noncommittal. Nevertheless, I invited him to join us. I then phoned Fred Upshaw, president of Ontario Public Service Employees Union (OPSEU), which represented about a hundred thousand members. He was interested in a meeting. I then contacted all the public-sector unions on the OFL executive board and informed them that OSSTF, OPSEU, and CUPE were interested in setting up a common front to fight Rae's Social Contract and invited them to a meeting on April 4, in the old Holiday Inn just off the Don Valley Parkway.

We quickly put together the nucleus of a formidable coalition, with CUPE Ontario's 140,000 members, OPSEU's 100,000, and OSSTF's 50,000, together with another 100,000 members from the Elementary Teachers' Federation of Ontario (ETFO) and the Ontario English Catholic Teachers' Association (OECTA). At a brief, preliminary meeting in Liz Barkley's office on the morning of the fourth, Liz Barkley, Fred Upshaw, Judy Darcy, and I decided to keep the agenda simple and just ask advice from whoever showed up. Our overriding objective was to preserve the principle of free collective bargaining and to protect public services. We hoped for a good showing from public-sector union leadership and the media. We were not let down.

Every major media outlet in the province was waiting for us at the hotel. Several hundred public-sector union leaders from big and small unions showed up. The mood was one of shock and disbelief.

Most who spoke at the meeting were furious that a social democratic government was forcing the unions to defend their long-held rights in a public arena against attacks from employers, right-wing media types, and the government itself. Every union leader in the room agreed that we had to fight back collectively. It was agreed that Liz Barkley, Fred Upshaw, and I would lead the coalition, joined later by Vanessa Kelly from the Canadian Union of Education Workers (CUEW) to ensure gender parity in the leadership. We called ourselves the Public Services Coalition (PSC). The brewing confrontation was the lead story on all the newscasts that evening and in the next morning's newspapers.

I awoke on April 5 around 6:00 a.m., eighteen years to the day since I bade farewell to my family and boarded a plane in Dublin bound for Toronto. I thought about my decision, what I had left behind, and I wondered what my life would have been like had I not emigrated. Would I still be a plumber, or would I have moved on to another career? What would have been different for Sheila and our three daughters? Then, as I always did, I reflected on how good Canada has been to us. Once I had ridden around Dublin on a scabber's bike. Now I was about to attend the premier's summit on behalf of 140,000 CUPE members and the 950,000 broader public-sector members of our Public Services Coalition. I left my home in Whitby with Helen O'Regan's words ringing in my ears: "Promise me you will never forget your roots."

CUPE's staff and elected leaders met at the Sutton Place Hotel, kitty-corner to the MacDonald Block where the summit was taking place. In the lobby I bumped into Judy Darcy, who was wearing a bright canary-yellow jacket. She noticed the look on my face and said, "We have an advantage over men in the range of colours we can wear." I smiled and said, "You won't be missed in the crowd," and she winked and said, "That's the point!"

We entered the main hall, where we found tables set out in a gigantic rectangle with microphones placed at intervals. Pandemonium ensued when it became clear that the seating capacity was for about fifty people max. More than 250 employer reps, union reps, and our PSC partners had shown up. The start was delayed while more chairs were brought in and decisions were made about who would be seated at the table and who would be relegated to the rear. In the end, CUPE was front and centre, directly across from the premier. Gord Wilson, who had shown up after all, was seated beside Judy Darcy and me. Others arranged themselves as best they could, but it was an unsatisfactory start to an unsatisfactory meeting.

Premier Rae entered the hall with a media entourage. He made his way around the tables as usual, his left hand stuffed into his suit pocket. He stopped to say a few words to Darcy, Wilson, and me, which made sense from a PR perspective: he wanted to demonstrate that we, among his most vocal critics, were still on somewhat friendly terms. Just the same, the initial chaos and subsequent glad-handing delay did not help the NDP come across as competent managers.

Of course, the entire summit was really just a public relations stunt. It gave Rae an opportunity to trot out his "three-legged stool" theory and send a signal to the media — and more importantly to the opposition parties — that he was getting tough with his union allies. Dennis Timbrell, the Tory president of the Ontario Hospital Association (OHA), knew what Rae was up to and mischievously presented a list of concessions he would like to see exacted from the hospital unions. Timbrell, ever a wily politician, also knew that people like Michael Hurley (OCHU) were sitting in the hall observing and listening to every comment from both employers and unions. In effect, Timbrell was using Rae's carnival to put pressure on his opposite number in the union. Rae announced that Michael Decter would be heading up the negotiations for the government. Decter, who had worked for the Howard Pawley government in Manitoba, was a self-made millionaire with a book about how he made his money in the stock market. He was a big proponent of outsourcing non-medical hospital services and had collaborated with Frances Lankin to reform Ontario's healthcare system. The reforms had led to hospital amalgamations and reductions in the number of hospital beds, especially in rural areas. The jobs he outsourced were jobs our CUPE, SEIU (Service Employees International Union), and OPSEU members were losing. This was the guy with whom we would be forced to negotiate to achieve Rae's Social Contract!

Decter and the Rae government had a serious problem: 90 percent of public-sector employees worked for the MUSH sectors and not directly for the Ontario government. Therefore, the government had no legal standing with respect to collective bargaining except in respect to its own employees who were members of OPSEU. This amounted to no more than 90,000 employees out of the 950,000 who could be impacted by a voluntary social contract. Both the premier and his finance minister had stated repeatedly that the public-sector employees had to find $2 billion in savings by taking unpaid days off and other such measures. How this was to be accomplished without legislation was unclear. Furthermore, CUPE is heavily decentralized; the collective bargaining rights rest with local unions in the five different sectors. CUPE had more than one thousand individual collective agreements in Ontario. My old local, CUPE 1000, rightly argued that they should not be covered by the Social Contract because Ontario Hydro did not receive transfer payments from the Ontario government — it was independent of the government. Rae's insistence that Hydro workers should also be forced to take unpaid days was an indication that the Social Contract was anything but voluntary.

The meeting broke up following an exchange with Rae over process. The unions wanted a central table, where we could keep an eye on organizations such as the Ontario Hospital Association, the Ontario Public School Boards' Association, and the Association of Municipalities of Ontario, which each viewed the Social Contract as a way to strip our collective agreements of basic rights and benefits. Needless to say, the employers wanted nothing to do with a central table, where consensus would have to be reached among all sectors and between employers and employees. The premier sided, not surprisingly, with the employers. He announced the formation of seven sectoral tables and indicated that he expected a progress report to be handed to the government on April 19, in time for Floyd Laughren's budget. The totally unrealistic time frame was just one more indication that Rae was willing to railroad us to his intended conclusion.

When the meeting adjourned, I was gobsmacked, not just by the sheer number of reporters waiting outside, but also by the diversity of organizations they represented. They came not just from Ontario, but from across Canada, the United States, and Europe. Their presence was another form of pressure. Clearly, there was no way on God's green earth that this negotiation was going to be a voluntary exercise, no matter what Bob Rae said to the contrary. He had put himself in a situation from which he either had to emerge with what he promised or become, in political terms, toast.

The leaders of the PSC decided to enter into discussions with the government only after we had hammered out a common position. We rejected the April 19 deadline as unrealistic, and we began internal discussions to develop a set of principles we wanted the government to agree to before we joined the talks. Meanwhile, the government negotiators, Michael Decter, Ross McClellan, and Peter Warrian, met with individual unions while the unions embarked on their own sectoral discussions.

It was a challenge to keep the coalition meetings on track as personalities and egos began to surface. Ted Roscoe, leader of SEIU, was viewed by most of the coalition partners as an unreliable ally, too willing to cave to Rae's demands. Roscoe had a bombastic personality and was given to shouting and pounding the table — he was not unlike the former Soviet leader Nikita Khrushchev, both in stature and in style. His tirades soon wore thin and, as he was launching into a tantrum at one early meeting, I stopped him mid-sentence and told him we had all had enough of his table-thumping and angry outbursts. The room erupted in spontaneous applause. To his credit, Roscoe apologized and became more constructive.

The relationship between OPSEU and CUPE was always competitive because the two unions represented workers in similar and overlapping professions, including hospitals, children's aid societies, paramedics, and so on. Fred Upshaw, president of OPSEU, was one of my co-leaders in the PSC, and everyone in the coalition was worried about what he and his union were up to in their discussions with the government. Hardly a meeting passed without Upshaw informing the rest of us that OPSEU was unique because the NDP government was their employer, and therefore they had an obligation to talk with them directly. While this was true, it nonetheless made everyone nervous that OPSEU would cut a deal with the government that would become the template for the rest.

Dr. Michael Thorburn, president of the Ontario Medical Association, showed up at one of our meetings. He was introduced as a guest and allowed to sit throughout the proceedings. This became a media story and a point of disagreement with Gord Wilson of the OFL. The OFL had not been a player during the Social Contract discussions, except when Julie Davis, OFL secretary-treasurer, arranged for Judy Darcy to talk with Minister Frances Lankin or another minister. Wilson was viewed with suspicion by most public-sector unions because of his tepid response to Rae's attack on collective bargaining rights. While Wilson was from the CAW, he had been at war with his own union for the previous ten years. He and Buzz Hargrove did not see eye to eye, nor did Wilson get along with Bob White. Consequently, Wilson sought alliances with the rest of the private-sector unions — or whomever he could separate from the coalition. He managed to bring Roscoe from SEIU and Upshaw from OPSEU into his camp. Thus,

Left to right: Me, Bob White, CLC president, and Fred Hahn, CUPE Ontario secretary treasurer, in Windsor in 2006.

the Public Services Coalition meetings became a complicated struggle between unions that wanted a genuine discussion aimed at finding a workable solution to the monumental problem Rae had created and those who were willing to cave so the NDP could save face. Wilson was seen as playing both sides of the street.

The coalition met weekly throughout April, while continuing to boycott the Social Contract talks. Through the media the government stated repeatedly that everything was on the table, and we took it at its word. Together, we developed a seventeen-page position paper in response to the government's three-legged stool demands. Our proposals included tax adjustments, a wage freeze, government downsizing through attrition, voluntary days off without pay, contracting-in of services to save money, and a joint task force to identify government waste.

Our research showed that twenty-three thousand profitable businesses had not paid a penny in taxes the previous year. Accordingly, we were looking for a minimum corporate tax. In addition, we felt it was time to bring in inheritance taxes and to increase the tax paid by the wealthiest 10 percent of the population. If these two measures — which were NDP policy — had been acted on, they would have yielded an additional $3.4 billion in government revenue annually. When added to the proposals we made for government downsizing through a temporary hiring freeze, a wage freeze, and voluntary time off without pay, the savings amounted to $6.4 billion — far more than the $2 billion the government was originally trying to achieve from public sector workers through their social contract and without cutting public services.

We asked the premier to meet with us so we could present our proposals to him. The meeting took place on May 7 in the Royal York Hotel. I distinctly recall sitting by the circular staircase in the foyer as I, along with a few of my colleagues, waited for the premier to show up. The hotel lobby was full of media with their cameras and microphones. My mind flashed back to 1975, when I had nervously waited in the same spot for my first Canadian job interview. How times had changed! The premier arrived and was immediately engulfed by a mob of photographers and reporters, and together we were ushered into the meeting room. The reporters got their photos, videos, and sound bites and then departed. Rae was cordial and talkative but he rejected our proposals for reforming the tax system outright. Liz Barkley leaned over while he was talking and whispered, "I can see light at the end of the tunnel. Unfortunately," she said, "it's another train." I laughed at the joke, but she was right, and it wasn't funny at all.

Following the meeting, Decter, and by extension the government, made the first in a series of mistakes. First, they issued an ultimatum to the unions. Negotiate a social contract by June 4, he said, with all the concessions demanded by the NDP, or face between twenty thousand and forty thousand layoffs.

This was just plain stupid. It was yet another indication that the government was clueless about the complexity involved in negotiating collective agreements with 950,000 public-sector workers over whom it had no legal jurisdiction. Floyd Laughren was still insisting that the government would not introduce legislation to extract the concessions, claiming they would be achieved by cutting transfer payments if the talks failed. But we had no doubt that this government was willing to use legislation against us. It seemed apparent, however, that Decter and Rae felt they were getting strong enough signals from some of the unions to risk rolling the dice by setting a deadline. I know that in their discussions with CUPE, Peter Warrian and Michael Decter conveyed the impression that it wasn't CUPE and its relatively low-paid workers they were going after, but rather the more highly paid teachers, nurses, doctors, and Hydro workers. Warrian, Decter, and the government implied that they were prepared to exempt low-paid workers from the provisions of the Social Contract — thereby driving a wedge between the different unions. As part of this strategy, the government negotiators moved the low income cut-off (LICO) up to $25,000 from $22,500 and eventually raised it to $30,000 to try to entice CUPE to break ranks. Workers earning less than $30,000 annually would be exempt from the Social Contract.

Finally, the PSC came up with our set of conditions to be met before we would enter formal discussions with the government. We demanded that the government acknowledge that they had no authority to unilaterally suspend collective bargaining in the broader public sector. Accordingly, we wanted a commitment that the government would not introduce legislation to impose a social contract in the event that the talks failed. We insisted that a central table be set up to ensure that government, employers, and unions could not engage in deal-making that undercut another coalition partner. And lastly, we had information that some employers were rushing to lay off workers before the Social Contract was agreed, and so we asked for a moratorium on layoffs while discussions were in progress. The government agreed to all four conditions.

The first central-table meeting was a farce held on May 12. Chairs were set out for thirty-three people, eleven each for representatives of government, the employers, and the unions. One hundred and fifty people showed up, resulting in an unseemly scramble as everyone tried to grab a seat at the table. Needless to say, no meaningful dialogue occurred. The employers used the chaos as an excuse to say they wouldn't be coming back, so there could be no central table. And this was the government's second serious mistake. A central table was one of labour's key demands, and yet they allowed this shamble to unfold.

Since the premier's announcement on March 30, CUPE met weekly with leaders from its five sectors. Because of the union's decentralized structure, the meetings involved more than one hundred leaders. The local leadership — not unnaturally — grew worried and suspicious when the media reported that progress was being made in discussions with the government. They were especially suspicious of the sectoral tables, the concern being that employers would make the greatest headway there in their drive for concessions. The CUPE locals were most worried about job security, but they were not prepared to take a 5 percent cut in compensation, either. They were, however, willing to take time off without pay. We all knew of individual members who wanted to take off as much as six months in order to work on a project or simply to travel. If their requests were pooled, they conceivably could be used either to eliminate or to greatly reduce the number of mandatory days off for other employees. The idea of setting up a jobs registry was also debated. In this proposal, a laid-off municipal worker in Hamilton could be hired from the registry in Toronto. The locals even were willing to consider a wage freeze or early retirement incentives that would have the effect of reducing the size of the public sector. With good will, there existed the basis for an agreement that would have provided the NDP and labour with the proverbial win-win result.

We floated these ideas at various times. Nothing ever came of them. The PSC continued to meet with the government week in and week out with the same lack of progress. My first CUPE Ontario convention since getting elected in 1992 was a raucous affair in Hamilton at the end of May. After my speech, which was well received, delegates were lined up six-deep at the microphones. I had been constantly in front of the media for almost three months, and CUPE Ontario was becoming a significant political presence. The membership voted in support of a resolution calling on CUPE not to go to the sectoral tables because the membership felt we would be knuckling under to the employers. In the hospital sector, for example, most of the bargaining on behalf of the hospitals is conducted between the Ontario Hospital Association and several healthcare-sector unions. Each hospital ratifies the collective agreement with its union based on the agreement hammered out at the central bargaining table. The CUPE locals were afraid that those collective agreements would be opened at a sectoral table. And who could blame them? The CUPE Ontario leadership was given clear instructions to suspend sectoral table discussions.

June 4 was approaching fast. CUPE had indicated that we would not sign any document ahead of the deadline, and that we would participate only at a central table or in one-on-one discussions. The hour of decision was drawing near.

All PSC member unions, except CUPE, were in discussion with the government at sectoral tables. CUPE continued to engage the government negotiators one on one on a daily basis. We floated the idea that if we accepted the government's wage- and hiring-freeze proposal, then we would expect concessions in return, namely job security and access to voluntary days off for members who wanted it, including long-term leaves of absence. In addition, we proposed that the government move the low income cut-off (LICO) from $25,000 to $30,000. Peter Warrian appeared to be open to the idea;

apparently, he had already run it by the number crunchers. From a fiscal standpoint, he said, it would work in achieving the government's stated goal; but, he added, "I want to be honest in that it may not be politically achievable as the opposition parties are calling for mandatory legislation."

As the government's deadline approached, the media camped inside the hotel, in the corridors and lobby, and outside, in the street. They knew the NDP government's future would be decided in the next forty-eight hours. The circumstances made it very difficult to conduct any sort of quiet diplomacy with the negotiators. CUPE continued to worry that one of the PSC unions would give in to the pressure and sign on the dotted line, dragging the entire 950,000-strong public sector down with them.

On the morning of June 3, CUPE was still optimistic. The day before, Peter Warrian told us to expect a visit from Michael Decter at 11:00 a.m. The CUPE delegation, consisting of Judy Darcy, Jim Anderson, me, and three staff advisors, arrived at the hotel at 9:00 a.m. in anticipation of his arrival. The tension was palpable. Television camera operators planted around the periphery of the hotel were watching for the clip that would make it onto prime time — one crew actually followed me into the men's room before I told them to beat it! Both Judy Darcy and I understood the significance of the mandate our members had given to us. We believed we had hammered out the basis for a constructive solution to the problem the government had presented. It hadn't been easy. Trying to negotiate an agreement with 950,000 public-sector workers, representing ninety different organizations, and 2,500 collective agreements involving thousands of local unions was madness — and all in front of the cameras. Yet we felt we had come through with solid ideas for cost savings, while also meeting the unions' goals of preserving our Charter rights and providing job security over the three-year life of the Social Contract.

Eleven a.m. rolled around, and then 11:30 and 11:45. There was no sign of Michael Decter. Gradually it dawned on us that we had been sucked into some sort of a Machiavellian manoeuvre by the government negotiators. And we were pissed.

Judy Darcy was furious when she phoned Peter Warrian and asked where the hell Decter was. Warrian had the gall to reply that Decter had knocked on our hotel room door and gotten no answer. I immediately opened the door and asked the reporters camped out there whether Decter had come by. Every one of them said no. Neither Decter nor anyone else had knocked on our door.

It was now clear the government was going around CUPE, calculating there was a better deal to be had at one of the sectoral tables. I went back to my room and turned on the television in time to see an interview with Liz Barkley from OSSTF. In her usual straightforward manner, she mused about the rumour that CUPE had cut a deal with the government! *The devious bastards!* I thought. Decter and his crew had segregated the unions into separate silos, feeding each a different story and fuelling the rumour mill! They were playing us off one another! From her comments and body language onscreen, I knew that Liz was royally ticked off. Between us, Liz and I represented 50 percent of the PSC leadership, and we were both feeling betrayed not only by the process but also the shenanigans of the government negotiators.

A meeting of the PSC was scheduled for 7:00 p.m. The six o'clock news on all television stations led with the same story: a deal between the public-sector unions and the NDP government was all but guaranteed. This claim could only have been planted by the government's spin doctors, unless, that is, a union had gotten a deal that they had not shared with other members of the PSC. At ten minutes to seven, I left my hotel room for the meeting room. As the elevator doors opened, I was enveloped by media in a blaze of television lights and camera flashes. As I made my way through the small army of reporters, I heard the unmistakable voice of the *Toronto Star*'s crusty Queen's Park reporter, Richard Brennan, yelling above the crowd, "Hey, Sid! Are you gonna sell out the workers tonight?" I whipped around, looked him directly in the eye, and said, "I've never sold out a worker in my life and I do not intend to begin tonight."

He smiled — he'd gotten the rise out of me that he'd hoped for — and then the media frenzy became more intense. "Mr. Ryan," bellowed a woman from the back of the pack. "Does this mean you will be voting against the government's Social Contract tonight?" I replied, "You will have to wait and see."

Judy Darcy was already seated in our meeting room. The tables were set up to form a rectangle, with seats for about forty people. Behind the head table, there was seating for about 150 local union leaders. Out of the corner of my eye I spotted Helen O'Regan. She grabbed me by the arm and said, "I'm so glad you're the leader in these times. I've heard CUPE will be voting no tonight and I just want you to know that I think you've made the right decision." Before she turned away, she squeezed my arm and whispered, "I knew you wouldn't forget."

At 7:00 p.m. the media was asked to leave the meeting room; the doors were locked and the meeting began. Liz Barkley acted as chair. (This duty was rotated among the four PSC leaders.) She had avoided me since I came into the room — still under the false impression that CUPE had cut a deal allowing collective agreements to be opened up and mandatory Rae Days imposed. She gave an impassioned speech explaining why OSSTF could not accept the Social Contract. All teachers were being hit hard. Young teachers who were frozen on the ten-year progression grid were especially under duress: it was estimated that the Social Contract would cost some of them as much as $80,000 over the course of their careers. When Liz finished her opening remarks, the room broke into thunderous applause and it was obvious that the Social Contract was in trouble.

I spoke next on behalf of CUPE. The room fell silent as I took the microphone. From the looks I received, it was clear that most of the people in the room had heard the same rumour that had earlier disturbed Liz. I began by recounting the day's events, not excepting Michael Decter's failure to show up as promised. I said that CUPE had kept the PSC informed of our discussions every step of the way. Our coalition partners knew that we had a mandate against going to sectoral tables, but that we were holding face-to-face discussions with the government negotiators. I explained that our primary goal was to achieve job security for the life of any social contract that we entered into.

I got to the heart of the matter. "No self-respecting trade union leader could sell out their membership by allowing signed collective agreements to be ripped open." My words were greeted by murmurs of approval. With passionate conviction, I ended by saying, "Especially not by a government we helped to elect! CUPE says no to the Social Contract!" This caused the room to erupt in hoots, hollers, table-thumping, and cheers.

Liz Barkley jumped up from the table and kissed me. Her eyes were full of tears. The die was cast. Fifty percent of the PSC leadership had said an emphatic no. Vanessa Kelly spoke next. The university sector was dead set against a social contract from the very beginning, and they were not about to change their minds now. Her members, too, were saying no to Rae's Social Contract.

All eyes turned to Fred Upshaw. In typical fashion, he talked about history and what had brought us to this point. He talked about his union and how they made decisions. He told us that he had summoned one hundred leaders from OPSEU to the Royal York Hotel and that they were in a room waiting to hear what the other unions were thinking. He asked that we not take any votes just yet, but allow him time to consult with his leadership group before making a decision. Everybody agreed. Fred left the meeting and we continued to hear from the different unions around the table. The pattern was the same: the leader spoke and the answer was no. Each time a "no" was recorded, the room erupted in applause.

Upshaw returned after about fifteen minutes. The room fell silent. He spoke slowly in his deep baritone voice and said, "My one hundred leaders are proud to join with the rest of the public-sector unions in saying no to Bob Rae's Social Contract!" Again, the union leaders in the room cheered, and we all began singing the union anthem, "Solidarity Forever." The media, overhearing the row, burst through the doors without invitation. In an instant, they were everywhere — a few photographers even jumped onto the tables as they sought the best vantage points for their pictures.

Eventually, the pandemonium died down. Reporters set up their mound of microphones at the head table and each of the union leaders spoke for a few minutes about what the refusal to endorse the Social Contract meant going forward. For my part, I talked about the hurt that trade unions were feeling, having been dragged through this sham process, and the damage it had done to the relationship between labour and the NDP. My final comment was played over and over on all the television and radio programs for the next forty-eight hours: "Bob Rae," I said, "I will never forgive you for what you have done to working men and women in this province."

While we may have been singing, and celebrating about our solidarity that June evening, I harboured no illusion about what this meant for the NDP government in Ontario. We had elected a government we expected to align itself with the fundamental principles of free collective bargaining. A freely negotiated collective agreement between two parties is sacrosanct, and no government should ever tamper with it. Equally important is the principle that if there is pain to be shared, for example, by cutting deficits, that pain will be shared across the board, not just by the workers, but also by corporations, high-income earners, and managers. Above all, unions have a right to expect such equal treatment from a government that claims to adhere to the principles of social democracy and workers' rights. Any violation of these principles is simply a betrayal of the working men and women who elected them.

Unfortunately, things went from bad to worse. The Rae government introduced legislation in the House that gave employers the power to rip open signed collective agreements. The message to public-sector unions was clear: either acquiesce to the demands of the NDP's Social Contract, or deal with the whims of every public-sector employer in Ontario. The one step the NDP promised at the beginning of the process never to take, they took at the end. This was the first time in Canadian labour history that any government had passed legislation to open signed collective agreements. And it was a step taken by a premier who had masqueraded as the champion of the working class.

The fallout from the debacle was almost immediate. Both Buzz Hargrove and I resigned from the Premier's Labour/Management Advisory Council. Julie Davis, secretary treasurer of the OFL, resigned as president of the Ontario NDP. Her resignation must have been a huge personal blow to Bob Rae because she co-chaired his victorious 1990 election campaign. Several unions and key individuals disaffiliated from the NDP and a major split developed in the labour movement. Most private-sector unions, including United Steelworkers, United Food and Commercial Workers (UFCW), Communications, Energy and Paperworkers (CEP), and a number of smaller unions, such as International Association of Machinists (IAM), sided with the NDP. On the other side stood the public-sector unions and the CAW.

The split played out in November at the OFL convention when an executive board motion to disaffiliate from the NDP caused a walkout by the private-sector unions supportive of the Rae government. The walkout meant the convention no longer met the quorum requirements of the constitution, so no further business could be conducted. A statement by the private-sector unions (mostly international unions) supporting the NDP and written on pink paper was circulated to the 1,500 delegates prior to the preplanned walkout. The document talked about the good pieces of legislation the NDP had passed and explained why the unions that signed the document would continue to support the NDP. The document made it clear that they did not support any shifting of union resources into the building of coalitions. It stated, "While coalitions and grassroots organizations have an important place in fighting the corporate agenda, we do not support a shift of scarce resources away from our party and towards other groups. We will not co-operate with a redirection of our per-capitas as called for in the Federation Policy." The wounds inflicted by the Social Contract were still too fresh for public-sector unions to forgive. The signatories to the document became known as the "pink paper unions." The rift has lasted to this very day and complicates efforts to initiate action whenever it's called for by the progressive wing of the labour movement. In 2009, as the newly elected president of the OFL, I learned that the pink paper unions were as adamantly opposed to social unionism today as they were back in 1993. This remains a major barrier in building the common front coalition of community allies required to challenge the current Ford government at Queen's Park.

In early 1995 the NDP government was coming to the end of its mandate. They waited as long as they legally could before calling an election. In midsummer, Bob Rae phoned me and said that he would like to explore the possibility of our working together to re-elect his government. Despite our differences over the Social Contract, he believed his government would be a better alternative to one headed by the Conservative leader, Mike Harris. Harris had released his party's platform months earlier. His so-called "Common Sense Revolution" would set a brutal agenda for the province. I agreed with Rae that it would be preferable to re-elect his government than see either the Tories or Liberals come to power, but I told him we had some serious issues to talk through. He agreed and said that he was talking to other people to arrange a meeting at his house the following Friday. He concluded the conversation by saying he would get back to me to confirm the date and time. The call never came.

About a month later, I received a phone call from a staffer in Mike Harris's office. He wanted to know if I'd be prepared to meet with Harris to discuss his platform. I was reluctant to agree. Frankly, I suspected Harris was up to no good. When I received another call from Harris's office a week later, I agreed to meet him in his office at Queen's Park, but I insisted there be no media in attendance. I took my communications person, Shannon McManus, with me because I suspected Harris would tip off the press in spite of our agreement to keep it private. Sure enough, when we arrived, we were met by a mob of photographers and reporters.

The meeting lasted about thirty minutes. Harris went over his platform, and I peppered him with questions about welfare cuts, and cuts to healthcare and education. Then he popped the question: Would I consider running for the Conservatives in the next election? I laughed out loud and said, "Sorry, Mike, you've got the wrong guy." After a few minutes of small talk, during which he admitted he would have been surprised had I accepted his offer, he asked to be excused for a moment, and I heard him whispering to his aides in the backroom. I knew we had to get out of there. I turned to Shannon and said, "We're being set up. We need to get to the media before he puts his spin on this."

We left. As I expected, the first question shouted out was, "Sid! Are you running for the Conservatives in the next election?" I answered: "Mr. Harris has indeed asked me to run for his party, but I turned him down, telling him he had a mean-spirited agenda that would hurt Ontario's most vulnerable."

The media scrum lasted about ten minutes, during which time Harris was left cooling his heels in his office as I pounded his platform. After I'd finished denouncing it, Harris emerged from his office. With stooped shoulders and his trademark aw-shucks, puppy-dog look, he said, "Well, I guess Mr. Ryan won't be running for the Progressive Conservatives anytime soon." He blathered for a minute or two about his platform and how good it would be for unionized workers and the hard-working men and women in Ontario. The incident ended in a sort of political standoff. Harris had set out to exploit the rift between me and Bob Rae, and I turned the tables by excoriating his disastrous platform. At best, mine was a hollow victory.

On June 8, 1995, Mike Harris won the election with a massive majority, with eighty-two seats. The NDP was reduced from seventy-four seats to seventeen, and Lyn McLeod's Liberals were reduced from thirty-six seats to thirty. Harris had a free hand to implement his agenda. On July 21, the new minister of finance, Ernie Eves, held a press conference and gave an economic update. Predictably, he said the books were in worse shape than the previous government had indicated. The deficit was much bigger and revenues much lower than predicted. He announced $1.9 billion in cuts to everything from healthcare to education and social programs. The cruellest of all cuts came to the most vulnerable on social assistance, whose rates were cut by a whopping 21.6 percent. In addition, a workfare program was announced that required those on welfare to find volunteer work in order to collect a welfare cheque. Workfare was the mean-spirited face of the Harris government, and I swore I would do everything in my power to kill this program. To my astonishment, the United Way announced they would partner with the Harris Tories to help implement his odious workfare program. I immediately called for a labour boycott of United Way, which set off a firestorm in the media.

It didn't take long for the United Way to back down when they realized I had the backing of most district labour councils. I next set my sights on municipal councils around the province and asked them to pass motions opposing workfare. Harris's mean-spirited program was more or less dead on arrival.

Bob Rae had blown his almost five years in office by turning against his base. In the process, he went where no premier in Canadian history had ever gone, giving employers the power to open signed collective agreements. A few months after losing the election, he resigned as leader of the Ontario NDP. He tore up his NDP membership and went home to the Liberal Party, a traitor to the cause. The "pink paper unions" who had supported him had egg splattered all over their faces.

Chapter 5
AT HOME IN THE WORLD

The labour movement has always had an international dimension: the injustices and inequities that unrestrained capitalism visits on workers in one country typically have analogues abroad. And sometimes issues of social justice transcend economics. At the turn of the last century, two of the world's greatest trade union leaders, Jim Larkin of Liverpool and James Connolly of Glasgow, were internationalists who found themselves fighting for liberty and social justice on the streets in Dublin and the shipyards of Belfast. In my years as a union leader, first with CUPE Ontario and later with the Ontario Federation of Labour, I often found myself making common cause with oppressed and disenfranchised peoples far outside Canada's borders. I believe it is important for Canadian union leaders to look beyond our borders and help fight injustice and intolerance wherever in the world we find it.

IRELAND DELEGATION, 1998

One cause close to my heart was the plight of the Irish Catholic minority in Northern Ireland. By 1998 a quarter of a century had passed since the grim afternoon when British paratroopers opened fire on a few thousand demonstrators in Derry. As mentioned, Bloody Sunday and the Troubles that followed were among the factors that led me to leave Ireland in 1975. There were many factors, of course, but the murderous sectarian confrontations in the North made the land of my forebears seem an inhospitable place for a young man starting out. For years, while I started a new life in Canada, nothing in Northern Ireland seemed to change — at least, not for the better. As the century drew to a close, the tensions got worse.

The violence associated with the Troubles was not tied to a single day, but the parades traditionally held annually on July 12 had become a flashpoint. These parades were organized by the Orange Lodge, a fraternal organization that brought together captains of industry, church leaders, politicians, and workers belonging to the three main Protestant denominations. The glue that kept its members together was their shared desire to maintain the political union with the government of the United Kingdom and to remain loyal subjects of the Crown. That notion was also shot through with fierce anti-Catholic dogma.

For the Orange Order, the Glorious Twelfth commemorated the victory in 1690 of William of Orange over the Catholic pretender, James II, in the Battle of the Boyne. That victory represents, in effect, Protestantism's triumph over Catholicism in Ireland. The annual marches, which often cut through Catholic neighbourhoods, inspired some participants to acts of provocation and violence against the Catholic community. A few years earlier, in 1994, the Garvaghy Road Residents' Coalition in Portadown, forty-five minutes west of Belfast, had given permission for a march by the Orange Order to pass through the Catholic community, on condition that the parade was respectful. The Reverend Ian Paisley, leader of the Democratic Unionist Party, and David Trimble, leader of the Ulster Unionist Party, dishonoured that commitment by linking arms and dancing a triumphalist jig down the lower portion of the Garvaghy Road. Two years later, in 1996, Mo Mowlam, secretary of state for Northern Ireland, allowed another parade down the Garvaghy Road. Two thousand British soldiers beat Catholic protesters off the streets before the march began. The British Army stationed armoured personnel carriers bumper to bumper along the entire length of the road, making most of the Catholic community residents virtual prisoners in their own homes. The parade sparked six straight days and nights of the worst riots in Northern Ireland since the 1970s. Homes and businesses were razed, cars were hijacked and set on fire, at least one man was killed, and scores of civilians and police were injured.

In 1998, spurred by the escalating violence, the British government made a concerted effort to resolve the conflict. In April a historic peace agreement that called for a power-sharing mechanism between Catholics and Protestants and between the Irish and British governments was signed by all parties in Northern Ireland. As part of the agreement, the British government also established a Parades Commission to regulate and approve the timing and route for future marches. There would, of course, be more marches. Not everyone was content to make peace.

In early 1998 Alan McConnell, a Toronto lawyer and president of the Information on Ireland Campaign, asked me if I would join an international delegation that would travel to Northern Ireland in early July to observe the Orange Order parades on the Garvaghy Road in Portadown and the Lower Ormeau Road in Belfast. Our purpose was to encourage dialogue and a peaceful resolution, to record events and incidents at flashpoints throughout our visit, and to write a report that would be handed over to the British, Irish, and Canadian governments. The delegation would also meet with senior Irish and British politicians to discuss the peace process. I agreed to go because I felt that, as Canadians, we would be viewed as more neutral than delegations from Britain or the United States.

On July 3, 1998, our delegation touched down at Belfast International Airport. Among the eighteen-member group were Warren Allmand, former solicitor general in the Pierre Trudeau government; Daniel Turp, Bloc Québécois MP; Cindy Wasser, criminal defence lawyer; John Murphy, president of the Power Workers Union; John O'Toole, Progressive Conservative MPP in the Harris government; and Cindy Stone, psychotherapist and author. I was happy to be back in Ireland, but I had a bad feeling in the pit of my stomach. This promised to be a very difficult trip.

On our way from the airport we passed several burnt-out cars, stark evidence of the tension and violence gripping the city. It was drizzling rain when we arrived at a tiny house on Hatfield Street, just off the Lower Ormeau Road, for a lunch provided by the Lower Ormeau Concerned Community (LOCC) organization. The bed and breakfast I had stayed in when I'd worked in Belfast as a teenager was within walking distance, and I once again felt the grave apprehension I had felt in 1968. I did not have to wait long for my concerns to be justified. Around 2:00 p.m., we set off for Portadown, travelling in two convoys so as not to draw undue attention. On our way into Portadown our own convoy was stopped twice by the Royal Ulster Constabulary (RUC) dressed in Darth Vader–type body armour and armed with automatic weapons. The RUC did not appear to welcome the presence of international observers.

We were driven to the Garvaghy Road Community Centre, a grey pebble-dashed one-storey structure teeming with kids and adults of all ages. The situation was chaotic and clearly the residents felt they were under siege and in danger. We were briefed by Rosemary Nelson, a lawyer, who had represented the family of a young Catholic man, Robert Hamill, who had been brutally kicked to death in Portadown earlier in the year while members of the RUC looked on and did nothing. Nelson gave the delegation a brief history of the area conflict. For more than 150 years, she said, the Orangemen marched from their lodge in Portadown to attend a service in the ancient and picturesque Drumcree Church, located on a hill overlooking the town. Following the service, they marched from the church down the Garvaghy Road, on their way back to their lodge. When the Garvaghy Road became heavily populated by Catholic families, who increasingly viewed the parades as an act of degrading triumphalism, problems arose. According to Nelson, the march normally took place one week prior to the twelfth, so this year the march was planned for Sunday, July 5. Prior to our arrival, however, the Parades Commission had announced the Orange Order would not be allowed to march down the Garvaghy Road on the return leg of their parade. This decree instantly became a test of political power between the British government and the Orange Order. Many people believed the turmoil created by the Orange Order over the Drumcree march was, in fact, a smokescreen meant to hide its real objective, which was to undermine the peace agreement. The Reverend Ian Paisley, among others, had made plain his vehement opposition to the agreement.

Each member of the Canadian delegation — with the exceptions of John Murphy and me — was assigned a family to billet with over the next three days. John and I, however, were sent to a small row house on the lower end of the Garvaghy Road, whose owner had gone on vacation to avoid the "marching season." Alarm bells didn't go off in our heads until we arrived at the block of tiny terraced houses. Our house was only a few hundred feet from the Loyalist community and members of the Orange Order had erected a massive arch in commemoration of the Battle of the Boyne right outside our front door. The British Army checkpoint, complete with armoured vehicles, was a hundred yards up the road, between us and the Catholic community, so in essence Murphy and I were on the wrong side of the dividing line. Murphy graciously offered me the larger front bedroom in the two-bedroom house. *What a nice guy*, I thought, until he winked at me and said, "I don't want a fuckin' petrol bomb coming through my window in the middle of the night." I hardly slept a wink until we left that house several days later.

Murphy, Cindy Stone, and I were assigned the shift between midnight and 6:00 a.m. to patrol and observe the community. We first made our way down to where the British Army had blockaded the road from Drumcree Church to the Garvaghy Road. It was a typically miserable Irish night: the temperature was in the low teens and there was a light drizzle, never heavy enough to warrant covering up, but just enough to make everything feel damp. The British Army had built a twelve-foot-high barricade that stretched from one side of the road to the other. In the fields adjacent to the road, they had dug a six-foot-deep trench and filled it with water. Behind this moat were strung three rows of razor wire that could rip a body to shreds. While we were speaking to the commanding officer we heard three loud cracks ring out in the midnight air. The officer warned us to move on; there were indications that a sniper was active in the area. The next day, the sniper was shown on television, crouched among the Orange Order protesters who were camped in the fields around Drumcree Church.

We spent the next few hours walking through the community, struck by how many people, including young children, were out on the streets. Nobody could sleep. One hundred thousand Orangemen were expected to descend on Drumcree from across Northern Ireland. People we encountered whispered about their fear of violence. A postman talked about the threats he received delivering mail in the Protestant part of the town. But the biggest fear of all was that the independent Parades Commission would cave in to the Orange Lodge pressure and allow one hundred thousand Orangemen to march down the Garvaghy Road.

At 12:30 p.m. on July 5 we heard the famous Lambeg drums, traditionally associated with Orange parades, beat in the distance as the Orangemen set out from their lodge. It was a rare warm sunny day in Portadown. We stood basking in the sunshine on the grounds of the Catholic church on the Garvaghy Road, along with about three hundred residents, police, army personnel, and priests. Soon we could see the bowler-hatted, white-gloved, and sashed Orangemen walking slowly past the Catholic church on their way up to Drumcree Church. For the most part the parade passed in silence. Just one idiot jumped up and down and made kicking motions as he shouted out "Robbie Hamill! Robbie Hamill!" — a crude re-enactment of the young man's brutal murder in Portadown. After the service, Harold Gracey, the grand master of the Portadown Orange Lodge, marched up to the army barricade with the throng of Orangemen behind him and handed the commanding officer a letter of protest. The rest of the afternoon was quiet.

The serenity of that beautiful summer day was broken when darkness fell. Several Orangemen attempted to climb over the army barricade and were repelled by the RUC. Riots erupted later, not just in Portadown, but across the six counties of Northern Ireland. The

RUC, backed up by the British Army, fought pitched battles with the Orangemen throughout the night. On the hill of Drumcree, Orangemen employed guns, petrol bombs, and nail bombs against the authorities. With each passing day, the crowds grew larger and angrier and their leaders more bellicose. Around the world, the bowler-hatted Orangemen were portrayed, accurately, as the bigoted remnants of a bygone era. Without doubt, they were losing the public relations battle with the Nationalist community. As observers, we, too, were astonished by — and carefully recording — the scenes unfolding before our eyes.

On Monday, July 6, the Canadian delegation headed back to Belfast for a series of meetings with leading politicians and organizations in Northern Ireland. We were going to stay in the Lower Ormeau Road area, a tiny Catholic enclave surrounded by Protestants. The neighbourhood had seen more than its share of the Troubles, some fifty-six murders over the years. The Canadian delegation met with Gerard Rice, a soft-spoken community organizer who worked primarily with youth. He had been a target for assassination on several occasions and had taken many precautions. He had one-inch-thick steel plates mounted on hinges on either side of the main window of his home. At night, he swung the plates across the window to stop petrol bombs from being tossed in. At the bottom of his stairs a padlocked steel gate stretched from floor to ceiling to prevent someone breaking in and murdering him and his young family while they slept. Security cameras were placed strategically around the outside of his house.

We received another briefing from Rosemary Nelson. The LOCC organization was in the courts trying to stop the Orange Order from Ballynafeigh in south Belfast from marching through their community on July 12, and Nelson focused her remarks on the legal issues raised by the challenge. The community felt that the commission had made a political calculation when it elected to allow the march in their neighbourhood, offering the permission as a kind of trade-off to the Orange Order for having disallowed the march in Portadown. Tensions were high among the residents on the Lower Ormeau Road.

Later that day, we were scheduled to meet with the deputy leader of the Democratic Unionist Party (DUP), Gregory Campbell. Ian Paisley, the party leader, was said to be unavailable. The meeting took place in Stormont Castle, one of the most majestic parliament buildings in Europe. As we made our way there, we saw the aftermath of the previous night's riots: burnt-out cars, makeshift barricades, and pavement blackened by petrol bombs. Police and army personnel were everywhere. The grounds of the castle, in contrast to the mayhem in the streets, were calm. As I walked up the steps, my thoughts flashed back to a time years ago, when as a naive sixteen-year-old, I had actually crossed paths with Ian Paisley outside his home.

Gregory Campbell entered the meeting room with a handful of DUP elected members, and we were joined by the American delegation of international observers. With a colleague, William Hay, Campbell reviewed the history of Unionism and the Orange Order, and the cultural significance of the parades to the Protestant community. We urged Campbell and his colleagues to enter into dialogue with the representatives of the Catholic communities across Northern Ireland, but the DUP refused to sit down with people who had been convicted of violence or were ex-prisoners. I pointed out that had the South African government adopted that position, there would have been no peace with Nelson Mandela and the ANC. We came to no agreement, but the exchange was civil. Campbell chastised the American delegation over a handout they had received prior to leaving the United States in which the Orange Order was compared to the Ku Klux Klan. The Americans apologized.

Later that night, more riots broke out in Belfast and across Northern Ireland. Children and teenagers engaged the RUC and British troops stationed at the two bridges spanning the River Lagan. John Murphy and I were billeted down on one of the side streets close to the Havelock bridge. The residents complained that during the marching season (from June to August) projectiles — and sometimes petrol bombs — came flying over the high wall behind the houses. Beyond the wall the Protestants were building the traditional Twelfth of July bonfire in an open area of wasteland. A typical bonfire pyre could reach a height of sixty feet of wooden pallets, old furniture, and construction materials. Its construction was a weeks-long social gathering at which children and young people, along with their parents, played their flutes, beat their drums, sang their songs, and drank copious amounts of beer.

Murphy and I had hardly slept since leaving Canada. Our three nights in Portadown were interrupted by our midnight-to-6:00-a.m. tours of the neighbourhood, and what little time remained for rest was punctuated by alarms and paranoia, as we each kept one eye open for a petrol bomb coming through the window. Our experience on the Ormeau Road was different but possibly even more stressful than on the Garvaghy Road because the Ormeau Road was wide open to traffic, and everybody talked about their fear of drive-by shootings. We wore royal blue windbreakers with the words "International Observer" emblazoned on the back. Some within our group felt the words made us a target, and as previously mentioned, the stretch of road had already seen fifty-six murders during the Troubles. Regardless, we stayed out on the street until everything quieted down for the night.

Murphy and I were billeted with a woman and her daughter in a house very similar to the one I had grown up in on Downpatrick Road in Dublin. When we got back to the house around 2:00 a.m. on our first night there, Pauline, the owner, made us a cup of tea, and we talked about how she hated the marching season. We were physically and mentally drained by the time we got to our room. I could hear the sound of pipes and drums from beyond the wall. It was hard to put them out of my mind, and I wondered how the residents coped with the noise and resultant tension for weeks on end. At last I fell into an uneasy sleep with the sounds of Loyalist music beginning to wane in the distance. My bed was positioned under the window, which was open to let in a bit of fresh air. In my half-awake condition, I thought I heard a noise, but I was unable to rouse myself to investigate. Over my head, I felt a presence and a distinct rustling sound and I knew I had to snap out of my semi-conscious state. The feeling was exactly the kind you get in the middle of a dream when you try to stop yourself from falling off a cliff. Something brushed against my head and landed on my chest. I let out a roar. Murphy leapt out of his bed, and Pauline charged into the room, her daughter close behind her. Someone switched on the light. My heart was pounding, ready to burst out of my chest. And there, sitting on the end of my bed, was a big friggin' cat that had been locked out. Somehow it had managed to climb onto the roof of the shed, leapt through the open window, and landed smack on my chest. And I, for a moment, thought I was being attacked by a murderous paramilitary operative.

I wasn't the only one who was wound up. Tension was building across Northern Ireland as July 12 drew closer. Rioting in the Protestant areas continued unabated and with increasing violence and ferocity. The Canadian delegation met with the Decommissioning Commission, whose mandate was to convince the paramilitary organizations, such as the IRA and the UVF, to destroy their weapons. Later that day our delegation got word that Ian Paisley wanted to meet with us in Belfast City Hall.

Belfast City Hall is a majestic old building smack in the centre of Donegall Square. Built between 1898 and 1906, it is regarded as the citadel of British and Protestant power in Northern Ireland. It was not until 1997 that the city elected its first Catholic lord mayor. The building itself is constructed in the Renaissance style with magnificent

July 1998, Belfast City Hall. Seated, Rev. Ian Paisley. Standing (left to right): John O'Toole, Conservative MPP; me; Arthur Sandborn, CSN Quebec; and John Murphy.

domes and a grand marble staircase. The last time I saw this building was in 1968–69 when I had witnessed the civil rights demonstrations.

The meeting with Paisley took place in a wood-panelled boardroom just off the main hallway. The boardroom table had enough seating to accommodate the entire eighteen-member Canadian delegation, and there was a raised dais on one side of the long, rectangular table. Members of our delegation joked that Paisley was probably pompous enough to come in and talk down to the great unwashed from the dais. When the door swung open, a tall burly man walked in, accompanied by the lord mayor of Belfast, who introduced him before leaving the room. Paisley bellowed a greeting and — inevitably — proceeded to mount the dais before addressing our delegation.

Paisley first gave us a rundown of the various elected positions he had held: member of the British parliament, member of the Assembly for Northern Ireland, member of the European parliament, member of the Orange Order, and leader of the Opposition in the previous Northern Ireland government. He wanted to impress upon us that he was a serious player in Northern Ireland politics. Then he got into the issues. His talking points with regard to the Parades Commission were the same as those of his deputy leader, Gregory Campbell: he questioned its legitimacy and stressed that Protestants had a right to march on the Queen's highways anywhere in Northern Ireland. He claimed that the British government bought the recent referendum on the Peace Accord by pumping £3 million into advertising, and he did not recognize the result. He and I got into a bit of a scrap over his unwillingness to sit down with his adversaries and try to find a workable solution. He insisted he would not sit and talk with "murderers and terrorists," which was how he regarded Sinn Féin and leaders of the Catholic residents' groups. I pointed out that he regularly sat with David Ervine, leader of the Progressive Unionist Party, who was a convicted member of a Protestant paramilitary group, although since reformed and a key player in the peace process. He denied having done so, but Ervine himself had told the Canadian delegation that he and Paisley had regular discussions. I left the Paisley meeting with mixed feelings. *Here is a man*, I thought, *who holds the future of*

Northern Ireland in his hands, yet he cannot bring himself to meet with the other great power in Northern Ireland politics, his nemesis, Sinn Féin. In later years, Paisley became the most powerful Protestant politician in Northern Ireland. His party went on to win the most seats in the new Northern Ireland Assembly. He eventually entered into power-sharing discussions with Sinn Féin and ended up becoming good friends with Sinn Féin's Martin McGuinness.

The morning of July 8 encompassed everything I love about Ireland. The sun was shining and bathing everything in that bright hue that I find is unique to Ireland. The delegation broke into two groups: one heading off to the courts, and the other, of which I was a part, to meet a bureaucrat from the office of Northern Ireland's secretary of state, Mo Mowlam. Mowlam's offices were situated in Stormont House in the grounds of the Stormont Castle estate. We were ushered into a stately room, which seemed opulent on first impression, but revealed signs of wear and tear in its scratched furnishings and frayed rugs upon closer examination. We were there to talk about the Parades Commission decisions, first to ban the Orange parade in Portadown, and then to allow it on the Lower Ormeau Road in South Belfast. We had expected to meet a senior civil servant, but when the door opened, Secretary of State Dr. Mo Mowlam herself walked in. She was fighting a cancerous brain tumour and refused to wear a wig or any head covering. At the time, she was the second most powerful politician in the United Kingdom, next to Prime Minister Tony Blair. After the introductions, she told us she had wanted to meet us personally so we could deliver her message directly to the residents of the Lower Ormeau Road. She wanted them to know the Nationalist community was winning the public relations battle all over the world, and it would be a big mistake for them to violently oppose the parade from marching down the Lower Ormeau Road. We told her we believed the community would be respectful and allow the parade to pass through without incident, but that there would be a large, visible silent protest. She talked about the Garvaghy Road parade being banned and said she would not give in to pressure from the Orange Order this year. As proof, she said, "that's why we've put all the furniture into Drumcree," a reference to the moat, razor wire, and massive barricade installed on the hill. In the banter that followed, she called Paisley a "wanker" as she joined the tips of her forefinger and thumb together to form a circle. As the meeting ended, she stressed the importance of her message to the Ormeau Road community to remain calm. Later that evening Arthur Sandborn, a member of our delegation from the CSN in Quebec, and I briefed representatives of the Lower Ormeau Road resident's association on our meetings.

After the meeting with Mowlam, we made our way back across the city to Falls Road to meet with Sinn Féin leaders. We were receiving a briefing from a senior member of Sinn Féin when Gerry Adams slipped into the room and sat at the back, listening. Eventually, to everyone's surprise, he spoke up. He talked for about thirty minutes, laying out his vision for a united Ireland. He was supportive of the Orange Order's right to march and to celebrate its history and culture. He just couldn't stomach the triumphalism that had become a part of so many recent parades.

Over the next few days the level of violence across Northern Ireland continued to escalate. Thousands more Orangemen poured into the fields around the church in Drumcree. At night, the security forces were assailed by sniping, nail bombs and petrol bombs, and small- and large-scale riots. In parts of Belfast the police used water cannons to quell the disorder. The scene was set for a doomsday confrontation between the mighty Orange Order that had ruled Northern Ireland for more than a century and the British government that was dug into Drumcree behind barricades, razor wire, and water-filled trenches. July 11 arrived with the Lower Ormeau Road residents readying for another RUC siege and the Orange Order preparing to light its monstrous bonfires. The sound of flutes, drums, and sectarian songs rang in our ears as we went to bed that night. We awoke to horrific news that shocked and sickened the world. At four thirty that morning, three young boys were murdered in their parents' home when a petrol bomb was thrown through the window. The children — Richard, Mark, and Jason — were unable to escape the flames that enveloped their house, and they were burned alive. Their mother, Christine Quinn, a

Catholic, and her partner, Raymond Craig, a Protestant, tried in vain to rescue the children. The ugliness of Northern Ireland's sectarianism was laid bare. At 8:00 a.m. I stood outside Sean Graham's betting shop on the Lower Ormeau Road along with our delegation and cried. I thought about my own three daughters in Canada and how horrific it must have been for the three young Quinns' parents.

The murder of the Quinn children led to calls from across Northern Ireland to abandon the protests in Drumcree. The Orange Order in Portadown was deaf to the plea. The parade, which normally takes place on the twelfth of July, was postponed to the thirteenth because the Sabbath fell on the twelfth.

The Lower Ormeau Road was decked out in black flags and black balloons, which created a sombre atmosphere. The sidewalks were lined with residents ten deep on either side of the street. In the distance, we heard the parade drawing closer. At the first bridge, the pipes and flutes stopped playing. The Orange Order marched, as agreed, to the sound of

International observers, Drumcree, Northern Ireland, 1999. Left to right: Svend Robinson, NDP MP; Dr. Carolyn Bennett, Liberal MP; me; and Warren Allmand, solicitor general from 1972 to 1976.

a solitary drumbeat. The parade passed without incident except for a few morons who gave a five-finger salute as they passed Sean Graham's shop, where five innocent people had been shot to death on February 5, 1992.

In Drumcree, as the enormity of the murder of the Quinn children sank in, the Orange Order's protests lost steam. The Reverend William Bingham, grand chaplain for the Orange Order's County Armagh wing, called for the end of the protests, saying that "after last night's atrocious act, a fifteen-minute walk down the Garvaghy Road by the Orange Order would be a very hollow victory because it would be in the shadow of three coffins of little boys who wouldn't even know what the Orange Order is." David Trimble, the leading Protestant politician in the North, and one that had previously danced a jig with Ian Paisley down the Garvaghy Road, called upon the protesters to go home. A couple of hundred diehard Orangemen continued their protest, but they had lost the support of mainstream Unionism in Northern Ireland.

Today, the picture is somewhat brighter. The Good Friday Agreement, which had been voted on in April 1998, set up the new governance model called the Northern Ireland Assembly, with representatives from both the Catholic and Protestant communities. The arrangement, astonishingly, worked. Ian Paisley's DUP ousted David Trimble's UUP as the leading Unionist political party and Gerry Adams's Sinn Féin supplanted the Social Democratic and Labour Party as the leading Nationalist party in Northern Ireland. Two arch-enemies, in fact, shared power. Ian Paisley became the leader of the assembly and Gerry Adams appointed Martin McGuinness as the deputy leader representing Sinn Féin.

Although incidents of sectarian violence and ethnic cleansing have dramatically declined over the years, Northern Ireland is still recovering from the trauma of the Troubles. The continuing volatility in the North was exemplified when, one month after our delegation had left Ireland, a massive car bomb exploded in the centre of the picturesque town of Omagh, murdering twenty-nine men, women, and children. A splinter group calling itself the Real Irish Republican Army had planted the bomb as a protest against the agreement.

Some six months after the Omagh bombing, in March 1999, Rosemary Nelson, the brave lawyer who briefed us on the legal issues affecting the Catholic and Protestant communities in Northern Ireland, was murdered. A bomb planted under her car exploded as she backed out of her driveway. She died in hospital with her husband and three young children at her side. And, sadly, Dr. Mo Mowlam died of her brain tumour in 2005. Both Ian Paisley and Martin McGuinness have since passed on, and the peace process is once again under stress with both sides unable to agree on how to govern the province. A dispute about energy subsidies embroiled the DUP in a major scandal, which led to Martin McGuinness and Sinn Féin collapsing the power-sharing government. Fresh elections in early 2017 saw Sinn Féin come within one vote of having the majority in the Northern Ireland assembly. Talks between the parties on power-sharing broke down over Sinn Féin's insistence on legislation to protect Irish language rights. The Brexit negotiations have also complicated the situation by threatening to install a hard border between the Republic of Ireland and Northern Ireland, which politicians on all sides say could lead to the unravelling of the Good Friday Agreement. The DUP are currently propping up the unpopular Tory government of Theresa May, which Sinn Féin say is a violation of the Good Friday Agreement under which the U.K. government is mandated to stay neutral. The people of Northern Ireland voted 56 percent to remain in the European Union. All of this uncertainty is leading people on both sides of the divide to take a serious look at a united Ireland. Recent polls have shown an appetite for the idea. The question of Northern Ireland is far from settled and certainly the horrors of sectarianism is never far from bubbling up to the surface again. Talk of a united Ireland is rife on both sides of the border.

CUPE AND THE MIDDLE EAST

CUPE Ontario has a proud history of engagement in international issues. We have spoken out on human rights abuses not only in South Africa and the Americas, but also in Iran, China, Darfur, Haiti, Iran, Bosnia, and many other regions of the world. For as long as I played an active role in CUPE Ontario's affairs, its influence as a union and as an advocate for social justice was steadily enlarged. Our organization's involvement with Palestine was not a departure from previous practice, but simply an expression of our continuing interest and concern.

In 1917 Palestine was under the control of the Turkish Ottoman Empire. My grandfather was among the thousands of British Army soldiers who brought an end to that empire. Palestine was one among several remnants of Turkey's shattered imperial domain that fell under Great Britain's jurisdiction. In November 1917 the British foreign secretary, Sir Arthur James Balfour, declared that Britain would look favourably on establishing a home for Jewish people in Palestine. Encouraged by what came to be called the Balfour Declaration and by the Zionist movement that had influenced it, Jews from around the world began to settle there. Their growing numbers raised tensions within Arab communities in the region and led to violence and uprisings until, finally, Britain washed its hands of the problem and handed responsibility for the protectorate to the United Nations. In 1947 the UN passed Resolution 181, which divided Palestine into two different states: 56 percent of the territory was given to the Jewish settlers; 44 percent to Palestinian Arabs.

In 1948 war broke out after the Jewish side declared its independence and set up the state of Israel. In the ensuing war, Israel captured an additional 22 percent of the territory, giving them 78 percent of the original Palestine. More than half the Palestinian population fled from the war or were expelled from their towns and villages.

War broke out again in 1967 and Israel occupied the remainder of the Palestinian territory, which is at the heart of the current conflict. At that point Israel controlled the West Bank, East Jerusalem, and Gaza. They also seized the Sinai Peninsula from Egypt and the Golan Heights from Syria. The UN passed resolutions 238 and 242 that same year, and the Security Council called upon Israel to withdraw from the occupied territories. Ever since 1967 the issue of the territories and the demand by Palestinians for the return of land in exchange for the promise of peace have been central to the numerous failed peace negotiations.

In the 1970s and 1980s Israel had a lot of support within the Canadian trade union movement, partly because Israel was understood to be building a social democratic society with its *kibbutzim*

With Peter Leibovitch, NDP campaign manager, Scarborough Centre, 1999.

(communes), and developing strong ties to the labour movement headed up by Histadrut, the governing body of the trade union movement in Israel. Additionally, the Israeli lobby in Canada was well organized and expended considerable resources promoting Israel as an egalitarian society in which the Israeli labour movement played an essential part. The Israelis shrewdly provided Canadian union leaders at all levels with the opportunity to visit Israel and witness the country's achievements. In addition, Dennis McDermott, the Canadian Labour Congress president through the late 1970s and 1980s, regarded himself as a Catholic Zionist, which had an enormous influence on the trade union movement in Canada. However, as the 1980s wore on, opinion within the Canadian labour movement began to shift, partly because of new immigrants entering Canada from the Middle East and other countries outside of Europe.

I first met Peter Leibovitch when he was a member of the United Steelworkers union in the 1980s. Peter came from an Orthodox Jewish family in Montreal and moved to Ontario when he was nineteen. He nearly always wore a blue denim jacket — it became a trademark of sorts — and a big smile. That smile could be quite disarming in the middle of a heated debate. Peter, despite his background, was passionate about his support for the Palestinians. He approached the complex problem from a social-justice perspective. This appealed to me: I saw the parallel between the Israeli occupation of Palestine and that of the Irish after eight hundred years of English rule and occupation.

The influence of activists like Peter — a principled activist with a world vision — led directly to the passage of an increasing number of pro-Palestinian resolutions by central labour bodies, including the Canadian Labour Congress and the Ontario Federation of Labour. The trend gathered steam when trade unions began to send delegations to Palestine and Israel to conduct independent investigations and report on their findings. The atrocities committed by the Israeli state, such as the demolition of people's homes as a form of collective punishment, was anathema to Canadian trade unionists. Similarly, denying people access to public roads because of their race or nationality and setting up roadblocks simply to make life miserable for people trying to commute to work constituted unacceptable violations of human rights. These abuses were ample grounds for the Canadian labour movement to examine critically its relationship with Israel.

In April 2000 I visited Israel as part of a Canadian labour delegation that included OFL president Wayne Samuelson; OSSTF president Earl Manners; lawyers Paul Cavalluzzo, Maurice Green, and Howard Goldblatt; and a host of construction trade union leaders. The trip was sponsored by the State of Israel Bonds/Canada in close co-operation with Israeli government officials. Ostensibly, the Israelis hoped to expose Canadian union pension plans to investment opportunities in Israel while at the same time telling their story to their visitors. As with the trip to Northern Ireland in 1998, our delegation was given excellent access to the political leaders of the day. The timing was propitious in that we arrived in the aftermath of a general election, and there was reason to think that an end to the conflict was in the offing. Ehud Barak, the newly elected prime minister and the most decorated soldier in Israeli history, had promised to negotiate an agreement with the Palestinians, Syrians, and the Lebanese that would finally enable Israel and its neighbours to live in peace and security.

During the course of our week in Israel, we met with the mayors of several cities and towns, including Shimon Shetreet, the senior deputy mayor of Jerusalem; Jacob Katz, the mayor of Metula; Menachem Ariav, the mayor of Upper Nazareth; and Zvi Zilker, the mayor of Ashdod. We also met with Brigadier General Oded Ben-Ami and Daniel Seaman, the director of the Foreign Press Department. Seaman was probably the most interesting and forthright of the diplomats we met. He gave us a sense of where the peace negotiations were at, but was very clear that Israel never would accept an absolute right of return provision for Palestinians. He envisioned a limited right of return "for some but not all Palestinians," and possible monetary compensation for the majority. He also said there would be a unilateral withdrawal of Israeli troops from southern Lebanon, and that discussions were underway with the Syrians regarding the Golan Heights, but Syria's desire for access to the Sea of Galilee was a stumbling block. Overall, his presentation left us with a sense that Israel and the Palestinians were on the cusp of a historic agreement.

We visited towns as far north as Metula on the southern Lebanon border and as far south as Masada. (Masada was the summer retreat of King Herod and the fortress where one thousand Jewish men, women, and children fought off the Roman army for three years before taking their own lives rather than surrender.) We sped between cities and towns along almost traffic-free and newly paved Israeli-only highways. Occasionally, we caught sight of the potholed and rubble-strewn Palestinian road system that exists in parallel to the Israeli network.

In the Druze village of Ussefiya in northern Israel, we spent several hours meeting with the village leaders, sharing a meal, and enjoying great conversations in their homes. In Metula we got to visit the Canada Centre — a full-sized ice hockey arena donated by the Canadian Jewish community. Metula, with a population of just 1,400, is nestled beneath the Golan Heights on the border with Lebanon, and the main source of income appears to be from the numerous apple orchards on the outskirts of what appeared to be a garrison town. Farther up in the hills we visited the Israeli checkpoint on the border with Lebanon. Young Israeli soldiers sat informally outside a small store, laughing and joking with the Canadian delegation. A month later, on May 2, 2000, Israel withdrew its army from southern Lebanon (just as Seaman had predicted), thus helping to ease tension in the region but not from the disputed Shebaa Farms, which Lebanon claims ownership of.

On April 2, the Canadian delegation was in Jerusalem. Because it was a beautiful, cool evening I decided to go for a walk rather than join the delegation at a Turkish restaurant. I stumbled upon the King David Hotel, a building steeped in history and controversy. More than fifty years earlier, the Israelis had been involved in a guerrilla war with the British occupying forces. The King David Hotel was the headquarters of the British Mandate secretariat and a portion of the British military command. It became the target of a terrorist act by the Irgun, a right-wing Zionist paramilitary organization headed by Menachem Begin, who later became prime minister of Israel. Just after 12:00 a.m. on July 22, 1946, a bomb planted by the Irgun exploded, blowing up the hotel's entire south wing. Ninety-one people were killed, among them Arabs, Palestinian Jews, and thirteen British personnel — mostly clerks and typists. As I stood in the lobby watching the hotel guests and staff go about their business, I imagined not only the mayhem and carnage that had occurred only a half century before but also the murderous bombing of the innocent in Dublin, Belfast, and Omagh.

A few days later, in Tel Aviv, I was about to enter a shopping mall when I was stopped and searched by a police officer. This was a stark reminder that, though the city was peaceful then, Palestinian suicide bombers had murdered scores of Israeli civilians in cafés and in the streets in the recent past. The incident again revived my memories of Dublin and Belfast during the Troubles, when personal searches were routine.

Of all the places we visited during our stay, two stood out as the most memorable. The first of these was the Western or Wailing Wall. It is the most sacred spot in the world for Jews, one of four magnificent walls built by King Herod to support an expansion of the Temple Mount plaza. The first temple was built by Solomon in the tenth century BCE and destroyed by the Babylonians. The Western Wall itself is 534 yards long but only 62 yards of it is visible and accessible to the public. Like so many others from all over the world, I placed a prayer note into one of the crevices between the stones. I was struck by the fervour with which people around me were praying. I could feel the reverence that the Jewish pilgrims felt for this holy place and the historical importance of the wall to the Jewish faith. The second site that left an enormous impression on me was Yad Vashem, the World Holocaust Remembrance Center. It leaves an indelible mark on anyone who enters its doors. The unspeakable horrors experienced by millions of Jews are laid bare for all to see in a stunning and sickening display of man's inhumanity to man. The haunting figures of emaciated men, women, and children burned their way into every fibre of my soul. The exit from the museum is the Hall of Names, where two million short biographies are stored, with room for six million altogether. Yad Vashem screams out, "Never again!" However, I did have one major regret about the entire trip and that was the lack of equal access to the Muslim holy sites and the broader Palestinian community.

That spring of 2000, Ehud Barak was in the throes of peace negotiations with the Palestinians. Talk of the imminent withdrawal of Israel Defense Forces from Lebanon was in the news. Everything appeared to be in place for a new beginning and — potentially — a peace agreement. Then, in the span of a few short months, everything fell apart. In July 2000 President Bill Clinton called Ehud Barak and the Palestinian leader, Yasser Arafat, to Camp David to try to hammer out the deal. The sticking points, as usual, were sovereignty over East Jerusalem and, from the Palestinian standpoint, sovereignty over the Temple Mount (a.k.a. Haram al-Sharif), among the holiest of shrines to both Jews and Muslims. Other issues included the right of return for refugees and the dismantling of illegal Jewish settlements that had been built on the Palestinian side of the Green Line (the boundary established in the armistice between Israel and its neighbours following the 1948 war). Eventually, Ehud Barak put an offer on the table that would cost him his job. In his proposal to Arafat, he suggested limited Palestinian sovereignty over a portion of East Jerusalem, which, for the right wing in Israeli politics, is the third rail. When word leaked out that Barak had been willing to trade a portion of east Jerusalem to Arafat in return for roughly 5 percent of Palestinian land along the Green Line, all hell broke loose in the Knesset (the Israeli parliament). It scarcely mattered that Arafat, who wanted complete sovereignty over all East Jerusalem, rejected the offer. Barak immediately began to lose support within his coalition government. After using up his political capital on the failed international peace process and largely ignoring domestic issues, he now found himself in choppy political waters.

Ariel Sharon, the hard-line leader of the right-wing Likud Party, knew he had Barak on the ropes. He pressed home his advantage by announcing he would visit the Temple Mount to visibly, and provocatively, demonstrate Israeli sovereignty over this most sensitive of religious sites. On September 28, 2000, he had several hundred police officers dressed in riot gear escort him to the site. Predictably, crowds of Palestinians, young and old, gathered to protest Sharon's action. They pelted the police with stones. The police responded with tear gas and rubber-coated metal bullets. The next day rioting broke out in the West Bank and East Jerusalem, five Palestinians were killed, and so began the Second Intifada. Within a year eight hundred people had died in the violence. Less than five months after his visit to the holy shrine, Sharon was sworn in as Israel's prime minister. He had promised to be tough on the Palestinians and not be bound by previous negotiations. Soon after his election, Sharon gave the green light to the building of a four-hundred-mile barrier wall that would separate the West Bank from Israel and, in the process, cut deeply into prime Palestinian land. The wall was ruled "inherently illegal" by the International Court of Justice, which went on to say the barrier's construction was "tantamount to annexation and impeded the Palestinian right to self determination."*

In 2004 CUPE Ontario held its annual convention in Windsor. My presidency was challenged by Bob Cullen, a union leader from the school-board sector in Sudbury. I was not particularly worried about the challenge, but I was ticked off that CUPE National was behind his

* *BBC News*, July 9, 2004.

campaign and had assisted in the production and printing of his campaign materials. CUPE National placed Cullen on the payroll as a temporary staff representative during the run-up to the election. It wasn't the first time that happened, and the standing joke in CUPE Ontario was that the best way to get a CUPE National staff position was to run against Sid for president. The election took place on the Friday morning of the convention and I won handily with an 80:20 split.

Prior to the convention it had come to my attention that CUPE Ontario's International Solidarity Committee wanted the union to place greater emphasis on the Middle East. In the past, we had paid a fair bit of attention to developments in South America and elsewhere, but neglected the Middle East. CUPE Ontario's committees are given a lot of latitude to focus on issues they feel are important, and I always encouraged them to challenge our membership and to prod us out of our comfort zone. The CUPE Ontario International Solidarity Committee had accepted that challenge by focusing on the plight of Iranian union activists. At our committee's invitation, Parviz Babaei, a veteran union activist

CUPE demonstration against P3 privatization, Ottawa, 2004. Left to right: Paul Moist, CUPE National president; Brian O'Keefe, CUPE Ontario secretary treasurer; me; and Ken Georgetti, CLC president.

and transit worker who had been imprisoned by the Iranian religious dictatorship for his activities, gave a brilliant speech about globalization to the convention linking free trade to the privatization of public services by multinational corporations. The result, he argued persuasively, was the erosion of workers' rights, wages, and benefits to maximize the profits of private corporations at the expense of services to the public. He gave the delegates a harrowing insight into the human rights abuses in Iran, and the torture and imprisonment of independent trade union leaders and activists. The Iranian delegation fully expected to be arrested on their return to Tehran. The CUPE Ontario members responded to brother Babaei's speech with a rousing and boisterous standing ovation.

The weekend following the convention, I addressed a larger delegation of Iranian worker representatives and the broader diaspora at Metro Hall in Toronto. The event was organized by the International Alliance in Support of Workers in Iran and sponsored by CLC, CUPE, CAW, and CUPW, and by Medhi Kouhestani-Nejad, an executive board member of CUPE Ontario. In my speech to the delegates, I was critical of the Iranian religious dictatorship and their abuse of workers. The tour by the Iranian workers was a huge success and ended with a resolution, passed at the Canadian Labour Congress convention in Toronto, calling for an international labour delegation to go to Iran and conduct an independent investigation into the human rights abuses there. Sadly, the CLC did not follow up on the resolution.

Canada, and by extension CUPE, is home to an increasing number of Muslims from around the world, so the committee felt it was appropriate for the convention to address the Islamophobia growing in the mainstream media and in our workplaces. It is impossible to have a dialogue about these issues without talking about root causes and the Israel-Palestine conflict is a significant source of anti-Muslim sentiment. The International Solidarity Committee proposed to kick-start the debate on the convention floor by introducing the delegates to two UN resolutions that Canada had already supported at the UN and made official Canadian policy. The idea was to take the guts of UN resolutions 242 and 338 and call for their implementation, in the process educating the membership with a good debate.

UN resolution 242 was passed by the UN Security Council in 1967. It deals with five principles: the withdrawal of Israeli forces from occupied territories, peace within secure and recognized boundaries, freedom of navigation, a just settlement of the refugee problem, and security measures including a demilitarized zone. UN resolution 338 is a companion to 242. On October 6, 1973, fighting broke out when Egypt attacked Israel from the Suez Canal area in the south and Syria attacked from the Golan Heights in the north. The resulting Yom Kippur War was won decisively by the Israelis. While it was still under way, however, the UN Security Council passed Resolution 338 calling for an end to the fighting and a start to negotiations to implement the five principles contained in Resolution 242.

The debate on the UN resolutions, which hit the convention floor on Friday afternoon, was vigorous. Mikael Swayze, a union rep for CUPE 3902 academic staff at the University of Toronto who identified himself as Jewish, spoke passionately against the resolution. I was proud of the membership for the respectful manner in which they argued the issues and came to a democratic decision, and the vote passed by a large majority. On Saturday morning, two women came to a microphone and identified themselves as delegates representing workers in the Canadian Jewish Congress — a CUPE local. They had been absent the day before and wanted to voice their concerns about the contents of the resolution and the fact CUPE Ontario was taking sides in the Middle East conflict. Under normal circumstances, once the convention has dealt with a resolution there is no mechanism to revisit it, especially if delegates are not in the convention hall during the debate. However, the delegates decided to allow the women to address the convention and make their points, listening respectfully to what they had to say before moving on to other business. It was clear the majority of delegates were happy with the previous day's vote.

Two years later, the 2006 CUPE Ontario convention became one of the most controversial conventions in the almost fifty-year history of the union. CUPE National, once again, encouraged a candidate, in this instance Gus Oliveira from the large municipal local in Hamilton, to run against me. And, in the now time-honoured tradition, he was given a temporary staff job with CUPE National prior to the convention.

As usual, I hosted a party for friends, supporters, and basically anybody who wished to show up in my hospitality suite on the night before the vote. My campaign team had rented a room with an enormous balcony overlooking the Parliament buildings. The place was hopping when, partway through the evening, I was pulled aside by CUPE members from the Toronto area: Katherine Nastovski, Adam Hanieh, Ali Mallah, Rafeef Ziadah, and David Kidd, an executive board member from CUPE local 79. They asked if I would support their resolution calling for CUPE Ontario to join the international Boycott, Divestment, Sanctions (BDS) campaign against the state of Israel, in order to hasten an end to the almost forty years of Israeli occupation of Palestinian lands. The central labour body in Palestine, the Palestinian General Trade Union (PGTU), along with seventy civil society and religious organizations had called upon labour around the world to support this campaign, which was similar to the one that helped bring an end to apartheid in South Africa. I gave them a commitment that if the resolution came to the floor for debate and if I felt it was in danger of not receiving sufficient support to pass, then I would relinquish the chair and speak in favour of the resolution. I could see they were pleased to have my support. I also understood, if the resolution was adopted by the members, it would be breaking new ground both for CUPE Ontario and the BDS campaign worldwide. No other union in Canada had tested its membership on the BDS campaign. Indeed, nowhere in the world had an organization with such a large membership (220,000 in the case of CUPE Ontario) supported the campaign. The 2006 election took place first thing on Friday morning and I easily won with an 80:20 split.

Resolution 50, dealing with the support for the BDS campaign, hit the floor around 11:00 a.m. on Saturday. Delegates at our conventions speak in favour of a resolution from a "pro" microphone and against it from a "con" microphone. I could see from the podium that the four pro microphones each had delegates lined up behind them, while there was no one waiting to speak for the con side. David Kidd was the leadoff speaker. He was both eloquent and forceful in describing his family's Jewish roots and the years he had spent living in Israel. He went on to describe the plight of the Palestinian people, the harassment to which they were subjected at military checkpoints, the illegal Israeli settlements on Palestinian lands, the building of the separation wall, and the demolition of Palestinian homes as collective punishment for entire communities. There were nine hundred delegates in the room but you could have heard a pin drop while he was speaking. He finished by reminding us all that we have an obligation to one another and, when it comes to matters of social justice, there is real meaning behind the old adage that an injury or injustice to one is an injury or injustice to all. The delegates erupted into thunderous applause when he was finished and a chorus was taken up, saying, "Question! Question!" indicating that the delegates had made up their mind and were ready to vote. I checked again to see if there were any speakers waiting at any of the con microphones. Seeing none, I asked for a show of hands (which is the normal practice) to end the debate. It was unanimous. I then called the vote on the resolution itself. I said: "All those in favour of the committee's recommendation of concurrence, please show." A sea of yellow voting cards shot into the air. I then said: "All those opposed to the committee's recommendation, please show." I didn't see a single card raised in opposition. I declared the motion passed with unanimous consent. Later in the week, after reviewing the video recording of the convention, I noticed the camera had captured two people off to my extreme left who had, in fact, raised their voting cards in opposition to the resolution. At the time of the vote they were out of my line of sight. I had my staff revise the result of the vote from "unanimous" to "almost unanimous."

The convention moved on to other business. About 11:30 a.m., I was approached by the CUPE Ontario communications rep Pat Daley on behalf of Katherine Nastovski, and was asked if I was okay with putting out a media release stating that CUPE Ontario had voted in favour of the international BDS campaign. I gave Katherine a look that basically said, "Sister, you are gonna get me into a pile of shit." And then I smiled and said, "Go for it." I figured, what's the point of taking a principled position and then hiding it under a bush? In any event, I knew the adopted resolution would be trumpeted around the world by the BDS campaign.

The convention lost quorum just before 1:00 p.m. and was adjourned. I was relieved to put it behind me. All conventions are stressful and, in this one, I had to fight an election as well as manage the usual mechanics involved in chairing such a large gathering. As always at CUPE conventions, several gigantic screens had been set up so delegates at the back of the hall could see and follow the proceedings. Because the president conducts the bulk of the chairing, I had been "onscreen" almost continuously from Wednesday to Saturday. Every move I made was scrutinized by the delegates. When it was all over, I was exhausted both physically and mentally. At 2:00 p.m. I went back to my room, turned off my cellphone, and napped for about ninety minutes. Later, I joined Brian O'Keefe for a light meal. My cellphone was still off and I was enjoying the few hours of relative peace. When finally, after we had eaten, I turned the phone on, my voice mail was full with messages from media outlets all over Canada. The press release on Resolution 50 had hit the fan.

The next morning, the news was full of the usual and predictable talking points from the Canadian Jewish Congress and B'nai Brith. It was suggested, for example, that the resolution was deliberately brought forward on a Saturday — the Jewish Sabbath — in order to avoid having Jewish activists speak against it. This was an insult to the many Jewish activists who were on the floor when the resolution was introduced, and a nonsense canard that is dragged out time and again to smear CUPE as supposed anti-Semites. I understood why they were upset: CUPE Ontario was the largest organization anywhere in the world to endorse the BDS campaign. The media, similarly, understood the significance of the vote. Before the weekend was over, I was in the eye of a very big storm. Synagogues across Canada denounced me. Emails filled my own and the CUPE inboxes. Columnists in the *National Post* and the *Toronto Sun* chimed in, along with right-wing radio talk-show hosts and the assorted nutbars who spew their vitriol over the air. It was a media storm.

Within two weeks, I received approximately thirty-five thousand emails, most from within Canada, but many from all over the world. They were split more or less evenly between opponents and supporters. Hundreds of the pro-Israel messages crossed the line separating civil discourse from hate mail. One woman wrote: "What of your CUPE membership … laden down with anti-capitalists, self loathers, labour-profiteers, anti-Semites, and 5th Column Muslim and mis-educated third world immigrants, taught from birth to hate Jews." Several blog postings were also beyond the pale. One blog in particular, *No Dhimmitude*, in a posting by "Dag" on July 25, said in part: "Ryan is a war criminal … he promotes terrorists, finances them, encourages them in word, deed, and with money. He should be killed … hang Sid Ryan from a lamp post." The blog went on for several pages, with dozens of comments, not one of them objecting to the lies and murderous threats. I made an official complaint to the police in 42 Division, who took down the particulars. A week later Staff Sergeant Dave Vickers phoned to tell me the police could do nothing, so I had my lawyer set up a press conference and announce that I was going to sue the site's perpetrators. The post and the comments were taken down within days.

Filth poured into my CUPE Ontario office for more than a month. My staff was subjected to vicious and vile phone calls from people calling them "whores" and "Nazis" and threatening to murder me. We did our best to ignore it but it was hard to endure. My main political concern remained the CUPE membership, whose responses I paid careful attention to. I received a small handful of phone calls and even fewer emails from CUPE members who complained about the resolution.

In defending the discriminatory actions taken against Palestinians in Israel, on the West Bank, and in Gaza, the Israel lobby tends to focus on the suggestion that they're not in any way comparable to the actions of the apartheid regime in South Africa. They are well aware that the BDS campaign has its analogue in the sanctions imposed on South Africa in the years before apartheid was defeated. Their sensitivity is not surprising. There's no question who occupied the moral high ground in South Africa's long struggle. If — or when — it becomes widely accepted that the situations are similar, and the Palestinians are seen to be oppressed in the same way that black South Africans were oppressed, the Israelis will have lost a hugely significant public-relations battle. This, presumably, explains the intensity of the vitriol that was directed at CUPE Ontario in the aftermath of the 2006 convention.

CUPE Ontario, however, is not exactly alone in making the comparison. The Harvard-based scholar and one-time leader of Canada's Liberal Party Michael Ignatieff described what he saw in a flight over the West Bank in an op-ed in the *Guardian* in 2002:

> When I looked down at the West Bank, at the settlements like Crusader forts occupying the high ground, at the Israeli security cordon along the Jordan river closing off the Palestinian lands from Jordan, I knew I was not looking down at a state or the beginnings of one, but at a Bantustan, one of those pseudo-states created in the dying years of apartheid to keep the African population under control.*

Similarly, South African archbishop and Nobel Laureate Desmond Tutu, who knows a thing or two about apartheid, expressed his disappointment at what he saw in the occupied territories. In 2002, he said,

> I've been very deeply distressed in my visit to the Holy Land; it reminded me so much of what happened to us black people in South Africa. I have seen the humiliation of the Palestinians at checkpoints and roadblocks, suffering like us when young white police officers prevented us from moving about.**

* Michael Ignatieff, "Why Bush Must Send In His Troops," *Guardian*, April 19, 2002, theguardian.com/world/2002/apr/19/israel3.

** Desmond Tutu, "Apartheid in the Holy Land," *Guardian*, April 29, 2002, theguardian.com/ world/2002/apr/29/comment.

Former President Jimmy Carter, another Nobel Peace Prize winner, used the expression in the subtitle of his book, *Palestine: Peace Not Apartheid*. In a December 2006 interview reported in the Israeli newspaper *Haaretz*, Carter said,

> When Israel does occupy this territory deep within the West Bank, and connects the 200-or-so illegal settlements with each other, with a road, and prohibits Palestinians from using that road, or in many cases even crossing the road, this perpetrates even worse instances of apartness, or apartheid, than we witnessed even in South Africa.*

From within Israel itself, B'Tselem, the highly respected Israeli Information Center for Human Rights in the Occupied Territories, issued a statement:

> Israel has created in the Occupied Territories a regime of separation based on discrimination, applying two separate systems of law in the same area and basing the rights of individuals on nationality. This regime is the only one of its kind in the world and is reminiscent of distasteful regimes in the past, such as the Apartheid regime in South Africa.**

Obviously, neither CUPE nor the organizers behind the BDS campaign were the only ones to see parallels between the apartheid regime in South Africa and the Israeli occupation of Palestine. Nevertheless, we were subjected to relentless attacks by partisans of the existing Israeli regime. Journalist Rex Murphy wrote a column for the *Globe and Mail*

---

* Jimmy Carter, quoted in "Jimmy Carter: Israel's 'Apartheid' Policies Worse Than South Africa's," *Haaretz*, December 11, 2006, haaretz.com/1.4938644.

** B'Tselem, "Land Grab: Israel's Settlement Policy in the West Bank," May 2002, btselem.org/publications/summaries/200205_land_grab.

entitled "Sid Ryan's Apartheid Smear."* The paper declined to publish my response. Natan Sharansky, former Israeli deputy prime minister and right-wing politician, also writing in the *Globe and Mail*, claimed that CUPE Ontario was using "code words" to call for the "dismantlement of … [the] Jewish State,"** which was a gross misrepresentation of our position. Attacks in the media like these, combined with the concerted letter- and email-writing campaign, reflected the sophistication and determination of an Israeli lobby bent on pushing back on criticism that stung.

CUPE Ontario never budged from its support for Resolution 50. I believed in the principles behind the resolution. I believed the Palestinian people were being subjected to cruel and inhumane treatment through the occupation and apartheid policies. As a leader of Ontario's largest union, I felt strongly that I had a moral obligation to use my platform and influence to speak out. I was aware that, in response to Israeli abuses, paramilitary organizations within the Palestinian community engaged in a vicious and inhumane campaign targeting Israeli civilians, using both suicide bombers and rockets fired from the Gaza Strip. I condemned these tactics unequivocally as the acts of terrorists. But, with equal force, I condemned Israel's disproportionate response to these attacks, a condemnation that has been endorsed by human rights groups around the world. Resolution 50 is an attempt by CUPE activists to use peaceful means to apply pressure to Israel to end the occupation and negotiate a peaceful settlement to the conflict. I have given my support many times to the two-state solution to the Middle East impasse even as that possibility is fast becoming a non-starter because of the proliferation of illegal settlements on Palestinian lands. I have not been alone.

Since CUPE Ontario's historic decision in May 2006, hundreds of BDS campaigns have been initiated around the world. Government bodies, ranging from the Norwegian government and the American

---

* Rex Murphy, "Sid Ryan's Apartheid Smear," *Globe and Mail*, June 3, 2006, theglobeandmail.com/news/national/sid-ryans-apartheid-smear/article729857.

** Natan Sharansky, "This Boycott Call Is Un-Canadian," *Globe and Mail*, June 1, 2006, theglobeandmail.com/opinion/this-boycott-call-is-un-canadian/article24424390.

Green Party to Sinn Féin and Dublin City Council have joined in. Artists and musicians, including Elvis Costello and Roger Waters (formerly of Pink Floyd), have initiated their own cultural boycott. The BDS campaign on its own will not bring about a two-state solution but it is most certainly having an impact. The issue has been debated in the Canadian, United Kingdom, and United States legislatures. One day, these grassroots efforts, combined with UN resolutions, and the possibility of Palestine taking Israel to the International Criminal Court for war crimes, will tip the balance in favour of a Free Palestine.

THE CAMPAIGN TO DEFEAT THE FTAA

The Battle in Seattle

Before the Quebec summit in 2001, which I described at the start of this book, there was Seattle in November 1999. As never before, the meeting of World Trade Organization (WTO) leaders in Seattle brought to public attention the outlines of the corporate plan for new rules affecting international trade, finance, privatization, low taxes, deregulation, sale of public assets, and investment laws that favoured corporate interests at the expense of civil society. Otherwise known as the Washington Consensus. In Seattle, civil society pushed back.

The WTO had been in existence for five years by then and boasted 135 permanent member countries with strong and legally enforced dispute settlement powers. It had replaced the old General Agreement on Tariffs and Trade (GATT), which had a provisional membership of 34 countries and no enforcement powers. The WTO exists to regulate and enforce trade agreements negotiated on behalf of transnational banks and corporations, backed up by member states.

The rulings of the WTO are final and binding. This is worrying, not least because we have seen many health-and-safety laws, labour laws, and environmental laws struck down by the WTO as "barriers to trade." Corporations and the global banks are at the table when countries negotiate trade deals. The old GATT system regulated tariffs and quotas, but their rulings were subject to challenges within sovereign states and were often overturned. The rulings of the WTO are not. One particularly egregious example of these corporate investor powers is contained within Chapter 11 of NAFTA: if a private sector corporation feels that their "investor rights or protections" have been violated, they can haul a member state before a secret trade tribunal, which has the power to award the complainant millions of dollars, paid for by the taxpayers of the offending member country.

This was just one of the most outrageous provisions that provided the impetus for the protest that found expression in Seattle. (Chapter 11 has since been removed from the newly negotiated USMCA that replaced NAFTA.) Hundreds of non-governmental organizations (NGOs) from around the world converged on the city. Environmentalists, educators, workers, farmers, anarchists, ecologists, students, and union members exploited the power of social media to respond rapidly and effectively in a powerful display of grassroots collaboration.

CUPE National kept a relatively low profile in the run-up to the protest, sending only a few staff members to Seattle: Morna Ballantyne, executive assistant to Judy Darcy, and CUPE researcher Catherine Louli. CUPE B.C. and B.C. Federation of Labour sent several busloads from the Vancouver area. A buzz was in the air, and my gut told me I should go to Seattle. I phoned every hotel within a wide radius of downtown Seattle before I found a motel twenty-eight miles away from the city centre. I arrived around eight on a cold and wet Monday evening. The taxi took an eternity to get from the airport to the motel.

Up by 6:30 a.m. on Tuesday, I switched on the TV and saw the beginnings of a historic battle. The talking heads and the people they interviewed presented two very different visions of the future. Corporations backed by compliant governments in developed countries wanted a global agreement on trade, goods, and services, regulated by a corporate constitution that overrode the laws of sovereign states. The NGOs, meanwhile, wanted no part of a trade agreement that jeopardized environmental laws, labour laws, or health-and-safety laws, or that privatized or commodified public healthcare, education, social programs, energy, or water. These assets are what make a society more equitable. They are the gifts we pass from generation to generation. In the middle of the divide were the developing countries that wanted to protect the meagre resources of their nations while gaining access to the lucrative markets in the developed world. The boys in suits from the developed world were having none of it.

I ordered a taxi and was about halfway to Seattle when my cellphone rang. It was a CBC reporter back in Toronto wanting to know if I was anywhere near the protesters who were blockading downtown streets. Twenty minutes later, I was in the city centre when all hell broke loose. I described the scene before me to CBC listeners as police and protesters clashed, and tear gas filled the air. Soon I was getting calls from other networks back in Canada. I spent most of the day giving hourly updates.

The organizational sophistication of the young protesters was impressive. Their short-term objective was to stop the WTO from meeting and thereby score worldwide media attention for their multitude of causes. Their underlying objective was to expose the secrecy in which corporations and world leaders conspired to establish the rules of globalization. The corporations and world leaders were inside a virtual fortress from which civil society was forcibly excluded. At every intersection, about fifty protesters gathered with no obvious leader. Every hour or so a "council meeting" was called, in which the activists formed a tight circle, shared intelligence from the other blockades, discussed strategy and safety, and decided on next steps.

The labour movement played no effective role in the protests. At some point that day, I discovered that the United States labour movement (AFL-CIO) was holding a rally in a football stadium twenty minutes out of downtown. I made my way there and found a large segment of the Canadian delegation listening to speeches. I bumped into Maude Barlow from the Council of Canadians and Tony Clarke from the Polaris Institute and told them what was happening on the streets outside the convention centre. I listened to the speeches for about ten minutes, decided it was a waste of time, and left. Maude and Tony rallied the Canadian delegation to do the same.

I was back downtown in time to see the police dressed in Darth Vader riot gear charging into the crowds. The air was thick with tear gas and smoke bombs. Every thirty minutes or so the police set off percussion bombs, which sound like car bomb explosions and are designed to spread fear. At one point, I came face to face with about a dozen black bloc protesters smashing plate glass windows and leaving a trail of destruction behind them. I grabbed one and tried to rip off his bandana. I called him a fucking idiot. Two of his friends intervened and pulled him away. I have no time for these morons, whose presence in legitimate protests give the police a reason to respond with overwhelming force. I also saw police provocateurs at work. I was running down a side street, attempting to escape from the tear gas, when a large police truck pulled up in front of me. The back doors opened and out jumped six or seven burly young men dressed as protesters. Two of them had sticks in their hands, which they beat against the ground. They called out to students and others on the sidewalks to join them as they made their way toward the main intersection at 6th and University. It is not unusual for police to embed themselves in crowds and pretend to be protesters. When they cross the line and incite protesters to commit acts of violence, they are no longer acting under the law. The police become lawbreakers themselves.

The protests raged into the night and for the next several days. Seattle was top of the news around the world throughout the entire week. The opening ceremonies and speeches had to be cancelled. The world was now watching what the corporations and governments were up to behind closed doors. The international delegations from the developing countries were encouraged by the protests and began to push back against the G7 countries. It was becoming clear the third meeting of the World Trade Organization was going to end without agreement. Civil society had flexed its muscles and sent a clear signal to the WTO, the IMF, World Bank, and the Organization of American States that life would not continue as before. The people were demanding a say in how trade agreements are negotiated. If noisy and boisterous protests were what it took, then so be it.

I came away from Seattle with the renewed conviction that if unions were to become effective agents of change, they had to join forces with civil society. In Seattle, the AFL-CIO was still mired in the old model of mass rallies of union members, isolated from community organizations, students, NGOs, and the like. It was clear to me that every successful mobilization that I had been involved in to date involved working closely with coalition partners from the community. The young protesters in Seattle had taken social unionism to a new level with their creative structures of leadership and communications.

The Cuban Connection

It was partly with this idea in mind that, earlier in 1999, I had hired Antoni Shelton as my executive assistant with special responsibilities for the legislative agenda of CUPE Ontario. At that time, Antoni was the director of the Urban Alliance on Race Relations and a former assistant to Zanana Akande, minister of social services in the Rae government. Antoni arranged a meeting between Edgar Godoy, an executive board member of CUPE local 2191, and me to discuss CUPE Ontario's international work. Edgar was born in Guatemala and made his way to Canada as a refugee along with his wife and two children. He felt strongly that CUPE needed to connect our local issues with the larger, international context. The policies contained in NAFTA and the FTAA have a direct impact on our public services, including the provision of clean water, healthcare, and education. I thought about Antoni's and Edgar's suggestions and realized they were correct. CUPE National was

Edgar Godoy at the healthcare rally, Queen's Park, October 2018.

spending a lot of time on international work, especially with the South Africans, yet we had very little connection with the labour movement in our own hemisphere. Following my trip to Seattle, I charged Edgar and Antoni with putting together an International Solidarity Committee. Edgar was elected chair, and over the next few months the committee made several recommendations that I took to the executive board. The primary recommendations were, first, to organize a conference focused on international trade agreements and their impact on Canada's social programs, and, second, to invite a delegation from Cuba to speak at our May 2000 convention in Windsor. The point was to develop links to the trade union movement in Central and South America and the Caribbean. Cuba would be a start.

We had hoped perhaps one hundred of our members would attend the conference on international trade agreements, but we ended up having to accommodate more than four hundred. Naomi Klein, who had just published her brilliant and hugely successful book *No Logo*, and Tony Clarke from the Polaris Institute agreed to be our guest speakers. Between them, they outlined the perils and politics of free trade agreements, the privatizations and loss of good-paying jobs that flow from them. These agreements were not just about the hollowing-out of Canada's manufacturing sector and the outsourcing of jobs to Mexico, China, and elsewhere, but they also posed a grave threat to the services delivered by the public sector. It was a sobering exposition.

As Edgar suggested, we invited Cuban labour leaders from the Workers Central Union of Cuba (CTC) to speak at our May 2000 convention. Roberto Cuesta Piz from the Public Administration Union (SINTAP) and Jose Suarez from the National Association of Innovators (ANIR) spoke about life in Cuba under the Batista regime, where black workers like them were discriminated against, many native Cubans were illiterate, and a universal healthcare system was non-existent. Today, Cuba boasts one of the highest literacy rates in the world, their universal healthcare system is second only to Canada's, and infant mortality rates are among the lowest in the world. All of this was achieved despite the United States' fifty-year blockade of the island. The bridges we were building with the Cuban labour movement would later become very important in the fight to kill the Free Trade Area of the Americas (FTAA).

Following the convention, I was invited by the CTC to visit Cuba, an invitation that was renewed after the anti-FTAA protests in Quebec City. Finally, in December 2003, I attended the SINTAP convention in Havana, which was much like the numerous labour conventions I had attended in Canada. Guests from several Latin American and European countries spoke, among them a strikingly articulate Bolivian activist, Evo Morales, whom I would encounter a few years later. I was somewhat concerned that the translation services were not simultaneous: each speaker would utter a few sentences and then pause, waiting for the translation, before proceeding. The effect was somewhat deadening. I asked Edgar if he would translate my speech for me. Edgar was familiar with my passionate style of public speaking and had translated for me on several occasions. He agreed and cleared it with the Cuban organizers. When my turn came, I spoke in warm terms of Cuba's achievements in the fields of health and education, and of how, despite the American embargo, Cuba still managed to provide its citizens with top-notch healthcare and education. I did my best to infuse my words with force and passion, which Edgar picked up on perfectly and I'm sure embellished. In concluding, I was pleased to note that their revolutionary hero, Che Guevara, had Irish blood, and that I was born on the most revered day in Cuban history, July 26, which marked the beginning of the Cuban revolution. The crowd roared its approval.

When we broke for lunch I met with the high-profile leader of the Argentinian labour delegation, Pablo Micheli. The year before, in 2002, CUPE Ontario had sponsored a visit by delegates from five South American countries to a healthcare workers' exchange in Niagara Falls. Pablo and I hit it off right from the very beginning. He was the leader of a progressive union not unlike CUPE. His union, ATE, is on the progressive and more radical wing of the labour movement in his country. A few years after our first meeting in Cuba, Micheli became the leader of CTA, a central labour body in Argentina. I would be seeing him again, in Buenos Aires, where his union would host the second healthcare workers' exchange.

Pablo Micheli (right), secretary general of CTA, one of two central labour bodies in Argentina.

I returned to Cuba a few months later in late January 2004 at the invitation of Manuel Monteros of the CTC to speak at the Third Hemispheric Encounter of Struggle against the FTAA. The timing of the Cuban conference was significant but purely coincidental in that Canada had arranged a mid-January Special Summit of the Americas in Monterrey to prepare for the fourth Summit of the Americas in Mar del Plata. Prior to the conference opening, I sat on a panel and delivered a presentation on the negative impacts of NAFTA on Canadian jobs. Seated next to me was Evo Morales, a Bolivian congressman and future president of Bolivia. The opening of the conference was memorable. The cavernous Palacio de Convenciones in Miramar, Havana, was jam-packed with two thousand delegates from thirty-four countries. No fewer than ten translation booths overlooked the main hall, reflecting the many languages and cultures of the attendees. Rumours circulated, whispered with a thrill of anticipation, that El Comandante himself, Fidel Castro, would make an appearance. He did, but in the most inconspicuous of ways. Just as proceedings got underway, a tall, bearded man in green army fatigues made his way onto the dais. The crowd erupted into a spontaneous chorus of "Fidel! Fidel! Fidel!" and "Long live the Revolution!" that lasted for about ten minutes. Castro simply waved and sat down. He took notes but did not speak during the opening ceremony.

I was approached by a young Colombian woman, Martha Cecilia Jordan Angulo, who told me that activist union leaders were under attack in her country. One in particular, Alexander López Maya, a former leader of her union and a member of parliament, had been forced to go into hiding after a veiled death threat by the president, Álvaro Uribe Vélez. During my own speech (a collaborative effort of Antoni, Edgar, and me) I asked the convention chair for permission to share some of my time with Sister Angulo. Her words left many of the delegates in tears. I ended my speech by moving a motion condemning the murder of union leaders in Colombia and sending a warning to President Uribe Vélez that if one hair on the head of Alexander López Maya was touched, then Vélez would be held personally responsible. The motion passed unanimously and formed part of the official convention statement.

Around 9:00 p.m. that night, Fidel Castro addressed the delegates. The Canadian delegation was pleased to discover that we were seated just six feet from the podium — that is, until his speech stretched out for almost five hours. Speaking without notes, he covered everything from baseball to the Bay of Pigs invasion and the FTAA. He was at times passionate, self-deprecating, funny, and proud of what Cuba had accomplished. But long-winded! People around us were falling asleep and the translators were so tired they were only completing half sentences by the time it came to an end.

The Argentine Connection and the Burial of FTAA

In November 2004, I led a Canadian delegation to Buenos Aires to co-chair the Second Healthcare Workers' Exchange along with my friend Pablo Micheli, general secretary of ATE. The conference was attended by more than one hundred delegates from a dozen countries, twice as many countries as had attended the inaugural meeting in

Niagara Falls. The FTAA dominated the agenda because of its potential to end up privatizing what was left of public healthcare in the hemisphere. The struggle is still far from being won.

President George W. Bush, along with a number of other national leaders who participated in the Quebec City summit, had marked 2005 as the year when the FTAA would finally be approved and come into force. But a lot had happened since Quebec. The protests highlighted civil society's opposition to these secret corporate deals. Cuba, which had been excluded from the negotiations, became a leading opposition force in the hemisphere, along with Venezuela. Venezuela's president, Hugo Chávez, emerged as the most visible public face of the opposition. In 2004 Castro and Chávez teamed up to announce the formation of the Bolivarian Alliance for the Americas (ALBA), effectively becoming the leaders in the fight against the FTAA. Also, in the aftermath of the Quebec summit, two more powerful left-wing leaders, Brazil's Luiz Inácio Lula da Silva and Argentina's Néstor Kirchner, came to power. Their two nations, both South American economic powerhouses, would play important roles in negotiations. Without them there could be no meaningful FTAA.

The Fourth Summit of the Americas took place in November 2005, in the resort city of Mar del Plata, Argentina, 250 miles south of Buenos Aires. The People's Summit took place at the same time. Canada was well represented with delegates from the CLC, CAW, CUPE National, and CUPE Ontario. The format of the protests was similar to the pattern set in Quebec City, with the People's Summit spread out across the city in university campuses and public spaces. The police and military buildup were even more severe than in Quebec City, with some ten thousand military and police personnel mobilized to ensure security. The conference site was surrounded by three concentric rings of fencing, covering twenty city blocks. The city had become a fortress.

The debates at the People's Summit were intense, as one would expect in a Latin American country. George W. Bush was the target of heated criticism. His war in Iraq was wildly unpopular. The president himself stayed well away from protesters, in private quarters on board a United States aircraft carrier, while his counterparts from other countries stayed in hotels inside the cordon. Hugo Chávez was the exception. He stayed in a modest hotel, coincidentally across the street from where I was staying with the CUPE Ontario delegation. Each morning he would exit the hotel and spend ten or fifteen minutes chatting with members of the public before heading to the summit. The contrast between Chávez in the street and Bush on his warship was not lost on anyone, including the media.

The FTAA talks did not go well. Néstor Kirchner, as host of the summit, opened up with a blistering speech. According to *Pagina/12*, an Argentinian newspaper, Kirchner railed against "international financial institutions, the Washington Consensus, the idea of the free market as a panacea, agricultural subsidies and the FTAA." "Simply signing an agreement will not lead to an easy and direct road to prosperity,"* he said, adding that the U.S., with its "role as first global power," needed to consider its policies toward the region as they "not only provoke misery and poverty, but also add to institutional instability." Kirchner finished by saying, "Our poor, our excluded, our countries, no longer accept that we have to keep talking in a low voice."

Bush listened attentively but was relatively quiet throughout the summit. He left the heavy lifting to Vicente Fox from Mexico, who did his best to push the FTAA agenda. Brazil's leader, Luiz Inácio Lula da Silva, however, insisted the FTAA had no chance of being approved unless the United States was prepared to eliminate the huge subsidies it provided to its own agricultural sector. The Brazilian and Argentinian agricultural sectors form a large part of their economies.

Outside the perimeter, the pressure from protest groups increased from one day to the next. An anti-FTAA, anti-Bush train packed with celebrities started its journey in Buenos Aires and slowly made its way to Mar del Plata, with several stops along the way. On board the "ALBA Express" and leading the protest was the football player Diego Maradona, along with Bolivian candidate for president Evo Morales, the Mothers of the Plaza de Mayo, and famous Cuban folksinger and poet Silvio Rodríguez. The train was met by

---

* *Pagina/12*, November 12, 2005.

the 1980 Nobel Peace Prize recipient, Adolfo Pérez Esquivel, who was the key organizer behind the twelve-thousand-strong alternative People's Summit.

The main protest march against the FTAA began in the pouring rain early on Friday, November 4, 2005, with sixty thousand protesters gathered in downtown Mar del Plata next to the outer perimeter fence of the FTAA negotiations. The march was led by the celebrities from the ALBA Express and a host of NGO leaders and community activists. Latin American protests, or even football matches, for that matter, are unlike anything else on the planet. The deafening sound of drums filled the air, intermittingly interrupted by the voices of thousands of activists singing and chanting slogans. The parade weaved through the rain-soaked streets to the Mundialista stadium. As we marched with the noisy crowd, I was approached by my friend Pablo Micheli, who told me I had a spot reserved on the main stage where Hugo Chávez, Evo Morales, and Diego Maradona would be speaking. Pablo said it was a "thank you" to CUPE for the role we played in helping to defeat the FTAA. I was provided with a translator and rushed from the march before it reached the stadium.

After an elaborate security check deep in the bowels of the stadium, we made our way onto the stage and watched, in awe, as sixty thousand protesters filled the stadium around us. The rain poured down, but it did nothing to dampen the spirits of the people. They held thousands of flags from every country in the hemisphere. Directly below the stage, Edgar Godoy, Antoni Shelton, and Claude Genereaux were flying the fuchsia flags of CUPE.

Hugo Chávez bounded up the steps from underneath the stand and onto the stage. A second or two passed before the crowd realized who it was, and then they roared. The cacophony of drums, whistles, chants, and singing was deafening. Chávez gave a rousing speech in which he declared that the Free Trade Area of the Americas (ALCA in Spanish) was dead. "ALCA has been defeated by the peoples of this continent," he told the crowd, "and today, in Mar del Plata, it is time to bury ALCA. The next thing we will bury is capitalism.... The battle against ALCA, we have undoubtedly won."

The program continued with short speeches from Maradona, Evo Morales, and the founder of the Mothers of the Plaza de Mayo, Hebe Bonafina, and with songs from Silvio Rodríguez. Following his short speech, Morales looked for a seat, spotted the empty chair beside me and sat down. We chatted briefly. I reminded him that we both had been part of a panel discussion in Cuba in 2003. One month after the defeat of the FTAA, he became the president of Bolivia.

As I look back at the incredible success we had in defeating FTAA, it is apparent to me that a number of factors were in play. The mobilization efforts of the Hemispheric Social Alliance (HSA) were instrumental in pulling together the trade unions and NGOs under one banner. The HSA enabled unions, environmental organizations, poverty activists, farmers, and others to talk to each other and hammer out a consensus on contentious issues. The concept of the alternative People's Summit was key in providing a space where members of the alliance could debate their issues at the summit site. The massive protests organized in each city where the Organization of American States (OAS) presidents were meeting was crucial to getting the message out to the millions of activists who were unable to attend. The involvement of Cuba and its willingness to host the People's Summit conventions and conferences in Havana were absolutely critical in expanding and building the movement. Because Cuba was outside of the OAS, Venezuela was key, on the inside, in connecting with the new leftist governments emerging in the southern part of the hemisphere. Hugo Chávez worked with four significant countries — Brazil, Argentina, Uruguay, and Paraguay — that turned down the Bush-led push for a new round of FTAA negotiations. These five countries together account for a huge chunk of the Latin American economy. Any hemispheric trade agreement signed without them would have been meaningless. A victory was achieved at Mar del Plata, but the fight against the corporate and state sponsors of the Washington Consensus is not over.

The mobilization that took place to defeat the FTAA was unprecedented in scope. Ever since the FTA was approved between Canada and the U.S. in 1989, and later, when NAFTA brought in Mexico, the left has been vilified by the media and politicians alike

From left: Denise Hammond, CUPE Ontario; me, CUPE Ontario president; and Candace Rennick, CUPE Ontario, at the York University strike, 2008.

as crackpots for opposing these agreements. Three decades later, everything we said was bad about free trade agreements has come to pass. The voters in America's Rust Belt states sent a strong and clear message to politicians that free trade agreements are killing our jobs and destroying our communities, just as we predicted. Donald Trump, a multibillionaire bigot, picked up on their pain and rode it all the way to the White House. Trump scrapped the Trans-Pacific Partnership (TPP) negotiations and threatened to rip up NAFTA. However, his bravado on NAFTA turned into mush when he recently merely renamed NAFTA, calling it the United States-Mexico-Canada Agreement (USMCA), with little discernable change for the protection of workers' rights. The AFL-CIO, the umbrella organization for labour in the U.S., said through their trade specialist Celeste Drake speaking on labour reforms, "It is not obvious that the improvements are sufficient to make a meaningful difference to jobs and wages or to Mexico's protection union regime … other rules in the agreement undermine the interests of working families." In Canada, the CLC and Unifor have both praised the agreement, whilst CUPE, USW, and other unions are highly critical. However, one thing is clear: Trump is no friend of the working class and for all his glib talk about bad trade agreements, his grandstanding rhetoric will do nothing to benefit workers. At the end of the day, the U.S. will continue to push globalization and sign onto trade agreements that are not in the interest of the average worker.

Canada so far has ignored the message heard in the Rust Belt of the United States. Prime Minister Justin Trudeau plowed ahead with the signing of CETA, a free trade agreement with the twenty-seven countries of the European Union. Buried inside CETA are the same clauses that have led to the hollowing-out of manufacturing jobs in North America. The trade unions in Europe put up a valiant battle to stop CETA. They took hundreds of thousands of their members into the streets in European capitals and did what they could to warn the public of the dangers. Sadly, they found no partner in Canada willing to match their mobilization. The Canadian Labour Congress gave the Trudeau Liberal government a free pass on CETA. The sum total of its opposition was a complaining press release and an old video posted to their website. Clearly, the leadership of the CLC has learned nothing from the historic battle to defeat the FTAA. Trudeau, emboldened by the lack of opposition from organized labour to his signing onto CETA, quickly moved without any public scrutiny to sign onto the much-hated TPP. Again, nothing but silence from the CLC. Canadian workers will pay a heavy price for this neglect.

Chapter 6
OFL PRESIDENT

I grew and matured as a union leader during my years as the head of CUPE Ontario and at the beginning of 2008 I felt my work there was coming to an end. I had been president for the better part of seventeen years and felt it was time to move on. During that period (1992–2009), I had taken CUPE Ontario from relative obscurity, operating out of a shabby office at the back of an industrial strip mall in Scarborough, and built it into a political powerhouse. In 2008, CUPE Ontario was at the forefront of every major union and political campaign in Ontario. Under my leadership, the union had grown from 140,000 members to over 220,000. We were by far the largest union in Ontario and our parent union CUPE National was the largest in Canada. CUPE Ontario had arrived and was now a major voice in Canadian politics. There was not a facet of public life that a CUPE member did not touch, from the healthcare system to education to the cleaning of our streets. After seventeen years as president, I noticed the big-ticket issues were beginning to repeat themselves. I did a lot of soul-searching in early 2008 and asked some tough questions of myself and about my future, trying to be objective about what was best for the organization. The answer became obvious.

I have always believed that the lifeblood of any organization rests in its ability to embrace change and to place trust in the next generation. I made up my mind to move on and allow new CUPE leadership to flourish and take over the running of the union. Throughout my leadership years in CUPE, I had been fortunate to work with some amazing and progressive leaders who both helped me grow as a union leader and supported me in implementing a progressive agenda. For example, Michael Hurley, the president of OCHU, has a brilliant mind and sharp wit that he uses effectively to advance the cause of CUPE's hospital workers. Brian O'Keefe is another leader that I was proud to have as my secretary treasurer for ten years. Brian holds a degree in economics from the prestigious London School of Economics, and he always managed to find resources to fund the plethora of campaigns that CUPE Ontario waged during our decade together. Edgar Godoy has a remarkable knowledge of Latin America and a big-picture vision of international organizing. I also surrounded myself with excellent and dedicated staff like my office administrator, Angela Kirby; Antoni Shelton, one of the brightest minds and strategic thinkers in the labour movement; and four of the best media people I know — Lynn Simmons, Shannon McManus, Pat Daley, and Stella Yeadon.

I loved every moment of the seventeen years I spent as CUPE Ontario president but it was time to hand off to the next generation of leaders. Fred Hahn had been the secretary treasurer of CUPE Ontario for six years and prior to that had led a progressive local union of social service workers in Toronto. Fred is an openly gay and very gregarious union leader who has always been loved by the membership. He was the obvious choice for leader given his work ethic and leadership skills. Candace Rennick was a very bright long-term-care-facility worker who had already been impressing people with her skill, knowledge, and feistiness for years despite her youth. She was growing into a mature young woman with a great future ahead of her. I never had a moment's hesitation in passing the torch to this dynamic duo, who have since gone on to blaze their own trails as leaders of what I see as the most progressive union in the country. I could have continued to lead CUPE Ontario for another ten years until my retirement, but I knew in my heart and soul I would not be doing justice to the job or to the membership. I was ready to move on.

I felt strongly about the skill set I could bring to the table at the Ontario Federation of Labour. I had one of the highest media profiles among union leaders in the country. I had been a regular guest on TV and radio talk shows during my career in CUPE. I was a guest columnist with the *Toronto Sun* for over two years, and my opinion pieces appeared in every major newspaper in the country. I deliberately cultivated a media presence in order to speak directly to the average union member or unorganized worker in the country. I know this pissed off a lot of my peers but it worked for me and, I believe, the movement, as well. I was an unabashed and unapologetic left-wing rabble-rousing union leader who knew how to garner free earned media better than most. I used my Irish "gift of the gab" to generate media stories on behalf of striking workers, fights against social injustice, cuts to public services, and to overall raise the profile of the labour movement. In 2009, the OFL had just about disappeared from public consciousness and I knew I could turn that situation around.

I spent the next several months consulting with mid-level union leaders and holding round-table sessions with disparate groups from the community. I knew from my experience with the Days of Action and the numerous campaigns I had organized in CUPE that Ontario's central labour body could not stand alone. It had to become the crossroads for social justice in Ontario where everybody felt they had a stake in the organization. In fall 2008, Antoni Shelton and I set up a series of eclectic round-table meetings with leaders from the childcare movement; poverty activists; housing activists; black, Latin, and Asian community activists; and many other organizations and individuals. The response from the community organizations was one of joy that, finally, somebody was going to pull together the "left" in Ontario to coordinate an intelligent resistance. From the meetings with individual union leaders and the community round-table sessions, the broad brush strokes of a program of change and action for the OFL began to emerge. The plan centred around four key pillars:

1. **Equity.** We need to build a new kind of labour movement that puts equity and equality for all at the heart of everything we do. But we need to also address systemic discrimination within our unions. That means we need to remove the barriers that advantage some groups over others. Indigenous workers and workers of colour need to see their race, language, and culture reflected in the union that wants their vote. We need to stand with these communities when they're battling fundamental human rights abuses like carding, missing Indigenous women, and the police use of force. This creates trust and a basis for others to join in.

2. **Engaging Government.** The OFL needs to re-engage with government such that we can have an impact on legislative and public policy development. There is a need to raise the minimum wage and initiate labour law reforms to address the preciousness and inequality that are driving thousands of families into poverty. Health and safety of workers must be placed front and centre on labour's agenda along with reforms of the Workplace Safety and Insurance Board (WSIB).

3. **Building the Movement.** The OFL needs to bring in new members, beginning with the CAW who have been outside the OFL for more than a decade. Establish a common front that represents a new kind of labour-movement organizing, one that opens our structures to the participation of community organizations, non-unionized workers, and the unemployed. Future OFL campaigns will need to reinvigorate the fighting spirit of organized labour and inspire the creation of an Ontario Common Front to address rising inequality and defend the interests of the next generation.

4. **Mobilizing the Membership.** We need to revert back to our roots and support demands for social justice and an end to inequality by putting tens of thousands of our members on the streets when necessary to back up our demands. When a local union is on strike anywhere in the province we need to get on the buses and lend them our support. If a worker is killed on the job we need to hold the employer and government accountable. We need a campaign to protect workers on the job.

I felt I had done my homework, consulted with local union leaders, district council presidents, and community organizations, but convincing more than fifty provincial and national union leaders to support my candidacy was an entirely different kettle of fish. The labour movement is often a cauldron of petty grievances that, in some cases, date back to the 1930s. It is also divided along political and ideological lines. As the leader of CUPE Ontario, I had made my views clear, and nobody had any illusions about where I stood on practically every political and ideological issue of the day. I had crossed swords with several of the union leaders I was now about to ask for support. However, I didn't really give a hoot how most national or provincial union leaders felt about me because I knew their members — who were coming to the convention to vote on the new OFL president — liked my politics and my willingness to fight and take CUPE members to the streets whenever the need arose. Notwithstanding my feelings, I now had to traverse the minefields of union politics and union leader egos to make a smooth transition and win the right to lead Ontario's one million unionized workers.

The Ontario Federation of Labour was formed in 1957 as a chartered organization of the Canadian Labour Congress. It consists of fifty-four unions, fifteen hundred local unions, and forty district labour councils. It represents approximately one million organized workers. Its main purpose is to provide a central labour body where the province's fifty-four unions can coordinate and share their resources around issues that impact all of labour in Ontario. This may include lobbying the provincial government on behalf of its membership, coordinating strike support, organizing mass demonstrations, and supporting social justice issues along with community allies, including LGBT, the Workers' Action Centre, and the Ontario Health Coalition, to name a few.

The OFL offices occupy one floor of an eight-storey building that was constructed in the 1960s by a group of unions who used it as their headquarters. Over the years, as union membership grew, 90 percent of the original unions left to construct their own head offices. The building is now primarily occupied by local unions, the OFL, and several miscellaneous small businesses. It is in a sad state of disrepair but it sits on a prime piece of real estate on Gervais Drive in Toronto at the intersection of Don Mills and Eglinton. It was sold in 2016 for a couple of million dollars less than what the OFL was offered in 2013, and the OFL now rents space in the building they once owned.

Over the years, central labour bodies such as the Canadian Labour Congress (CLC) and the OFL have become the battlegrounds where old grievances and rivalries between the various unions are sometimes fought out to the detriment of the entire labour movement. These battles have led some union leaders to adopt unsavoury and undemocratic tactics to get their way, including withholding per capita taxes (union dues), disaffiliation from central labour bodies, refusal to join central labour bodies such as the OFL and district labour councils, and under-reporting membership numbers. All of these practices are a direct violation of the CLC constitution but penalties are never enforced by the CLC leadership. These undemocratic practices have left federations and district labour councils grossly underfunded. As a result, funds for community outreach and necessary campaigns to enhance and protect the gains made by the labour movement are inadequate or non-existent. The CLC's refusal to enforce its own constitution weakens the labour movement.

No less serious are the rifts between unions. In particular, the battles between the United Steelworkers and the Canadian Auto Workers (formerly the UAW, now Unifor) are legendary. The animosity and the rivalry can be traced back to the 1930s, between the traditionally communist-led Mine, Mill and Smelter Workers' union, Local 598, and the USW. Mine, Mill spurned the Steelworkers (which represented the employees of Inco, one of the main mining companies in the Sudbury area) to merge in 1993 with the Canadian Auto Workers. This became a sore point with Leo Gerard, the USW Canadian director at the time. (Gerard has since moved on to become the USW International president.) He complained bitterly to Buzz Hargrove about this intrusion into what he regarded as the USW's backyard, and Hargrove did not hide his delight at the CAW's coup.

The internationally based industrial unions, such as USW, UFCW, SEIU, ATU, and IAM, are leery of Unifor (CAW). Some of the rhetoric deployed in past disputes, in which Canadian union leaders accused American branch unions of being puppets, manipulated by their head offices, is remembered with rancour. Unifor recently trotted out similar rhetoric, using it as part of their justification for raiding the Amalgamated Transit Union (ATU) in Toronto and Unite Here 75. The argument is, frankly, disingenuous, but it allows Unifor to cloak itself in the Canadian flag while enlarging its membership at international unions' expense.

The splits in the labour movement can also be ideological. This was certainly the case when the pink paper unions sided with the Rae Government over the Social Contract. The pink paper document was unrestrained in singing Rae's praises while criticizing the progressive unions that opposed it. In effect, the controversy nearly split the OFL in half. Of course, I sided with the progressives.

The ideological rupture between the two factions widened further after the Ontario Conservative Party's victory in 1995. The progressive unions responded to the Harris government's savage cuts to social programs and attacks on collective bargaining rights by organizing Days of Action, in which selected cities were shut down on a rotating basis over a two-year period. The pink paper unions went along with the strategy reluctantly, at best, not shutting down any of their own workplaces and participating only in a few large demonstrations. They also distributed buttons with the slogan, "Don't blame me, I voted NDP" — a clear shot at the unions that had opposed the Social Contract.

In 1997 Gord Wilson retired as OFL president, likely because he knew he would not be re-elected after the divisive role he had played over the previous two years. Paul Forder announced his intention to run to replace Wilson, sending the leadership of the pink paper unions into fits. Wilson scoured the entire labour movement looking for a candidate to run against Forder. Many names were floated, including Dave Christopherson (CAW), a decent guy who had been a member of Bob Rae's cabinet and was current MP for Hamilton. In a Machiavellian spirit, Wilson figured Christopherson would split the CAW vote. However, Wilson and the pink paper faction eventually settled on Wayne Samuelson, an OFL director. Forder, who was also an OFL director, was a militant who wanted to mobilize the membership for political action, whereas Samuelson sought to rebuild the NDP, whatever that meant. The campaign was nasty. It culminated with unions on both sides busing over a thousand extra delegates into the convention on the day of the election in an effort to tilt the final result. This practice, it need hardly be said, is profoundly antidemocratic. In the end, Samuelson won the election by 205 votes out of a total of 2,220 ballots cast.

In the aftermath of the election, the OFL was once again under the control of the conservative unions, and though the convention delegates voted to continue with the Days of Action, plans to build to a general strike fizzled under Samuelson's leadership. A few more Days of Action were held but no general strike. The pink paper unions had succeeded in shutting down any visible resistance to the attacks on social programs and workers' rights, opting instead to put resources into the Ontario NDP — but even that was a dubious claim.

The labour movement was still reeling from the splits following the Bob Rae years when, in early 2000, the CAW became embroiled

At the Kingston Day of Action in June 1998. Left to right: Ethel LaValley, OFL secretary treasurer; Irene Harris, OFL executive vice-president; me, CUPE Ontario president; Bob White, CLC president; Ken Brown, SEIU Canadian director; and Howard Hampton, Ontario NDP leader.

in a raiding dispute with the Service Employees International Union (SEIU). Eight SEIU locals, covering seventeen thousand members, declared their intention to move to the CAW. The CAW argued that union members should be allowed to move from one union to another, provided they democratically voted to do so. The SEIU argued that the CAW had violated the CLC constitution by contacting their membership without their permission. The SEIU won the argument and demanded the CAW be kicked out of the CLC. Ken Georgetti tried in vain to mediate but, in the end, the CLC executive imposed sanctions that basically kicked the CAW out. The CAW eventually made amends and were readmitted to the CLC but refused to rejoin the OFL. The reasons were debatable but, regardless, the loss in revenue to the OFL amounted to more than $7 million over the twelve years they were out. CUPE National pulled the same stunt, withholding per capita dues from the CLC when a disagreement erupted in 2005 over a raiding dispute between the International Woodworkers of America-Canada

(IWA) union in B.C. and CUPE's Hospital Employees' Union. This tactic is the antithesis of trade union principles. It deprives the central labour bodies of the resources to carry out their mandate and disproportionately hurts the most vulnerable workers in smaller unions and workers who do not belong to a union. In his 1998 memoir, *Labour of Love*, Buzz Hargrove lays the blame at the feet of the non-progressive union leaders: "The OFL leadership does not share our passion for social equality, reform, and preservation of workers rights … as a provincial umbrella organization, it's largely irrelevant to working people."

In my opinion, Hargrove's assessment of the CAW's role as the progressives in Ontario's labour movement is overblown. There is no doubt the union was a much more militant and progressive force under his early leadership and, before him, Bob White's leadership. However, all that changed when Hargrove shifted to the mushy middle occupied by the federal and provincial Liberal parties. In the late 1990s and early 2000s, after surveying their membership, the CAW formally shifted their exclusive support away from the NDP in favour of so-called "strategic voting." On the surface, this "new" strategy was intended to maximize the political clout of the CAW by supporting both Liberals and NDP candidates, but, in practice, strategic voting became a dog-whistle summons to vote Liberal. Hargrove's rhetoric hardened to the point of hostility toward the NDP, which eventually got him kicked out of the party.

Sam Gindin, the left-leaning chief economist for the CAW during this period, opined bitterly about Hargrove's embrace of Liberal prime minister Paul Martin at the CAW's annual convention in Toronto in 2006, publicly breaking with his former boss in a scathing letter posted on social media. Gindin challenged Hargrove's motives for cozying up to the Liberals: "Was this really about what was best for the Canadian working class — a legitimate debate — or simply about a new relationship to the Liberals and more subsidies to the auto industry?"* Gindin's words were prophetic. Hargrove went on to lobby for hundreds of millions of dollars in taxpayer subsidies for the enormously profitable auto

* Sam Gindin, "The CAW's Direction: Some Questions," *Bullet*, December 14, 2005, socialistproject.ca/2005/12/b10.

corporations. His assault on the NDP took a turn for the worse when he openly attacked Howard Hampton, Ontario NDP leader, during the 2007 provincial election. He was quoted by the *Toronto Star* saying Hampton had "lost complete touch" with the people of the province, and "I see absolutely no reason to vote NDP."* In the eyes of the vast majority of unions in the labour movement the CAW were now solid Liberal supporters and champions of "corporate welfare bums," which ironically was the subject of a 1972 book by NDP leader David Lewis.

I was under no illusion that my past working relationship with Hargrove and the CAW was not going to help me win the support of provincial and national union leaders with whom I had done battle over Rae's Social Contract and the Harris Days of Action. I decided to start with Wayne Fraser, director of the Steelworkers in Ontario. Fraser and I had not seen eye to eye for many years, but the flare-ups were relatively infrequent and usually involved a difference of opinion around the OFL executive board meetings. When I met with him, he had Marie Kelly with him. Kelly was a staff lawyer with USW and also a member of the OFL executive board. To my surprise, Fraser gave me his support and asked if I would consider supporting Kelly for secretary treasurer, the number-two position in the OFL. I had not given any serious consideration to my running partner, but it made sense that the person should come from the private sector. I also liked that Kelly was from USW because I felt it would be good to bring CUPE and USW closer together. I also felt strongly that the OFL should have a woman or person of colour in the top leadership ranks. Kelly was a bright, feisty, and capable union leader, but I was also aware she had some powerful detractors within her own union. I left the meeting agreeing to support Marie Kelly.

Next on my list were Smokey Thomas of OPSEU and Sharleen Stewart of SEIU. I knew it would be difficult to get support from both these leaders. In the late 1990s the Harris government had gone on a rampage of amalgamating municipalities, schools, and hospitals, and forced the merger of bargaining units at the same time. This pitted

* Linda Diebel, "Hargrove: 'No Reason to Vote NDP,'" *Toronto Star*, October 5, 2007.

three unions — CUPE Ontario, OPSEU, and SEIU — against one another in runoff votes to see which union would represent the workers in each workplace. I had spent a lot of my time, along with Michael Hurley, first vice-president of CUPE Ontario and OCHU president, visiting all of the affected hospital workplaces. CUPE won several major representation votes and added thousands of new members to its ranks at the expense of OPSEU and SEIU. Not unnaturally, neither Thomas nor Stewart were happy about these changes. But they weren't raids; they were government-mandated mergers. Neither Thomas nor Stewart committed to supporting my candidacy, waffling about consulting their executive boards.

Most other union leaders were supportive or their union was split, with the exception of Linda Haslam-Stroud from the Ontario Nurses' Association (ONA), who said she did not like my overt support for the NDP or my militant ways. I knew Fred LeBlanc of the Ontario Fire Fighters would not be supportive. A few years earlier LeBlanc had publicly objected when I threatened to pull off a province-wide strike to pressure Premier Dalton McGuinty into giving CUPE members the same sweetheart deal he had given firefighters on their OMERS pension plan. The last noncommittal person was Rod Sheppard of the International Federation of Professional and Technical Engineers (IFPTE), commonly referred to as the Society. I was not concerned about any of these leaders' influence on the election, with the exception of OPSEU, as they brought very few delegates to the convention. However, at the time, I had no idea the damage that Fraser, Kelly, Thomas, Stewart, Haslam-Stroud, Sheppard, and LeBlanc would inflict upon the OFL during my six-year presidency.

In December 2008 Israel launched the Gaza War against Hamas and the civilian population of Gaza. I strongly condemned the bombing of UN schools and a university in Gaza. In an interview with a *National Post* reporter, I inappropriately compared the bombing of Palestinian schools to the Nazi campaign of burning books during the Second

World War. I apologized for my remarks but was attacked by the Israeli lobby. The Jewish Defence League (JDL), an extremist Israeli lobby group, protested outside my CUPE office. The story blew over in a few days but not before USW District 6 director Wayne Fraser seized the opportunity to tell me I could no longer count on his support. He was now supporting Marie Kelly for OFL president. It was not that he was a supporter of Israel. To my knowledge he had never publicly expressed an opinion on the Middle East. Rather, he was exploiting my misstep to implement a plan to promote Kelly. I checked around to see how other union leaders felt about my widely reported remarks. Most were unconcerned, but I detected a hardening of opinion among the pink paper leadership.

The question of Kelly's candidacy came to a head at the OPSEU convention in April 2009. Kelly and Fraser asked me to meet them in the Sheraton hotel. Fraser did most of the talking. According to him, he and a number of other union leaders had agreed that we should all meet and decide among ourselves who would lead the OFL. He suggested everyone should agree to go along with whatever decision the union leaders came to. I was stunned.

The audacity to even make the proposal was remarkable, but I also saw it as a sign of weakness. I knew which union leaders were opposed to my candidacy but, more importantly, I also knew they did not have the horses to beat me on the floor of the convention. I politely refused to cut a backroom deal with union leaders and told Fraser to tell whoever he was consulting with that the presidency of the OFL would be decided by a free vote of the membership on the floor of the 2009 convention. I left them to think things over for a few minutes. When I returned, they both agreed that Marie wanted to be on the ticket as a candidate for secretary treasurer.

The convention was exciting. Antoni Shelton arranged a hospitality event that involved, among other things, a saxophone player in the hallway leading into the ballroom. Faith Nolan, the protest singer and gay rights activist, was onstage with her band. She wrote a song for the occasion titled "Here Comes Sid." The next morning, when the convention opened, Antoni had a team of fifty volunteers handing out hats and scarves as delegates entered the hall. I came down the escalator to be greeted by a gantlet of sisters from Faith Nolan's choir singing Bob Marley's "Stir It Up." I danced with them for a few minutes to a lot of hooting and hollering before entering the cavernous convention hall and taking my place in the CUPE Ontario section. Antoni whispered for me to look over my left shoulder. Behind us were four tables reserved for SEIU, with ten delegates to a table: every single one of them was wearing my scarves and hats. The same held true for ONA, the Society, and large portions of the delegations from OPSEU and USW. The membership knew nothing of the machinations of their leaders from behind the scenes aimed at denying my candidacy. I was acclaimed president of the Ontario Federation of Labour on November 27, 2009. My father had died on that date in 1988 and I felt him with me as I made my acceptance speech. Marie Kelly was acclaimed secretary treasurer, and Terry Downey from OPSEU was acclaimed executive vice-president.

In mid-December, two weeks after the OFL convention, I paid a visit to the OFL offices on Gervais Drive in North York. Elizabeth Smith-VanBeek, a forty-three-year employee of the OFL and the director of administration, showed me around the office and gave me a tour of the eight-storey building. I was shocked by the state of disrepair the building was in and even more horrified when Elizabeth told me of the several million dollars of outstanding repairs required to fix the heating and cooling systems. The elevators were like something out of the Dickens era and held together with spare parts scavenged from an elevator that was out of service. The steps leading up to the building had safety railings missing and rust stains on the concrete. The parking lot was a mess of humungous potholes. To top it off, Elizabeth said the basement had flooded so many times that the insurance company was refusing to pay for future repairs unless the flooding problem was fixed. The building was 80 percent occupied, but some of the tenants were constantly behind or withholding their rent. The previous administrations had not set any funds aside for repairs or capital costs, thereby handing off to me a building in a horrible state of disrepair and quite frankly a health-and-safety hazard for those working in it.

Following the meeting with Elizabeth, I dropped by to visit with Marie Kelly and Terry Downey to discuss our future plans for the OFL, but we never got to that part of the discussion. Instead, the meeting was derailed over my hiring of Antoni Shelton as OFL executive director. The two officers raised the budget as their primary objection to the hiring of Shelton, but the OFL wasn't responsible for Antoni's salary for the remainder of the budget period, as CUPE Ontario had agreed to keep him on their payroll for the remainder of the OFL fiscal year. Over the course of the one-hour meeting, it became clear to me that their issue had nothing to do with the budget. Rather, it was an attempt to ensure I would not be effective in my role as OFL president by cutting off my access to one of the best organizers in the labour movement. The minor issue of hiring a staff member turned into a phony war that embroiled the OFL leadership as Kelly and Downey kept up the drumbeat for months. They had a roadblock for every initative I tried to get off the ground. Three months following my election, the leadership of OPSEU, SIEU, ONA, Fire Fighters, and the Society began cutting their per capita payments to the OFL in half. Within eighteen months, they had stopped paying altogether. At the June executive board meeting, seven months into my term and after they had cut their per capita tax in half, these same unions voted to fire Antoni Shelton because, they argued, the OFL was running a deficit and could not afford to pay him. I had heard from a number of sources shortly after my election that there was a small cabal of five or six union leaders who were plotting to undermine my presidency by cutting their per capita tax and eventually withdrawing from the OFL if I became president. Bob Huget, former NDP cabinet minister and Ontario region vice-president of the Communications, Energy and Paperworkers Union (CEP), said, "He was in attendance at a number of meetings of union leaders prior to Ryan's election where it was suggested by some that if Ryan was elected as president, their strategy would be to withdraw from the Federation and/or withheld their per capita tax."

The straight-shooting Huget objected to this strategy because he felt it would severely damage the federation, and withholding per capita tax would violate the OFL constitution. He further said, "If some of you don't like Ryan and don't want him to be president then mount a campaign and run a candidate against him. That's what our democratic elections are about." Instead of running a candidate against me they set out to sabotage my leadership and damn the consequences for the OFL, the movement, or its community allies.

The collective loss in revenue to the OFL was about $1 million per year on a $5 million annual budget. So, the financial hit was huge. During this period, I was in constant touch with Ken Lewenza, the national president of the CAW. I had known Ken from his days as president of CAW local 444 in Windsor. He was a powerhouse of a union leader with an outgoing, larger-than-life personality. I watched him work a roomful of politicians packed to the rafters with ex-premiers, cabinet ministers, and the captains of industry, and I also saw him on picket lines hugging and embracing workers fighting for a decent standard of living. He was a tough union leader with a heart of gold, which he often wore on his sleeve. Ken had promised me that if I became president of the OFL he would reaffiliate the CAW with the OFL. He was good to his word. In June 2010, I was proud to swear in Ken Lewenza and Peggy Nash as OFL vice-presidents. I was also pleased to be able to keep a key election promise. Lewenza had an immediate impact on the OFL executive board with his no-nonsense approach to business. Besides being a staunch ally of mine, he was also in a position to be able to bridge the gap between the CAW and USW. The unstated war between these two unions went back decades and was at the heart of a lot of the labour movement division. Ken Neumann, the Canadian director of USW, is an affable and likeable union leader, and I truly believed that Neumann and Lewenza could change the course of labour history. However, I still had concerns about the Ontario director of USW, Wayne Fraser.

I was absolutely determined not to be knocked off the agenda I had campaigned on because of the shenanigans of a handful of union leaders who had their own agendas and who never supported me from the get-go. I had a plan for the OFL and I was going to see it implemented regardless of the opposition from some quarters. Part of that plan was to ignite excitement within the membership and to get them out to support striking workers and engage in acts of solidarity with community allies. My first year as OFL president was jam-packed, full of events that began to strike a chord not only with union members: social justice organizations on the outside were also beginning to take note. The OFL office was a buzz of activity with meetings of community organizations and OFL committees that had a new lease on life and a mandate to be active and innovative — every other day the media were calling for interviews or showing up in the office with TV cameras. The OFL was laying the seeds for the emergence of a common front, and it all started within one month of my becoming the OFL president.

KILL A WORKER, GO TO JAIL

Health and safety is one of the major driving forces within the labour movement. Many union activists will say they first became involved in their workplace or union as a result of unsafe working conditions, and my experiences in the Hydro nuclear power plants reinforced that. It was an issue I had promised to elevate in importance to government and employers alike and an area in which the OFL could have a significant impact.

On Christmas Eve, 2009, four migrant workers from Uzbekistan were making repairs to an apartment building balcony in the west end of Toronto when the scaffolding they were standing on collapsed. All four died. I had personal experience working on high scaffolding during my years as a mechanical maintainer in Ontario Hydro, so the death of these workers affected me greatly. I decided to do something about it.

I called Antoni Shelton on Boxing Day to pull together a hard-hitting press release in which we called for a criminal investigation into the incident. Our demand was not unprecedented: there was federal legislation dating back to the 1990s. In 1992, twenty-one miners at the Westray Mine in Nova Scotia lost their lives as a result of an underground gas explosion. The ensuing legislation that received unanimous consent in the House of Commons called for criminal charges to be laid if an employer was found guilty of negligence in the death or serious injury of a worker. This law had never been successfully used in Ontario despite several hundred workers having been killed on the job since the law was enacted in 1992.

The fact that the tragic event happened on Christmas Eve and the shameful nature of the incident meant that the deaths of the four migrant workers received a lot of media attention. I attended a candlelight vigil for the workers just after Christmas and gave several media interviews to demand that the police conduct a criminal investigation. I put further pressure on the Ministry of Labour and the Toronto police by kicking off a campaign tagged with the slogan "Kill a Worker, Go to Jail." Our goal was, first and foremost, to have the police do their job whenever there was a workplace fatality. Usually, after making sure there was no foul play involved, the police simply handed the investigation over to the Ministry of Labour. If the ministry found evidence of obvious negligence, the employer sometimes pleaded guilty and paid a small fine. This practice had to change. I wanted to see the police follow the federal criminal code and lay charges. The only way to stop the carnage in Ontario workplaces was to see the CEOs of negligent employers marched out of their boardrooms in handcuffs. In far too many cases, the guilty employers receive a fine and a slap on the wrist for killing a worker and then build the fine into the cost of doing business. In some cases, the OFL discovered some employers found guilty of maiming or killing a worker on the job had been found eligible in subsequent years to receive rebates from the WSIB.

Eventually, our agitation yielded results. The Peel Regional Police called an outdoor press conference and invited me to attend. They announced criminal charges would be laid against the owner of the construction company, Metron, and the supervisor involved. The case wound its way through the courts and the owner was assessed a $50,000 fine for the death of each worker. I was livid that the judge pegged the worth of a human life at this paltry sum. I begged the Crown attorney to appeal. She did, and on appeal the fine was upped to $750,000. It was the largest health-and-safety fine handed down in Canadian history, but I still wasn't happy, I wanted the employer to go to jail. After a long trial, the supervisor on the site, not the owner, received a jail sentence — another first in such cases — but I would sooner have seen the owner doing time.

Over the next several years, the Kill a Worker, Go to Jail campaign took off across Canada. In Ontario, we met with the solicitor general and got a commitment that police training for investigating workplace fatalities would be updated to include the changes made to the Canadian Criminal Code. I had made a commitment to the membership that, if elected president, I would put health and safety back on the front burner for the labour movement. I made good on that promise. The Kill a Worker, Go to Jail campaign was one of my proudest accomplishments as OFL president.

USW 6500 STRIKE SUPPORT

The OFL had not been seen in the forefront of visible membership mobilization since the Days of Action ended in 1998. There was a malaise about the movement and it appeared every union was content to work away in its own silo. If my vision of an Ontario Common Front was to see the light of day, then it was imperative to break out of this malaise by encouraging unions to support each other. Within the movement there is never any shortage of strikes and lockouts — the perfect vehicle to get unions and activists working together.

In the waning days of my CUPE Ontario presidency, I was on a province-wide tour with Maude Barlow from the Council of Canadians to promote the idea of banning the use of bottled water from our public institutions. As we travelled from North Bay to a meeting in Sudbury one cold and miserable afternoon in October 2009, I asked Maude if she would like to join me in visiting a picket line. USW local 6500's three thousand members had been on strike against Vale Inco since July. Vale, a Brazilian-owned mining company, had recently purchased Inco for $19 billion while promising the federal and provincial governments they would maintain the existing workforce for at least three years. Within months Vale Inco had broken the agreement, laying off workers and basically thumbing their nose at the federal government, which had approved the sale of Inco under the foreign investment

Maude Barlow, Council of Canadians, and me at the 2008 CUPE Ontario convention.

guidelines. In July 2009 Vale Inco demanded major concessions in pensions for new hires, seniority rights, and profit-sharing programs. The workers resisted and were pushed out on strike.

Eight months after the strike began, Ken Neumann invited me — in my capacity as the newly elected president of the OFL — to speak at a rally organized by the national Steelworker office in support of the USW local 6500 strikers. The Toronto demonstration was designed to put pressure on Premier Dalton McGuinty to intervene and use government pressure on the company to end the strike. Vale Inco had brought in scabs for the first time in the history of labour relations between mine owners and steelworkers in Sudbury. Anti-scab legislation has been a bedrock demand of labour since the Harris government scrapped the NDP's anti-scab legislation in 1995. The steelworkers have a history of being willing to take long strikes in defence of key union principles such as the right to a decent pension plan and benefits for retirees. One such strike was the ten-year battle in Quebec that culminated in the Quebec government passing legislation that outlaws two-tier pension and benefit plans.

I was delighted to help organize support for the Sudbury steelworkers. This was precisely what I had promised I would do. In my mind, this is the single most important function of the OFL — or of the CLC, for that matter — to rally support behind affiliates when they strike.

On March 19, 2010, twenty busloads of supporters from across the GTA and beyond rolled into the Sudbury Community Arena parking lot. It was an impressive show of support — all the more impressive given that it was a weekday, and many of the people who attended took time off work for the event. Leo Gerard, international president of USW, was ecstatic when he saw the turnout. Together with the striking USW 6500 members and their supporters, we filled the 5,100-seat arena to the rafters, with a couple of thousand more seated on the floor. Jack Layton was on hand to lend support and gave a rousing speech, promising to take the fight into the House of Commons. Leo Gerard showed his frustration by threatening to shut down the Trans-Canada Highway if progress was not made in negotiations. The strike dragged on for four more months before settling in July 2010.

The mobilization for Sudbury was a modest event and carried out with very little notice, but it energized the OFL staff and those who made the journey. They wanted more of it. The union leadership around the province and on my executive board also took note that I had arranged the event on behalf of steelworkers despite the relationship I had with Wayne Fraser, the Ontario director of USW. But I had a good relationship with the rank and file of the USW and their national leadership, and the event support was an important way to demonstrate that.

G20

In June of 2010, the G20 came to Toronto. It was one more opportunity to mobilize thousands of union members and community activists to protest against globalization and the resultant austerity programs that are causing so much inequality worldwide. The OFL teamed up with the CLC and People First, a collection of community organizations, to mobilize thirty thousand protesters from the GTA and the province. The G20 was the second mass mobilization of the OFL membership within the first six months of my presidency. The week before the G20, I attended a press conference to kick off a week of protests and warned about the possibility of police violence and provocateurs to justify the outrageous spending of $1.8 billion on security. My words turned out to be somewhat prophetic.

The G20 meeting turned into another grotesque spectacle in which the power of the state was brought to bear with wildly disproportionate force against citizens exercising their democratic right to protest. The government spent $1.8 billion on a security fence that snaked its way through several miles of the downtown core, deployed a militarized force of twenty thousand police officers onto the streets of Toronto, and effectively deprived its citizens of their constitutional rights. Peaceful protesters became enemies of the state for little more than exercising citizens' rights. The police excesses included the use of "kettling" and the unlawful arrest of more than a thousand citizens. Police clad in full dystopian Darth Vader getup surrounded peaceful citizens for hours, in the pouring rain, for no reason other than intimidation. Tear gas and rubber bullets were used on the streets of Toronto for the first time in history. In the weeks prior to the G20, the OFL had worked with the police to designate Queen's Park as a safe zone, but a handful of youthful protesters were brutally beaten there by police who had illegally removed the badges that would have made it possible to identify them.

In the months that followed, investigations were conducted into the instances of police brutality, the human rights violations, and the suspension of civil rights. Much later a damning report was released by the Office of the Independent Police Review Director, Gerry McNally, confirming that "police made unlawful arrests, Charter Rights infringements and violations of prisoner rights during an unprecedented campaign of excessive force."* To date, only two officers have faced criminal charges for these assaults and the hundred officers who removed their name tags to disguise their identities have received only

---

* Colin Perkel, "G20 Report Blasts Police for 'Unlawful' Arrests, Civil Rights Violations," *Globe and Mail*, May 16, 2012, updated May 1, 2018, theglobeandmail.com/news/toronto/g20-report-blasts-police-for-unlawful-arrests-civil-rights-violations/article4179372.

minor sanctions. One of the police officers was given a short prison sentence for assaulting a peaceful protester, but the sentence was commuted to seventy-five hours of community service. Toronto's chief of police, Bill Blair, eventually quit his job and went on to become a Liberal MP.

OFL GROWTH

The OFL began to see a bump in new affiliations and our provincial media profile was sky-high. Our news clipping service was chockablock full of OFL hits on all the mainstream media outlets. In August 2010, I negotiated a $2 million, two-and-a-half-year contract with the WSIB for the OFL's program to support reintegration of injured workers into the workplace. The WSIB provides funding to the OFL and employer organizations to run programs and classroom training on the complexities of the return-to-work protocols following an injured worker's long absence from the workplace. This was the first new WSIB money for labour's injured worker program in more than ten years.

Though I had my differences with WSIB chair Steve Mahoney during my years as president of CUPE Ontario, I had a professional respect for him. I made it clear that the OFL had issues with the way the WSIB conducted its affairs vis-à-vis labour, but we did not want to see the WSIB privatized, and we shared common ground. I could also phone him whenever an urgent situation arose, and he usually was able to resolve the problem. Unfortunately, the $2 million was later jeopardized as a consequence when some unions stopped paying per capita and pushed the OFL into financial crisis. Senior WSIB bureaucrats began to withhold the funds when stories about the OFL finances were constantly leaked to the *Toronto Star*.

New members were pouring into the OFL every month, and not just from the CAW. In the first five months following my election we added twenty-six thousand new members from CAW, CUPE, CEP, ATU, and Queen's University Faculty Association. This was in addition to the fourteen thousand CUPE members who joined the OFL just prior to my election. The OFL was making headway, despite all the behind-the-scenes shenanigans. But the new members did not make up for the loss of union dues from the hundred and forty thousand who had stopped paying.

We had arranged quarterly meetings with the Liberal government that were cordial but sometimes testy. Fifteen union leaders on the OFL executive board got to grill the minister of finance and the minister of labour and their senior staffs. I liked the idea of union leaders meeting with the government. There would be no backroom deals so long as I was in office. I always briefed NDP leader Andrea Horwath on the outcome of these discussions; however, that relationship was not a two-way street.

I felt the OFL was injecting a new sense of energy into the movement. I was pleased with the magnificent turnouts for our rallies and demonstrations. Our mainstream media and social media profiles were excellent and our new quarterly "President's Report" and weekly "Updates" were big hits with the membership.

THE BRANTFORD ECP BLOCKADE

In September 2010, Carolyn Egan, USW Toronto area council president, and Don Guest, USW local 1-500 president, two very progressive union leaders, approached me about a two-year-long USW strike in the Brantford area. The issue was that Engineered Coated Products (ECP), a Florida-based company, had locked out its workers and was demanding major concessions. The company had hired a strike-breaking company to tie the union up with court injunctions restricting the number of picketers on the line at any given time. This made the picket line meaningless and allowed the employer to bus scabs across. Consequently, the strike was entering its third year.

The OFL planned a three-day blockade of the plant with the local leadership of Don Guest and Garry MacDonald, president of the Brantford District Labour Council. The strategy was simple but effective: "nobody in and nobody out" for three straight days, with the help of unions who did not have court injunctions prohibiting them from mass picketing. The CAW would sponsor the first day and CUPE Ontario the second.

On the first day of the blockade no scabs showed up, but there was a great turnout from the CAW and good media interest. The picket line was jammed with hundreds of workers who came to show support from several other unions. Day two also passed without incident, with CUPE members singing songs of solidarity and listening to music from speakers set up under a makeshift tent. That night after most of the CUPE members had gone home, a skeleton crew of women from CUPE local 966, led by their president Mary Jo Falle, remained on the line while the rest of the women from the local hunkered down in sleeping bags on the floor of the district labour council union hall. Around midnight, a call for help came from the picket line, and the women in the union hall hurriedly dressed and charged down the road to find four of their sisters doing their best to stop a busload of scabs from entering the plant. The bus driver was clearly agitated as the CUPE women draped their CUPE flags over his windshield, preventing him from moving the bus, and the scabs in the bus tried to hide their faces. Out of the blue, two more buses arrived and stopped short of the picket line. Out stepped silver-haired Carolyn Egan with two busloads of steelworkers behind her. A cheer went up as the steelworkers added their heft to the picket line and the chant began: "Nobody in, nobody out!" An hour later, the busload of scabs backed away and disappeared into the night. My good friend Mike Seaward (who shockingly and unexpectedly passed away in June 2017) loved to tell the tale of the night the CUPE sisters teamed up with the steelworkers in Brantford to chase away a busload of scabs.

On day three of the blockade, a huge crowd of USW members and supporters gathered outside the Brantford courthouse to hear USW national director Ken Neumann announce that, for the first time in fifteen months, ECP had agreed to return to the bargaining table. The blockade tactic worked. The courthouse location was deliberately chosen to demonstrate the unions' disgust at the way ECP had abused the courts to harass its workers and circumvent their right to strike. The blockade of the ECP plant was the first such militant action the OFL and its affiliates had undertaken in decades. In the absence of anti-scab legislation, cross-picketing, in my opinion, is the only way to stop employers from using the courts to undermine legal picket lines.

It seemed the steelworkers were constantly under attack and in need of some serious help in 2010. On November 6, nine hundred USW 1005 members in Hamilton were locked out by U.S. Steel in an attempt to end indexing of the pension benefits for nine thousand pensioners and to replace the defined-benefit pension plan for new hires with a glorified savings plan. To their credit, the USW took the battle over pension plans for younger workers very seriously. A defined-benefit pension plan guarantees a worker a set pension, based on a formula, for life, and is backstopped by the employer. A defined-contribution pension plan, on the other hand, is dependent on the vagaries of the stock market, and the employer has no obligation once the employee retires. USW local union 1005 was having none of it, and they called me for help. I put the OFL machine at their disposal and informed the OFL affiliates that we would be organizing a Day of Action in Hamilton on January 29, 2011, to support the steelworkers. The OFL and CLC staffs, working together, did an amazing job of organizing buses from across the province. The OFL worked closely with Mary Long, president of Hamilton and District Labour Council, Jake Lombardo, a vice-president in USW 1005, and Eddie St Marie from the CLC to coordinate the campaign from the Hamilton end. A week before the event, we already had forty-six busloads of union members registered.

On January 29, a bitterly cold and snowy day, fifty-eight busloads of union members from across Ontario rolled into Hamilton to stand in solidarity with nine hundred locked-out steelworkers and nine thousand pensioners. We marched through the streets of Hamilton with Jack Layton; Andrea Horwath; Rolf Gerstenberger, the president of USW 1005; Ken Neumann; Leo Gerard; and Wayne Fraser. Later we were joined by Bob Bratina, the mayor of Hamilton, who gave a brilliant speech calling out U.S. Steel executives for their treatment of their employees. The massive demonstration was splashed across the front page of the following day's *Hamilton Spectator*. It was an amazing show of solidarity for the locked-out workers, the nine thousand retirees, and the community. In my first twelve months in office, I had organized three mass mobilizations of the membership in support of USW. None of these events would have been possible without local union activists such as Carolyn Egan, Don Guest, Rolf Gerstenberger, Jamie West, Peter Liebervitch, and so many others.

HARASSMENT ALLEGATION

Although the year started off with sisters and brothers marching in solidarity with those who were locked out, within some quarters of the house of labour, there was very little solidarity.

At the executive board meeting in February 2011, Terry Downey, OFL executive vice-president, informed the board she was laying charges of harassment and discrimination against me. It was a bombshell. She had a letter from her lawyer but was not at liberty to show it to the executive board, nor would she show it to me. Nevertheless, she demanded that the executive board launch a full investigation into allegations that she refused to disclose. I was speechless. In the course of the ensuing discussion, it became obvious that some members of the executive board had at least partial knowledge of the contents of her letter. Needless to say, I was furious. Anybody who knew anything about my past, my stance on human rights, my life's work on minority rights, or my thirty-year career in the labour movement would know her allegations were totally baseless.

Of course, Smokey Thomas, Wayne Fraser, and the rest of the usual suspects jumped all over the issue. The board voted to hire a lawyer, who would appoint an independent arbitrator. The OFL constitution allows for the president to hire the services of a lawyer to defend against lawsuits, but it does not cover the person making the allegations. Thomas moved to have the board pay Downey's legal fees, as well as mine, up to a maximum of $100,000 each. The OFL's lawyer hired retired judge Patrick LeSage to conduct the investigation. I hired David Jacob to defend me, and Downey hired Raj Anand, a renowned lawyer on minority rights. Maliciously, the complaint was leaked to the *Toronto Star*, who splashed it above the fold on their front page. My political enemies were prepared to stop at nothing to damage my reputation. Judge LeSage and his team interviewed just about the entire OFL staff, as well as several others outside the organization, in an investigation that dragged on for several weeks.

LeSage's report cleared me. As the *Toronto Star* put it: "Ontario's biggest labour body recently spent more than $350,000 to exonerate president Sid Ryan of racial discrimination and harassment complaints by one of its top officers."* Under the terms of LeSage's brief, I am prohibited from discussing the details, but the *Star* reported LeSage's written public comments as follows: "'I conclude there was neither individually nor collectively discrimination, harassment or reprisals on the basis of race or gender by Mr. Ryan against Ms Downey.'" The *Star* went on to say:

> The case reflects an internal power struggle that has marred the federation for more than a year. Insiders say some unions have been actively trying to undermine Ryan, who won office in 2009 and has raised the public profile of organized labour despite the internal bickering. It has reached the point where some unions slashed their funding to the OFL.

The *Star* reported that Ken Lewenza said that the case turned into a distraction for the federation and wasted funds and valuable staff time.

UNION DUES STRIKE

By the end of summer 2011, we were deeply involved in the preparations for the upcoming OFL convention. I felt that previous conventions had been dull affairs, and I had it in mind to change things up. Plus, I wanted the equity committees to make their presentations directly to all twelve hundred delegates, rather than just to the fifty or sixty delegates who showed up to a caucus meeting outside of convention hours. We had made relatively little use of technology in the past,

---

* Tony Van Alphen, "Rights Complaint Exposes Deep Rifts at OFL," *Toronto Star*, August 25, 2011, thestar.com/news/gta/2011/08/25/rights_complaint_exposes_deep_rifts_at_ofl.html.

so delegates had been left to stare at a boring banner at the back of the stage for six days. I decided to revamp both the overall look and the method for committee presentations by introducing music and videos. Instead of a banner, we'd have several giant screens behind the podium to highlight the topic under discussion. The convention would be livelier and the delegates more engaged in interactive discussion with panellists or guest speakers.

Meanwhile, the campaign by a handful of unions to bankrupt the OFL was in full swing. As the convention date approached, however, it began to dawn on the leaders of the campaign that they may have outwitted themselves. The OFL constitution stipulates that only fully paid-up unions can send delegates to the convention. The four unions withholding their per capita tax would not be eligible to attend if they refused to pay up their arrears. Neither Marie Kelly nor Terry Downey had a snowball's chance in hell of getting re-elected if the four unions they had aligned themselves with were ineligible to attend the convention. As the understanding of their dilemma spread to local unions across the province, names of individuals who might challenge Kelly and Downey were floated. Two names kept popping up: Nancy Hutchison from USW and Irwin Nanda from CUPW.

I knew Irwin Nanda from his years on the OFL executive board, so I asked him directly if the rumours were true. He said he was running but needed to talk with his national union before making any public declaration. Nancy Hutchison also said she needed to consult with USW leadership because she could potentially be running against Marie Kelly who was also from USW. A month prior to the November convention she said she was running.

A few days before the opening of convention, Smokey Thomas issued a press release. His union would not be attending the OFL convention, instead holding an OPSEU convention. He was quoted in the *Toronto Sun* saying OPSEU was on a "dues strike" against the OFL. It was clear from his statement that Kelly and Downey had been tossed under the bus. The day before the convention opened, both Kelly and Downey announced they would not seek re-election. On November 22, 2011, Nancy Hutchison was elected OFL secretary

With Nancy Hutchison and Irwin Nanda at a student strike in Montreal, 2012.

treasurer, Irwin Nanda was elected OFL executive vice-president, and I was re-elected president.

THE WORK OF BUILDING A MOVEMENT

In the spring of 2012, I re-hired Antoni Shelton. One of his key functions was to ensure every element of our strategic plan was moving forward on all fronts leading up to the 2013 convention. The overall goal was to change the OFL model, from business unionism to social movement unionism. Given our limited resources, this meant empowering our committees and district labour councils. We had to both provide support to striking unions and develop policy papers in consultation with our community allies to move our agenda forward. At the same time, the government had to see us as being a credible organization that could give valuable and strategic input to government policy. Above all, they needed to know we could mobilize our membership if the need arose. We got to work on several campaigns that are still at the heart of the OFL's work today.

The campaign to raise the minimum wage was getting off the ground and beginning to resonate with the public. One of the key players in the early days of the Workers' Action Centre's campaign was Pam Frache, the OFL director of research. We helped Antoni get appointed to the Liberal government's advisory panel on the subject. The panel recommended raising the minimum hourly wage from $10.25 to $11.25, but the big breakthrough came when Antoni's work on the panel paid off and they recommended that the government tie the minimum wage to a cost of living allowance (COLA). Under these terms, the minimum wage would no longer be frozen, as it had been for eight years under the previous Conservative government.

Overall, we were pleased that the government was once again consulting with labour and accepting our people as appointees to important committees. The previous year, they appointed the OFL health and safety director to an expert panel on health-and-safety issues following the Metron scaffolding disaster in which four workers lost their lives.

We made a priority of getting the Common Front organization up and running again. I accepted the recommendation to appoint Carol Baker, a community activist and past OFL vice-president, to be the community co-chair along with Nancy Hutchison. Antoni Shelton was working on the digital infrastructure to support the program and working on a policy paper with Edgar Godoy. The Common Front held three summits dealing with poverty, austerity, and inequality over the next two years. The turnouts for these events from community activists and union members was inspiring, but very few provincial or national union leaders showed up to these grassroots organizing events, except for Fred Hahn and maybe one or two others. If there is ever going to be a serious and lasting effort to build a common front in Ontario, union leaders will have to come to the table and be prepared to pony up the resources to fund and staff such a large undertaking.

Natalie Mehra, president of the Ontario Health Coalition and one of our community partners, pitched in to write a brilliant paper for the Common Front titled "Falling Behind." The paper demonstrated how poorly funded Ontario's social programs were when compared to those in the rest of the country. The report measured ten key indices such as housing, poverty, and funding for health and education. Ontario was dead last on all fronts but one (B.C. had a more severe problem with child poverty than Ontario). Natalie and I spent the rest of the week presenting our message on TV and radio across the country.

Despite the gruelling workload in the office, we still managed to provide tremendous strike support to our affiliates. Halfway through the year, the Liberal government went to war with teachers and support staff in the education sector by introducing and passing Bill 115, an act to deprive unions of their democratic right to free collective bargaining and their right to strike. The Liberals wanted the unions to voluntarily agree to concessions and wage freezes or else have them imposed by government legislation. This was reminiscent of the Rae Government's Social Contract, which had caused so much upheaval, and I was more than surprised to see that the Liberals had not learned any lessons from that debacle. McGuinty was given the same answer we gave to Bob Rae — take a hike. On October 15, 2012, Ontario premier Dalton McGuinty announced he would be resigning as premier and proroguing the legislature until his successor was selected at the end of January. McGuinty had been embroiled in a scandal over the cancellation of two gas plants in the suburbs west of Toronto, allegedly to save the seats of some Liberal candidates in the previous year's election. The Liberals would hold a convention at the end of January to pick McGuinty's successor. I immediately called for a mass demonstration of unions and our Common Front partners to be held outside the Liberal convention at Maple Leaf Gardens on January 26, 2013.

That morning was a sight to behold. Thirty thousand protesters arrived at the historic Allan Gardens on 131 buses from across Ontario. Others came on foot, by bicycle, and in cars. Union members, poverty activists, environmentalists, and Indigenous people all gathered in unison to send a message to the Liberals. The people of Ontario had had enough of their austerity agenda, and we wanted a commitment from the new premier that Liberal attacks on workers' rights would end. The drama inside and outside the convention was televised live. Kathleen Wynne's speech sent a message to the protesters outside that, if elected premier, she would fix the problems with

Bill 115 and be willing to negotiate with the unions in the education sector. We believe this happened, in large measure, because the OFL worked with our affiliates and mobilized thirty thousand union members, including Common Front allies, to show their strength to fifteen hundred Liberals as they made the decision about the next premier of Ontario.

Further into the year the dues strike began to bite. The bills were beginning to mount, especially the important ones such as paying into the pension and benefit plans for current staff and retirees. Tenants complained when the antiquated elevators at the OFL office were constantly breaking down. The oversized computer printer systems cost a small fortune to keep operational, and we were constantly worried about meeting payroll. To make matters worse, some locals were affiliated but chronically several months behind in arrears, leading to serious cash flow problems. With Nancy Hutchison's election as secretary treasurer, I hoped she would tackle some of these problems, especially the arrears. This never happened in a meaningful way. To be fair, Nancy had no experience in finance before becoming the secretary treasurer, so she was on a steep learning curve. Instead of working with me to combat the financial challenges, however, she grew oppositional and teamed up with the unions who were withholding their per capita. Her change in attitude took place around the same time Wayne Fraser retired and his protegé Marty Warren took over as USW Ontario director. I sincerely believe Nancy was used by the same cabal of union leaders who had threatened to undermine my leadership back in 2009.

Meanwhile, Tory opposition leader Tim Hudak started to worry many union leaders, especially in Ontario, with his musings about introducing "right to work" legislation if elected premier. He had been leading in the polls for the previous twelve months. At the federal level, Prime Minister Stephen Harper launched several broadsides at the labour movement in ordering CAW and CUPW back to work. In the CAW case, Harper prevented a strike in the private sector, which was unheard-of in the history of labour-employer relations. The news south of the border was not encouraging either, as several states introduced right-to-work laws. The climate for labour was not good.

A few weeks prior to the November 2013 OFL convention, I met with Rob Fairley about the potential dangers of Tim Hudak as premier of Ontario. Rob suggested we set aside some time at the upcoming OFL convention to talk about the threat to workers' rights posed by Hudak's Conservative Party. Later, I brought Antoni Shelton and Joel Duff into the discussions with Rob, and over a two-week period we developed a "Workers' Rights" campaign. Our goal was to reduce the themes for the campaign to a single sheet of paper, printed back and front, on which the main actions would be highlighted. We developed a comprehensive narrative to accompany the handouts. The idea was to give the delegates a list of realistic and achievable things they could do, such as holding meetings to alert their local union executive to the consequences of a Tim Hudak victory, workplace coffee shop round-tables, and talking to family members and neighbours about what right-to-work laws actually mean to the average worker.

At the convention, we conducted a two-hour workshop for all twelve hundred delegates, which in itself was a departure from previous conventions. It was a huge success. We gave delegates real information about a serious and imminent threat, and we provided a plan to combat it. We knew that 30 percent of union members and their families voted Conservative, and we had to drive that number down if we were to swing the tight electoral races away from the Conservatives. The plan was unanimously accepted. I received a mandate from the membership to mobilize for the June 2014 provincial election.

The OFL has what is arguably the most progressive and inclusive executive board in the entire labour movement. It has thirty-nine members with representation from big and small unions, district labour councils, guaranteed seats for five equity-seeking groups (Indigenous, youth, LGBTQ, visible minority, and disabled), and women. The board members representing the equity groups or labour councils have the same weight of voice and vote as the president of the country's largest union. During the convention, there was an attempt to undermine this democratic governance model. Some leaders of the big unions felt that "we pay the freight; therefore, we call the shots." To circumvent the elected executive board, a group of those union leaders, led by Hassan Yussuff, concocted a plan to bypass the board and install an unelected and unaccountable "executive committee" to oversee the board's work. Before the convention Yussuff sent a letter to every local union in Ontario calling for such a committee. He neither consulted with nor sent a copy to the OFL's elected officers.

Convention delegates figured out the game pretty quickly and voted down Yussuff's plan. Most of the union leaders pushing the resolution behind the scenes were embarrassed when the majority of their members voted to reject it. Jerry Dias stood in support of the resolution, but more than half his three hundred delegates sat on their hands; the same for USW's Marty Warren, who looked like a lost soul as half his delegation did not support his position. The grassroots district labour councils, led by Durham, London, Guelph, and Kenora, mobilized the floor to defeat the resolution. Two years later an almost identical resolution passed by a one-vote majority. I suspect this is a resolution that future OFL conventions will revisit.

But after the 2013 convention, my adversaries were madder than hell that they had failed to wrestle control of the OFL executive board away from the progressives. USW delegates to the board became openly hostile and disruptive, putting Nancy Hutchison in a difficult position. Executive board meetings once again became a battle ground for petty grievances and endless arguments about the finances. Nancy had taken to bringing stacks of unpaid bills she piled in front of herself as a prop while she gave her report to the executive board. The USW union reps on the board also began to talk about withholding their per capita tax. After all of the work I had put into supporting USW locals on strike, I was very disappointed.

Confidential financial reports were leaked to the *Toronto Star* and *Toronto Sun* following each executive board meeting. Every issue and campaign effort brought the organization to a halt. The campaign to stop Hudak was no exception. In January 2014 I had to challenge the entire leadership structure of the CLC in order to fulfill the mandate I received from the 2013 convention to mobilize the OFL membership in a Workers' Rights campaign. In early January the CLC held a meeting with a group of unions to talk about putting on a Working Families Coalition campaign in Ontario. The Working Families group is led by Pat Dillon, chair of the Provincial Building and Construction Trades Council of Ontario and a lifelong Liberal. I was not invited to the CLC meeting, and, according to journalist Martin Regg Cohn, it was because of my pro-NDP leanings:

> One of the underlying concerns about Ryan's role is that his pro-NDP leanings might get in the way of strategic support for the Liberals in ridings where they are better positioned to defeat the Tories. But the OFL leader is determined to lead the charge …
>
> If union leaders flirt with a "parallel" campaign, "I can guarantee you we will be decimated as a trade union movement following the next election."*

Neo-conservatives often resort to Orwellian terminology to conceal the true intent of their policies. A perennial favourite is the demand for so-called right-to-work legislation, a deliberately misleading phrase for an approach to union-busting. Tim Hudak, who took over as leader of the Ontario Conservatives when John Tory stepped down, made the attack on unions central to his campaign leading up to the 2014 provincial election. He blamed the Conservatives' poor showing in the 2011 election on union-sponsored negative advertising, even bringing a court case against a group of unions. When that failed, he began pushing the right-to-work concept, the idea that workers in a

* Martin Regg Cohn, "Unions Slide from Unity to Enmity Over Tim Hudak: Cohn," *Toronto Star*, January 21, 2014, thestar.com/news/canada/2014/01/21/unions_slide_from_unity_to_emnity_over_tim_hudak_cohn.html.

unionized workplace be allowed to opt out of paying union dues while reaping the rewards of the union-negotiated wages and benefits (the irony of this concept was not lost on me). In short, he argued that the law should promote worker freeloading at union expense, basically threatening to undo 130 years of union struggle and progress. I vowed it would never happen on my watch.

On January 21 I held a meeting of all the Ontario union leaders represented on the OFL executive board, along with their communications staff and political advisors. The CLC hired EKOS Research Associates to conduct daily polling of the fifty-four ridings we had identified as being in play. Antoni Shelton set up a war room at the OFL office, plastering the boardroom walls from floor to ceiling with riding maps and data. He was able to match the geography covered by district labour councils and riding boundaries, and we discovered most of the targeted labour councils covered three or four ridings. Through this process we identified sixteen labour councils within whose boundaries the provincial election would be won or lost. We contacted all sixteen district council presidents to get their buy-in for our Workers' Rights campaign. These labour council presidents and their membership played key roles in the success of campaign that followed.

I asked each leader on the OFL executive board to free up one staff person to assist with the monumental task of reaching out to one million union members. Five unions responded: Unifor provided Mike Shields; CUPW gave us Alan McMahon; the Society of Professional Engineers sent Richard Long; the Sheet Metal Workers provided Jim Moffat; and CUPE Ontario booked off a staff rep for every one of the sixteen meetings. In addition, Carol Baker, the Common Front co-chair, was released to help us by Goldblatt Partners, the labour law firm. Through the magnificent efforts of these team members and the OFL staff, we trained an army of ten thousand activists in sixteen meetings across the province. These activists then reached out to their local union executives and members, and their families, friends, and neighbours. The wide reach of having ten thousand trained activists spreading the word not to vote Tory was mind blowing. I had not witnessed an energy like this since the Days of Action back in the 1990s.

As soon as the writ was dropped, the OFL assembled two teams of fourteen students from the university sector, whom we'd trained to be super-duper canvassers. Their job was to knock on doors in the NDP-held ridings we had identified from our polling. When word got around that the OFL had two teams of "poll cats" working from 10:00 a.m. to 9:00 p.m., seven days a week, campaign managers swamped us with requests for assistance. The students' efforts were of inestimable value.

In the middle of the campaign, Hudak announced that, if elected premier, he intended to lay off a hundred thousand public-sector workers. We pounced on the promise straightaway. Toby Sanger, the CUPE economist, broke down the impact of the layoffs in each of our key ridings. We could show the precise number of layoffs in places like Oshawa, Windsor, and Peterborough and how they would contribute to further increases in unemployment in already struggling local economies. We prepared dozens of press releases targeted to each community, and the effect was almost immediate. Tory candidates were on the defensive. Talk radio shows were inundated with angry callers and public-sector workers venting at the Conservatives. The tide was turning.

At the same time, the NDP was in serious trouble in downtown Toronto. Andrea Horwath had designed her campaign to appeal to soft Tories by deliberately highlighting fiscal conservatism that amounted to a rebranding of the party. She gambled that voters would buy into an NDP campaign platform that was a repudiation of traditional left-of-centre NDP policy, in favour of mealy-mouthed centrist positions that never resonated with the NDP base, never mind voters at large. The OFL Workers' Rights campaign created a wide space on the left for the NDP, which the party failed to capitalize on. The NDP had to be embarrassed into supporting an increase in the minimum wage, which it agreed to by also promising to give the small business community a tax cut. Unsurprisingly, this NDP campaign was ineffective.

The Liberals won a majority government. Tim Hudak's Conservatives were soundly defeated. The NDP finished up with the same number of seats they had before, losing three in Toronto, but picking up seats in Oshawa, Windsor, and Kitchener. A week after the election, Tim Hudak resigned as Conservative Party leader. The Workers' Rights campaign had achieved its goal by driving down the Conservative vote among union members from 30 percent to 19 percent. From the moment we introduced it at the 2013 convention straight through to the election night results, the OFL's campaign was a model of participatory democracy, demonstrating what a united labour movement could achieve. Our members were jubilant.

Jerry Dias and Hassan Yussuff were effusive in their praise, basically crediting the OFL for the defeat of Hudak and his anti-union agenda. A few critics, such as Marty Warren from USW, claimed that Hudak "defeated himself," and Smokey Thomas accused union leaders of "selling their souls" to the Liberals. Perhaps he had forgotten about the Working Families meeting he had attended in January. A handful of diehard NDP supporters attempted to blame the OFL for the NDP's underwhelming performance, but the firing of several key staff and advisors around NDP leader Andrea Horwath was a more accurate indicator of the truth. I find it tragic when the NDP leadership forgets what the party stands for. Horwath redeemed herself for me with her performance and party platform in the 2018 election. I was proud, then, to knock on doors in Oshawa with Jenn French and talk about the progressive NDP platform.

In the spring of 2014, Hassan Yussuff called me and made a pitch for my support in his bid to unseat Ken Georgetti as CLC president. I was surprised, both that he was entertaining a run against Georgetti and that he was leaving it so late. Yussuff's stance was that he had a higher profile than Hassan Husseini, a candidate with a campaign already up and running who was picking up momentum. I liked Husseni's politics and his campaign of "taking back the CLC," a not-so-subtle jab at the business-unionism model practised by Georgetti over his fifteen years in the job. Yussuff promised to lead a progressive and activist CLC and to mobilize the membership around labour's key demands, and specifically to fight free trade agreements. His sense that he had a better chance of defeating Georgetti than Hassan Husseini made sense to me.

I thought it over and decided to support him, despite my reservations about his sneaky attempt to undermine the OFL executive board. I phoned Hassan Husseini and explained my rationale. He was gracious and said he understood. He, too, would eventually drop out of the race and throw his support behind Yussuff.

The CLC convention was held in Montreal in May 2014. It was a raucous convention with two clearly defined camps. On one side of the cavernous hall sat the pink paper unions, and on the opposite side were mostly public-sector unions and Unifor. The leadership of the National Union of Public and General Employees (NUPGE) and CUPE National were with Georgetti, but because of the decentralized structures of those two unions, the membership was split. Both sides bused in hundreds of delegates from across Quebec and nearby Ontario. Yussuff pulled out a squeaker of a victory, winning by a mere forty votes out of 4,600 ballots cast. I worked my butt off and brought a lot of support to Yussuff from Ontario and across the country. Professor Larry Savage, director of Brock University Centre for Labour Studies, who attended the CLC convention, wrote in his blog:

> Ontario Federation of Labour President Sid Ryan (also a former president of CUPE Ontario) played a pivotal role in Yussuff's campaign....
>
> Ryan was able to garner support for Yussuff from key components of CUPE's Ontario delegation and helped to shake loose committed voters from a broad cross-section of unions by strategically and tactfully taking aim at Georgetti's record as CLC President at the convention microphones during the course of debate.
>
> For example, in a speech that gained him a standing ovation from delegates, Ryan accused the CLC leadership of not having done enough to stand up and oppose the discontinuation of home mail delivery by Canada Post. Ryan's intervention

> reminded delegates that the labour movement must do better, in order to resist and ultimately defeat the Harper government's agenda.*

WE NEVER FORGET OUR FRIENDS

A few weeks after the 2014 CLC convention, I was in a downtown Toronto hotel when I came across a party thrown by Unifor to thank the workers on the Yussuff campaign. (I was not invited.) As soon as Jerry Dias spotted me he sheepishly stood up to toast me and say what a great job I had done and that I was the only federation leader with the "balls" to come out publicly and support Hassan Yussuff. He was critical of the Federation of Labour presidents who were Unifor members but would not openly support Yussuff. He went on to say, "We never forget our friends."

At the OFL, we were feeling pretty good about the Workers' Rights campaign and the outcome of the CLC convention. At the executive board meeting in June 2014, the usual squabbles over the finances took centre stage. USW reps made their usual complaints about quarterly deficits while still telling their locals not to pay their per capita. Nancy gave her usual report with the stack of unpaid bills in front of her while never calling out her union for being in arrears. John Cartwright moved a motion to have BDO conduct an audit of every penny the OFL had taken in over the previous twelve months and every penny it spent over the same period. When the auditor presented his report at the September meeting, it showed the OFL had a modest surplus for the period audited and was, in fact, managing the finances in a responsible manner. The surplus came at the cost of not filling seven vacancies on staff and spreading the workload out as best we could. But we were managing.

The BDO report was not what my adversaries on the board were hoping for. As soon as the BDO auditor left the board meeting, USW vice-president Tony DePaulo read a statement that, to paraphrase,

---

* Larry Savage, "How Hassan Yussuff Won the CLC Presidency," rabble.ca, May 14, 2014, rabble.ca/blogs/bloggers/views-expressed/2014/05/how-hassan-yussuff-won-clc-presidency.

the international president Leo Gerard gave the USW leadership in Canada the go-ahead to cut their per capita to the OFL. In November, Hassan Yussuff ordered a second audit, which would be conducted by Deloitte Touche.

The following January, Hassan Yussuff set up a meeting with five unions, ostensibly to discuss ending their dues strike against the OFL and paying up their arrears. Neither I nor CUPE Ontario president Fred Hahn were allowed to attend. Several more larger meetings followed in rapid succession until the Deloitte Touche audit came down in early March. From a cursory examination of the report, it was clear to me that Deloitte Touche had not been given the real numbers, underreporting OFL revenue by $500,000, and I put my concerns in writing to Hassan Yussuff and his bookkeeper Jasen Murphy. Both insisted there would be no change to the report despite the obvious discrepancy.

Now I knew what was afoot. The secret CLC meetings I had been barred from attending had nothing to do with rogue unions paying up their per capita arrears but, rather, had to do with regime change. The cabal had the report they'd been itching for all along, and they used it to demand the OFL be placed under financial administration. At the end of April 2015, Hassan Yussuff sent me a letter to this effect; his bookkeeper, Jasen Murphy, would be the administrator. The next day, his executive assistant Chris MacDonald called with facetious "good news" for me: Unifor was sending Chris Buckley into my office, allegedly to help Jasen Murphy with OFL political issues. Over the next three months, under CLC financial administration, the OFL arrears grew higher than it had been in years. Instead of fixing the per capita problem, as was said to be the reason for financial administration, the CLC was presiding over an expansion of unions refusing to pay per capita. Fifty percent of USW locals had now joined the per capita boycott, along with IAM and some UFCW locals. Buckley's own local, Unifor 222, was three months in arrears.

In late August Hassan Yussuff asked to meet for dinner, at which he begged me not to run again for president. He called me a "working-class hero," and said if I ran again "they" (whoever they were) would destroy my reputation. Prior to the dinner with Yussuff, I had a lunch meeting with Jerry Dias in mid-August at the Sheraton Hotel in Toronto where he broached the subject of me not running again but pledged his support to me regardless of what my decision would be. Both Yussuff and Dias offered me jobs as incentive not to run. Yussuff said he would guarantee me a multi-year appointment with the NDP if they won the federal election, or a one year CLC appointment if they did not. I knew Yussuff was blowing smoke up my ass, as he had no juice with the NDP, and in any event it was stupid of him to be offering anybody a job with the party without their express permission. Dias on the other hand was a different kettle of fish: he offered me a job looking after Unifor's Social Justice Fund, which he said was poorly run, and the union had basically no idea what international projects were worth keeping and which ones should be scrapped. I instinctively knew this was not a genuine offer from Dias, as Ken Lewenza, the founding president of Unifor, had not been offered a commensurate position upon his retirement. At the time of Dias's offer, I shared the details with Ken Lewenza as a courtesy to a good friend. Meanwhile, it had been reported to me several times that Buckley was badmouthing me with union members around the province, and I asked Yussuff at our dinner meeting to get him under control. The next morning, Irwin Nanda called to say Buckley was at the office shaking hands with OFL staff and telling them he was going back to Unifor. Later that day, the *Toronto Star* phoned and asked my opinion about Buckley running against me. I was stunned, so my answer was blunt and honest:

> I'd be very naive not to believe Mr. Buckley had ulterior motives from the beginning. I was upset that the CLC had not vetted properly nor performed their due diligence on the person they had placed in my organization in a position of absolute trust.... Mr. Buckley's decision has got to go down as one of the most unethical and self-serving moves I've seen in my 30 years as a labour leader.*

* Richard J. Brennan, "Bitter Battle for OFL's Top Job Taking Shape," *Toronto Star*, August 26, 2015, thestar.com/news/queenspark/2015/08/26/bitter-battle-for-ofls-top-job-taking-shape.html.

At the CUPE Ontario 2006 convention with Fred Hahn, newly elected CUPE Ontario secretary treasurer.

My conversation with Yussuff the night before clearly meant the jig was up. Buckley had been no more helping Jasen Murphy with the OFL politics than the man in the moon. Buckley's presence was about access to OFL information in preparation for his run against me. On Labour Day in Toronto, a CBC reporter approached me to say that Jerry Dias had just announced on the radio that he would not be supporting me for OFL president. My immediate thought was Dias's phrase at Yussuff's victory dinner: "We never forget our friends." I still find it hard to believe that a union leader would use Labour Day — the most sacred of days for the working class — to call out a fellow union leader.

At this point, I had a decision to make. I had previously beaten back this cabal of union leaders several times. Would I put my faith in the membership and run again? I had two years left to go before mandatory retirement kicked in at age sixty-five. Around this time, Fred Hahn came to see me. "If you run," he said, "I believe you will win, but by winning, I believe you will lose. We will all lose the OFL because these guys will financially destroy it." Unfortunately, he was right. Were I to run again and win, I had no doubt that the handful of union leaders withholding their union dues, now joined by USW and UFCW, would bankrupt the OFL.

I had always understood the labour movement was bigger than any one person, so I made the difficult decision to retire, rather than see the OFL run into the ground by a group of union leaders with no respect for the OFL and CLC constitutions. I informed the membership of my intent to retire in an open letter in the newspaper* addressing the thousands of rank-and-file activists and local union leaders who had supported me over the previous thirty years.

While I still believe I made the right decision, I am disheartened by the labour movement's lack of response to the current threats to workers' rights posed by the election of Doug Ford and his Conservative government. I hope they will yet rally together to demand better.

---

* Sid Ryan, "Open Letter: Sid Ryan Announces He Is Leaving OFL Job After Six Years," *Hamilton Spectator*, September 22, 2015, thespec.com/opinion-story/5925572-open-letter-sid-ryan-announces-he-is-leaving-ofl-job-after-six-years.

Chapter 7
THE GRANDER VISION

During my six years as president of the OFL, my team and I worked tirelessly to implement a progressive agenda that would equip labour activists with the skills to tackle the challenges of neo-liberalism and austerity. We believed we needed to connect with activist allies within our local communities and outside our borders, and we drew heavily on our decades of experience organizing campaigns such as the Ontario Days of Action and the fight to bury the FTAA. The "community service organizations" model championed by Cesar Chavez and Dolores Huerta of the United Farm Workers in California, and CUPE Ontario's "social unionism" model were the inspiration behind our strategic plans. Our goal was to infuse the labour movement with a newfound sense of energy and ability to mobilize its one million members. The CLC, OFL, and district labour councils, as central labour bodies, have an enormous responsibility to reach out beyond the confines of organized labour. Their mandate can be as broad or as narrow as they decide. They don't have responsibility for collective bargaining negotiations (except with their own staff), but practically

United Farm Workers march from Delano, CA, to Sacramento, CA, in 1994 to retrace the steps of Cesar Chavez, who died a year earlier. Left to right: Daniel DeLeon (USW), Arturo S. Rodriguez (UFW president), me, Dolores Huerta (co-founder of UFW along with Cesar Chavez), and Cliff Andstein (CLC director).

everything else falls within their bailiwick. The concept of social movement unionism (SMU) is tailor-made to complement community campaigns that have broad social appeal. Social movement unionism can best be described as a movement of movements, where class struggle intersects with issues of race, poverty, the environment, the oppression of Indigenous Peoples, the antiwar movement, global climate change, or the struggle for domestic and international human rights.

SMU is the polar opposite of business unionism. Most of Canada's unions concentrate almost exclusively on negotiating wage and benefit improvements for their members. They are comfortable in a system where the bargaining process is established by labour laws and enforced by the courts, which are nearly always stacked against workers' rights. They run on a business model when they could, instead, apply their considerable resources to challenging the system that gives us neo-liberal austerity and the resulting inequality. Business unionism plays into the hands of the corporate sector, right-wing governments, conservative think tanks, and politicians who claim the only role for unions is to negotiate wages and benefits and leave the business of politics to the politicians. This proposition gives rise to the notion that unions are obsolete, that their opinions are irrelevant, and that they have no business commenting on international affairs, police shootings, climate change, and Indigenous or minority rights. But if unions don't speak for their members, who will?

Very few unions admit to being business-model unions; most profess to believe in "social unionism." In reality, their record in publicly supporting and mobilizing their members behind big campaigns such as the Days of Action, Idle No More, Occupy, or Black Lives Matter tells a different story.

Some unions use community organizations, on occasion, to further their collective-bargaining agendas, but using a community organization in this way hardly makes them part of the movement. A temporary alliance like this may not be a bad thing, if it can be shown to benefit all parties. This has been the case, for example, in teachers' collective bargaining, where the well-being of students is usually and genuinely uppermost in the mind of both teachers and support staff unions. This was the case in the 1990s, when teachers' unions took on the Mike Harris government over class size and the wider attack on public education. The problem occurs later, when there is no significant follow-up with the student body or parent organizations that supported the strike in the first place. The militancy exhibited by the teacher unions in the midnineties and their coalitions with students, parents, and community organizations has essentially petered out. A big part of the problem is the cozy love-hate relationship some teacher unions have with the Ontario Liberals and a top-down business-unionism style of leadership. The one thing we know for certain is that when teachers mobilize their membership, they can effect change and sometimes even change governments. The Chicago Teachers Union (CTU) had the same malaise that teachers across Canada are experiencing today. They revolutionized their union in 2010 by electing leadership that adopted a social-movement model of unionism. A group of activist teachers formed a group they called the Caucus of Rank and File Educators (CORE), forming committees in every school in Chicago.

Eventually, they took control of the twenty-seven-thousand-member union and gave the boot to stale leadership drawing exorbitant salaries and gold-plated pensions. A new, empowered, grassroots, local leadership built alliances with community organizations, as well as black, Hispanic, and poverty activists, and took on the all-powerful Chicago City Hall in a seven-day strike and won. On April 1, 2016, the union went on a one-day political strike — a Day of Action — in support of more funding for their schools so that working-class kids and those living in poverty could have access to decent education. This is the kind of transformation we need in Canada's labour movement.

One way, and possibly the only way, to build that sort of a coalition and momentum going forward is for every national, provincial, and local union to fully participate in and fund province-wide Common Fronts. Ideally, all local unions will become engaged in their local community to eradicate poverty, build affordable housing, and work with the local coalitions to campaign for legislative changes that range well beyond their own workplace agenda. We have to move away from the model of narrowly defined self-interest bargaining that only benefits union members. On far too many occasions, I have heard poverty activists disparagingly refer to union members as the elite among workers, with their good wages, benefits, and pension plans. The reality is that many, perhaps most, unorganized workers do not see unions as their allies. They rarely see unions step up to the plate to fund resource campaigns waged on behalf of the homeless or the working poor. The paltry amount of funds that unions put into the WAC campaign to raise the minimum wage demonstrates how far unions have yet to go to be true allies in the war on poverty.

Currently, most national unions and central labour bodies operate in silos. Too often, they are hindered by a top-down, hierarchical model of leadership. And, too often, they cut themselves off from their natural allies in civil society. Small wonder, then, that they are losing union density. They can step up — or be left behind.

TOWARD A COMMON FRONT

Central labour bodies represent 3.4 million unionized workers in Canada. The labour movement is by far the largest self-funded organization in the country, dwarfing many times over the combined membership of all the Canadian political parties. Likewise, the collective revenue stream of the labour movement far outstrips the combined resources of all the right-wing organizations aligned against us, such as the Fraser Institute, the C.D. Howe Institute, the Canadian Taxpayers Federation, or the Manning Centre. Unfortunately, instead of using these resources to fund really effective campaigns that could change so many people's lives for the better, they're locked up in fifty-four national union silos. Worse, far too often, these resources are used to fuel petty internal wars instead of being directed against the real enemies of the working class.

The union movement needs to adopt the deep organizing models that are employed by groups such as the Association of Community Organizations for Reform Now (ACORN), or the Workers' Action Centre (WAC). Organizing province-wide rallies and protests is a great exercise in building solidarity among union members and for applying pressure on governments at all levels, but protests alone are a poor instrument for reaching the millions of workers and activists who don't belong to a union. Similarly, while the traditional tools — door knocking, phone banks — are still effective, Obama-style social media campaigns could expand our reach exponentially.

During my time at the OFL we decided to broaden our base of support and build upon the many mass demonstrations we were organizing. We came to realize that, on any given day, a local union was either on strike or holding a demonstration somewhere in the province. Similarly, somewhere a community organization or NGO was launching a protest. Surely it made sense to connect these different campaigns — thereby enhancing their power to bring about change. One way to connect them was digital mapping. The concept was to provide individual activists or organizations within a city or town the ability to log on to the map and describe the nature of the campaign they were conducting within their own community. There were a number of benefits to developing this device. First, it allowed activists to see what campaigns were taking place where they lived. Second, it provided them with details of each campaign and the contact information of the people who were leading them. Third, the interactive map facilitated the formation of a local common front, bringing labour and community organizations together. Fourth, it provided the OFL with an overview of all SMU activities taking place in Ontario. Finally, and importantly, it changed the top-down, hierarchical dynamic that traditionally typified union activism by giving local unions and community organizations the ability to enter their own data into the program with minimal oversight from the OFL. It empowered the grassroots.

The digital map was one initiative. Another was our effort to build up our database of activist contacts by utilizing NationBuilder, a software program designed to merge contacts from a multitude of social media sources, such as Facebook, Twitter, Instagram, Snapchat, and email lists, plus the new interactive map and good old-fashioned sign-up sheets gathered at OFL events. Within a matter of weeks, we grew our contact list by more than ten thousand entries. We developed a workshop on the use of social media and the new interactive map as organizing tools, and delivered it to all forty district labour councils in Ontario as well as the ninety Common Front partners. The workshop became a feature of all OFL-sponsored events province-wide.

On the deep organizing front, the OFL teamed up with Judy Duncan, the Canadian director of ACORN, to conduct three pilot door-knocking exercises in Scarborough, Windsor, and Oshawa. The objective was to talk to people face to face about poverty and related issues. ACORN knocked on a thousand doors in Scarborough alone, received more than 450 positive responses, and signed up sixty activists who were willing to engage in some form of action. This was straight out of the Cesar Chavez playbook. Within months, four Common Front chapters involving labour and community organizations sprang up in Windsor, Kitchener-Waterloo, Oshawa, and London. The Kitchener-Waterloo common front was active in a provincial by-election that saw Catherine Fife win the seat for the NDP in an upset win over the Liberals. In Oshawa and London, the common front was immersed in the $15 per hour minimum wage campaign, while also active on the political scene, especially around pension reform. The OFL deployed the transformative model of social movement unionism that encapsulated the concept of deep organizing, interactive mapping, social media campaigning, and the formation of the Common Front bringing together ninety community organizations and labour unions.

On Friday, April 20, 2013, we held the inaugural Common Front assembly meeting in the Church of the Holy Trinity beside the Eaton Centre with representatives from more than a hundred organizations and labour unions attending. The discussion and workshops on structure and governance went on well into the night and resulted in agreement on forming an interim governance steering committee. On Saturday, we introduced the Common Front to the public under the banner of "We Are Ontario." One hundred busloads of protesters rolled into Queen's Park to join ten thousand activists already assembled on the lawns of the pink palace. Two buses drove through the night from Timmins to show the Liberals how ticked off they were with Bill 115 and Liberal austerity.

The Common Front inaugural demonstration marching along Bloor Street, Toronto. Left to right: Nancy Hutchison, OFL secretary treasurer; Irwin Nanda, OFL executive vice-president; me, OFL president; an unknown fellow demonstrator; Patti Dalton, president, London and District Labour Council; Mary Long, president, Hamilton and District Labour Council; and Geraldine McMullen, vice-president Hamilton and District Labour Council.

Teachers, poverty activists, healthcare workers, environmentalists, seniors, childcare workers, and parents came together to demonstrate the power of social movement unionism in action. Following the speeches, we marched up Bay Street, along the ritzy shopping district of Bloor Street and back to Queen's Park. The next day a photo of the demonstration was splashed across the front page of the *Toronto Sun*, with the massive sidewalk-to-sidewalk-sized banner emblazoned with the words *We Are Ontario* dominating the photo. The *Toronto Star* and other media outlets carried similar photos inside. We had pulled off a hugely successful launch of the Common Front and garnered tons of free media in the process, causing the Liberal government to feel some heat. The massive turnout — a total of twenty thousand citizens — was impossible to ignore.

The Common Front was a spectacular success but its success engendered a responsibility to those who joined it, a responsibility to continue to grow and engage all its members in campaigns and community-building exercises. This means providing resources, including seed money, so that member organizations can get their campaigns off the ground. Success also means hiring staff to administer the entire operation as it grows. Tragically, the dues strike by a handful of unions kept this from happening. The Common Front stalled.

Going forward, I envision a labour movement that forms a common front with community organizations that are driven by values and principles similar to our own. We can begin by identifying the larger causes that are important to us, some of which have implications that stretch far beyond national boundaries. I hope to see a social union movement (SUM) that applies its formidable resources — its funds, its people, and its organizational expertise — to causes that reflect our deeply held beliefs and let us reach out to our allies in many corners of civil society. Some of these causes seem obvious to me. We need to support those engaged in precarious work, embrace the Leap Manifesto (which I'll discuss momentarily), take up the cause of migrant workers, address the issue of food security, and renew our commitment to the New Democratic Party. This list of causes may not be exhaustive, but it is a beginning, and in current circumstances, it may represent challenge enough.

Common Cause: Precarious Work

One of the great successes of SMU-style organizing was the grassroots campaign to raise the minimum wage led by the Workers' Action Centre (WAC). Deena Ladd, WAC organizing director, was an executive member of the Ontario Common Front steering committee. Their community organizing was textbook perfect: they built alliances and public support through street theatre, demonstrations, and savvy lobbying of government politicians in their constituency offices. The campaign was built in steps over a three-year period utilizing the skills of Pam Frache, past director of research for the OFL, along with hundreds of young community organizers. The OFL provided a little seed money and services in kind, such as printing flyers and leaflets. One important milestone was getting Antoni Shelton appointed to the Ontario Government's Minimum Wage Advisory Panel, which the Liberal government had set up to hold public hearings. The WAC was instrumental in pressuring the Liberals to hold these consultations. Out of that review came the recommendation to raise the minimum hourly wage — which had been frozen since 2010 at $10.25 — by a modest amount, but the big leap forward was the decision by the committee to fully index future increases in the minimum wage. The OFL coordinated its submission to the panel with the WAC.

The campaign intensified during the 2014 provincial election. On December 14, 2014, several thousand protesters, organized under the banners of WAC and We Are Ontario, filled Dundas Square in downtown Toronto before flooding into the Eaton Centre across the street, where most, if not all, the retail workers earned less than $15 an hour. The media had a feeding frenzy. The pressure on Liberal politicians ramped up and public support was growing by the week. Parents, in particular, understood the precarious nature of modern jobs. They saw first-hand that their university-educated kids were returning home to live with mom and dad because of the lack of decent jobs.

Gradually, the tide of public opinion was turning. Finally, in January 2018, the Liberal government announced they would raise the minimum wage to $14 an hour immediately, and to $15 in January 2019 — fully indexed to inflation. This was a stunning victory and a tribute to the hard work of the WAC. Fully one-third of all Ontario workers (1.7 million) will receive an increase in wages. This tiny, underfunded organization had shown the entire labour movement, with its formidable human and financial resources, what a community-based campaign of unorganized workers can achieve.

A key component of the minimum wage campaign was the outreach to an army of young, energized, and educated workers. The WAC invested heavily in training these workers, not only to fight for a living wage, but also, more importantly, to be the leaders of tomorrow's labour movement. These activists, many of whom are people of colour, have tasted success. They are the future of Canada's labour movement.

The plight of young workers is deplorable at present. There are far too few opportunities for young people to break into leadership roles. Union conventions are populated with a disproportionate number of grey-haired activists who should consider making space for the next generation. At a recent OFL convention, a motion both sad and hilarious was put on the floor calling for a "young" worker to be redefined as one who is under thirty-five, instead of under thirty, which is currently the case. The motion was rejected after it was pointed out that a thirty-five-year-old could be a grandparent. But clearly something is wrong when genuinely youthful workers have no place at a union convention. This is especially true now, when young workers have the most to lose from neo-liberalism and the austerity policies that come with it. They have inherited a world of precarious part-time work without benefits or pensions, often while carrying a mountain of debt from their post-secondary education. They watch helplessly from the margins as some baby boom–era leaders sell them out, by setting up two-tier wage systems and eliminating their opportunity to retire with a defined-benefit pension. The fuse has been lit, for example, in Ontario's auto sector, which is certain to explode as new, younger workers earning $17 per hour find themselves working side-by-side with older colleagues taking home $30 per hour. To rub salt into the wound, the baby boomers will retire with a comfortable defined-benefit pension, while the millennials will most likely retire into relative poverty with their defined-contribution plan. The day will come when these marginalized workers will form a majority inside the auto plants. When that happens, we can anticipate a new breed of militants rising up to challenge the power structure within their unions and the corporate bosses who reign over them.

There are a number of key lessons to be learned from the minimum wage campaign. The first and primary lesson is that what seems impossible at the outset often proves to be achievable over a relatively short period of time, provided the campaign excites people at the community level. This is especially true if the campaign involves and is inclusive of young workers. The second lesson is that the fight to raise the minimum wage should have been the focus of every union in the province and every union in the province should have supported the WAC with financial and human resources. Instead, the campaign was powered by the sheer tenacity and conviction of the activists, with relatively little union backing. According to the annual report of the WAC, unions contributed only 5 percent of their funding in the fiscal year 2015–16. The third lesson is that the labour movement missed an opportunity to more fully engage with young and immigrant workers by actively participating in the campaign — and I don't mean by merely showing up at a rally. The growth of unions depends directly on reaching out to these populations. These are the workers who can be found in entry-level jobs in factories and workplaces similar to the plant where I started working as a young immigrant in 1975.

Common Cause: The Leap Manifesto

> The new social movements bring a lot to the table — the ability to mobilize huge numbers of people, real diversity, a willingness to take big risks, as well as new methods of organizing including a commitment to deep democracy.
>
> But these movements also need you — they need your institutional strength, your radical history, and

> perhaps most of all, your ability to act as an anchor so that we don't keep rising up and floating away.
>
> We need you to be our fixed address, our base, so that next time we are impossible to evict.
>
> And we also need your organizing skills. We need to figure out together how to build sturdy new collective structures in the rubble of neoliberalism.
>
> — Naomi Klein in a speech to the Unifor founding convention, 2013

In September 2013 I sat in the front row at the founding convention of Unifor, the new private-sector union that came about as a result of a merger between the Canadian Auto Workers and the Canadian Communications, Energy and Paperworkers unions. Naomi Klein delivered the keynote speech. At the time, I did not realize she was foreshadowing the broad brush strokes of the Leap Manifesto, a document calling for a radical restructuring of Canada's economy by ending our dependence on fossil fuels. She surprised many in the hall with a powerful appeal for the new, supersized union to assume a leadership role in meeting the challenge of climate change. She was venturing into a minefield. Ninety percent of the workers in the audience earned their living either in the extractive oil industry or in the auto industry that still mostly relies on petroleum products. Klein offered up a different vision of a low-carbon-based economy. She said that we need to end our dependence on fossil fuels and look to the new, renewable energy industries that are locally controlled. Workers need to be trained and transitioned to the good-paying jobs involved in building and installing wind turbines, solar energy systems, and geothermal projects. Our communities need to be restructured with massive investments in old and new infrastructure, new subways, and high-speed electric trains, where affordable and energy-efficient housing gets built along transit routes. She called for investment in the existing low-carbon green jobs of nursing care, teaching, homecare, social services, public transit, and sanitation. She argued that the multitude of social movements and community organizations need

Naomi Klein and me at the inaugural planning session for the Leap Manifesto, University of Toronto.

the labour movement to become their anchor and to provide them with organizational skills and resources. The structure she described was not unlike the social movement unionism envisioned by the OFL's Common Front and launched a year earlier — but better funded.

Klein faced a tough audience. The labour movement is not known for its long-range vision. Union leaders generally focus on the short-term bargaining cycle. Few will risk the wrath of their members by taking a leadership position on climate change. The battles within the labour movement in years gone by, over the abolition of asbestos and tobacco products, for example, are proof that the preservation of existing jobs wins out every time, even over threats to the health and safety of union members or the community.

But change is coming, no matter how much some union leaders may pretend otherwise. Earlier technological revolutions, like the coming of the cotton gin or, later, the triumph of the combustion engine, led the world into new eras of growth and prosperity. The transition from a carbon-based economy similarly will present enormous opportunities for a changed future. Naomi Klein may not have convinced the union delegates with her brave foray into the heart of Unifor politics, but she laid down an important marker.

That marker is encapsulated in the principles of the Leap Manifesto. On a beautiful sunny day in spring of 2015, representatives from sixty community-based organizations, Indigenous Peoples, and labour unions came together for two days at the University of Toronto to discuss climate change, energy democracy, Indigenous rights, pipelines, free trade agreements, neo-liberalism, poverty, austerity, and the inequality that flows from our market-driven capitalist economy. Out of that forum a consensus emerged, which was then turned into the Leap Manifesto. The document has sparked intense debate around the country and especially within the NDP and the labour movement. The manifesto calls for

- respect for the rights of Indigenous Peoples;
- a radical shift away from fossil fuels and for Canada to produce 100 percent of its own electricity needs from renewable sources by 2050;
- no new pipelines or increases in the extractive industries;
- heavy investment in green, low-carbon-footprint jobs in areas such as healthcare, education, and childcare;
- an end to all subsidies for extraction industries and a reinvestment in training and retraining of workers for the jobs of the future;
- the building of electric cars and trains alongside affordable housing and transportation routes; and
- a plan to pay for it all by ending subsidies, raising taxes on corporations, and implementing taxes on wealth and financial transactions.

The urgency with which this transformation has to happen cannot be emphasized enough. Bill McKibben, the award-winning author, environmentalist, and co-founder of 350.org has broken down the crisis facing the planet into three simple but frightening numbers:*

- **2°C.** This is the most warming the Earth can endure before we suffer catastrophic consequences in the form of extreme weather and its consequences — hurricanes, wildfires, floods, and drought. We are already 40 percent of the way to that number.
- **565 gigatons.** This is the amount of carbon dioxide that, if pumped into the atmosphere between now and 2050, will lead to the planet exceeding the 2°C limit. If we continue on our current path we will hit 6°C of warming when 2050 rolls around.
- **2,795 gigatons.** This is the quantity of worldwide oil, gas, and coal sitting in the ground, waiting to be extracted and burned. The number is five times greater than the 565 gigatons that will already push us past the point of no return. If we are not to exceed the 2°C upper limit then 80 percent of the identified reserves has to be left in the ground.

The value of these assets to the ExxonMobils of the world is $27 trillion. If we abide by the 565-gigaton limit noted above, it means leaving $22 trillion worth of fossil fuels in the ground. Based on the numbers, and the mind-blowing value of stranded fossil-fuel assets, these corporations are not going to allow a shift away from fossil fuels without one hell of a fight. They now have an ally in the White House, a president who is a climate change denier.

The problems facing the labour movement, which most union leaders have yet to come to grips with, are twofold. First, the world has no choice but to dramatically and quickly shift away from a carbon-based economy toward one based on renewable energy sources

* Bill McKibben, "Do the Math: The Science of Climate Change," June 25, 2013, video, 5:46, excerpt from *Do the Math*, produced by Kelly Nyks and Jared P. Scott, youtube.com/watch?v=HEpbYGZKrC4.

within the next two decades. Other nations are racing to make the shift. Germany and India have recently announced plans to phase out internal combustion engine (ICE) vehicles by 2030, and to go electric instead. Norway and the Netherlands hope to make the switch by 2025. China has a strategic plan to become the world's leader in the manufacture of electric vehicles and a goal of 60 percent penetration of electric vehicles in all its major cities by 2030. Seven other countries have a similar goal. The changes go beyond the phasing out of ICE vehicles. Germany is producing 36 percent of its daily electricity needs through renewable sources of energy and is leading the world in solar photovoltaic (PV) capacity. "On Sunday, May 8, Germany hit a new high in renewable energy generation. Thanks to a sunny and windy day, at one point around 1pm the country's solar, wind, hydro and biomass plants were supplying about 55 GW of the 63 GW being consumed, or 87%."*

China leads the world with the most installed wind power capacity, currently totalling 114,000 megawatts. (That is the equivalent of 211 Pickering-size nuclear reactors!) Jobs in the oil, gas, and coal industries, including pipelines and oil refineries, will take a major hit as the worldwide demand for fossil fuels declines, as it surely will.

The second problem will be the potential insolvency of major Canadian pension plans that are invested to some degree in fossil fuel and related industries. Pension plan managers take the long view (thirty to forty years). If the world appears to be weaning itself off fossil fuels by 2030, it makes no sense to be building or investing in pipelines that lock us into the old sources of dirty energy for the next forty to fifty years. Environmentalists have started a global divestment movement (GDM) calling on pension plans worldwide to divest from the fossil fuel industry. On the same day late last year, both New York State and New York City announced their intention to divest their pension funds from dirty energy sources. The president of France, Emmanuel

* Michael J. Coren, "Germany Had So Much Renewable Energy on Sunday That It Had to Pay People to Use Electricity," *Quartz*, May 10, 2016, qz.com/680661/germany-had-so-much-renewable-energy-on-sunday-that-it-had-to-pay-people-to-use-electricity.

Macron, has announced that France will no longer issue licences for oil and gas exploration on any of its territories. He also used the hashtag #LeaveItInTheGround, the rallying cry of environmentalists, in making his announcement. Hundreds of faith organizations, a number of educational institutions, and pension plans around the world have signed on to the campaign. So far, no major Canadian pension plan has done so. This is a mistake. Canadian unions need to step up their game. The jobs of the future will not be in the extractive industries.

According to the U.S. Department of Energy, in 2016 there were 3.4 million workers employed in the clean-energy sector, compared to 2.9 million workers in oil and gas and related industries. In Canada, according to a report from Clean Energy Canada released in March 2017, there were 23,700 direct jobs in the clean energy sector, compared to 22,300 in oil and gas. Union leaders in Canada are missing the boat when they argue against the Leap Manifesto. Jerry Dias, the leader of Canada's largest private-sector union with members in the auto and extractive industries is not doing his members any favours when he ignores the science and the reality that the world is moving away from fossil fuels. According to him,

> You can't just come out with a statement that says we are going to eliminate all the use off fossil fuels, there is going to be a major reduction by this date and we're going to be fossil fuel-free in 2050.... People are not going to think that makes a lot of sense, especially if there isn't a realistic plan to achieve those goals.*

Notwithstanding, Jerry Dias's skepticism, Canada has a realistic shot at producing 100 percent of its electricity requirements from low-carbon renewable energy sources by 2035, according

---

* Althia Raj, "Unifor President Jerry Dias: Leap Manifesto Debate at NDP Convention Was Thoughtless," *HuffPost*, April 13, 2016, huffingtonpost.ca/2016/04/13/jerry-dias-leap-manifesto-ndp-rachel-notley_n_9682484.html.

Jane Fonda and me at the Jobs, Justice, and Climate rally in Toronto, 2015.

to sixty Canadian energy scholars who wrote a consensus report for Sustainable Canada Dialogues.* Currently, the report says, 68 percent of Canadian electricity need is generated by hydroelectric sources (rivers and dams), which could be shared between provinces with the development of an east-west smart grid, 15 percent is produced by nuclear energy, and 23 percent by fossil fuels. Change is not only needed; it's within our grasp.

The labour movement should be mounting an aggressive campaign to divest their pension plans of their (now risky) fossil fuel investments. In addition, they should lead the charge to stop the $2.9 billion annual

* C. Potvin et al., *Acting on Climate Change: Solutions from Canadian Scholars* (Montreal: Sustainable Canada Dialogues, 2015), sustainablecanadadialogues.ca/files/PDF_DOCS/SDC_EN_30marchlr.pdf.

taxpayer subsidies going into a dying industry and invest that money instead in renewable-energy technology. Why on earth are Canadian taxpayers giving subsidies to the world's richest corporations at a time when the healthcare system is crumbling under the weight of cutbacks? Lastly, they should give serious thought to the type of jobs, in wind and solar energy, that the Germans and the Danes are championing. Denmark, a small country with a population one-sixth of Canada's, has thirty thousand jobs in the wind-energy sector alone. Germany has created 347,000 jobs, the bulk of which are in the photovoltaic (solar) sector. A single wind turbine involves the manufacture of hundreds of moving parts, the provision of several hundred tons of steel, and highly skilled engineers, technicians, electricians, millwrights, welders, and ironworkers to design, build, install, and maintain them. These are the valued-added jobs of the future. We can, and should, be keeping them in Canada, rather than shipping them abroad.

At their 2016 convention in Edmonton, the NDP passed a resolution endorsing, in principle, the Leap Manifesto. The Manifesto was put out for discussion among the NDP ridings with the intention to debate it at the 2018 convention. That never happened. The party insiders decided it was too controversial and buried any notion of the NDP supporting the principles of the Leap document. It is now up to the progressives in the labour movement and their community allies to breathe life into the Leap Manifesto. The Canadian Labour Congress, eleven Federations of Labour, and fifty-four national unions need to step up to the plate — now more than ever — and put climate change at the top of their agendas. Bill McKibben has laid out the stark reality of what will happen to the planet if we stick our heads in the sand.

Common Cause: Migrant Workers

The year 2016 marked the fiftieth anniversary of Canada's Seasonal Agricultural Workers Program (SAWP). A program designed to allow thirty thousand migrant workers from Mexico, South America, and the Caribbean to enter Canada to toil in our fields and harvest the crops — back-breaking work that Canadians are allegedly not prepared to do.

SAWP is similar in design to the hated, and racist, Bracero Program employed by the United States government from 1942 to 1964, by which Mexican migrant workers were admitted into the States on temporary work permits and treated like indentured slaves.

Today, Canada's SAWP and a number of other programs that fall under the Temporary Foreign Worker Program, such as live-in caregivers and the so-called low- and high-skilled worker streams are not much better than the Bracero scheme. In 2006, the Conservative government took the relatively small TFWP and expanded it to include all occupations in Canada, and opened it up to accept workers from every country on the planet. Employers took full advantage of the opening, with its fast-track approval process, and went on a hiring binge, bringing in migrants to work in restaurants, construction sites, gas stations, meat-packing plants, the banking industry, and a multitude of other sectors — including the Olympic Village in Vancouver. Employers were given the right to pay "high-skilled" workers 15 percent less than the prevailing rate, and "low-skilled" workers 5 percent less. To no one's amazement, employers abused the system, flooding their workplaces with thousands of migrant workers. The effect was supressed wages for all workers in the affected workplaces, which was likely an intended, if unstated, goal of the Conservative government.

Prior to their arrival in Canada, migrant workers under the TFWP have to agree to be tied to a single employer who basically possesses the same control over their hours of work, working and living conditions as slave owners did in the American South. The employer can have a worker sent back to their country of origin without any form of an appeal process, just the word of the owner. Repatriation has devastating consequences for the worker: he or she often not only loses the family's only source of income, but also is frequently in debt, to the tune of thousands of dollars, to the unscrupulous agents who recruit them in the first place. Between 2001 and 2013 there were 710 repatriations. It's no wonder migrant workers are afraid to complain about the abuses they often endure. The employer has the whip hand.

The situation is complicated by the split jurisdiction between the federal and provincial governments. The federal government has the responsibility for immigration policy and therefore gets to design the program; the provincial governments have the responsibility to enforce employment standards and health-and-safety laws. The federal government approves all of the applications for employer work permits, and under the Conservative government from 2006 to 2015 they refused to share the list of employers and the names of migrant workers with the provinces. This made it practically impossible to conduct workplace inspections for employment standards or health-and-safety violations. The result could be fatal.

In February 2012 ten migrant workers from Peru were killed in Hampstead, Ontario, when the 15-seat van they were travelling in collided with another vehicle. The driver of the truck was also killed.

The *Waterloo Record* reported:

> Workers' rights advocates said the crash in Hampstead, a hamlet north of Shakespeare, has brought to light the hazards faced by tens of thousands of migrant workers toiling on Ontario's farms. Long shifts under gruelling conditions leave workers exhausted and vulnerable to accidents such as Monday's devastating collision, said Stan Raper of the Agriculture Workers Alliance. Chris Ramsaroop of the group Justicia for Migrant Workers said fear of deportation prevents most workers from flagging safety issues on the job or in transit.*

The issue was ignored for years; but eventually, beginning around 2013, the media began to report on the abuses associated with the program. The controversy reached something like boiling point when the Alberta Federation of Labour received a report under a Freedom of Information request listing the names of five thousand Canadian employers who had received TFWP work permits. Never had anyone in power acknowledged that the program was being so widely used.

* "Horrific Crash That Killed Workers Raises Concerns Over Labour Rights," *Hamilton Spectator*, February 7, 2012.

The Tories, suddenly finding themselves in damage-control mode, blamed the employers. As if the situation came as a surprise!

The political fix they came up with was to split the TFWP into two parts. One part retained the TFWP name and covered migrant farm workers and live-in caregivers. The majority of these workers are from developing countries and remain tied to one employer with all the associated problems. The second part is called the International Mobility Program (IMP). Its supposed purpose is to fill gaps in high- and so-called low-skilled jobs, where no qualified Canadian worker can be found. "The sleight of hand involved in splitting the program into two parts, is it allows the government to report the number of Temporary Foreign Workers in the country at a much lower level than the actual number," according to Karl Flecker, former director of research for the CLC. He gave an example: "In 2013, the government announced the number of 2013 TFW permits issued was 83,740 compared to 65,457 work permits in 2006. This gave the false impression the TFW program had grown only marginally since 2006, when in fact, the government issued an astonishing 630,000 temporary work permits when the International Mobility Program work permits were added to the number."

All of this points to a major problem for Canada's workforce and the labour movement in general. According to Statistics Canada the Canadian workforce is about nineteen million strong; the 630,000 TFWP and International Mobility Program combine to make up about 3 percent of this total. Both components of the program are rife with documented abuse of basic workers' rights. The IMP in many instances is used by employers to supress wages in the hospitality and other sectors, and to supply themselves with a pool of compliant, precariously employed workers. Both programs are exploitative and potentially inhumane.

This situation cannot be allowed to continue. Unfortunately, the response from organized labour is befuddled and hampered by business-unionism. The United Food and Commercial Workers (UFCW) union has effectively taken the lead in the fight for the rights of migrant workers. They have won some significant battles in the courts and put a lot of resources into assisting migrant farm workers by setting up resource centres to assist them with health-and-safety and wage claims, and dealing with language barriers. The problem with their approach is it's all very much behind the scenes. The UFCW is the second largest private-sector union in Canada, but it is not known for its ability to mobilize its members. If they were to adopt social movement unionism and pump their resources into the plethora of community-based organizations, such as Justice for Migrant Workers, No One is Illegal, the Latin American Trade Unionists Coalition, and Migrant Workers Alliance for Change, their impact would be magnified many times over.

There is near unanimity on what needs to be done to fix the problems with the migrant worker programs. In 2013, the OFL developed a Workers' Bill of Rights that calls for a path to citizenship for migrant workers who come to Canada year after year to harvest the crops. This would eliminate the fear of repatriation and the illegal recruitment fees charged by crooks who prey on migrant workers. It would give the workers clear and unambiguous access to health-and-safety laws, unemployment insurance, decent housing, workers compensation, minimum wage, and the right to join a union. Most importantly, it would clear the way for regular workplace inspections. The UFCW, CLC, and the community organizations all have similar-type policy papers in place, but what's lacking is the spark that would bring it all together. That, I believe, is the role the labour movement should be playing. Fighting in the courts and lobbying government officials behind the scenes is essential, but without the common front with community organizations, political street theatre, demonstrations, and mass mobilizations to educate the public, not much is going to change.

Common Cause: Food Security

The fight to raise the minimum wage was just one battle among the many that need to be fought to deal with the greatest scourge of our time in developed countries, and that's the massive growth in inequality. Tens of millions of workers and their families around the world are just barely making ends meet. Access to fresh and safe food has become a significant challenge for many. Just look at the lines at food banks and the number of homeless people in every major city in Canada. Unions can have a significant impact in the fight against poverty by using their resources to ensure low-income and minority residents living in urban areas have access to affordable and nutritious food. Many urban-centre residents live in "food deserts," that is, areas not served within a reasonable distance by a supermarket stocked with fresh fruit and vegetables. The individual or family living in a food desert ends up having to eat processed, dried, and canned foods with low nutritional value, a condition that contributes to negative health outcomes, such as obesity and diabetes.

Strategically located supermarkets are one solution. A more creative solution is reflected in the operation of a New York City organization called 596 Acres. This group conducted a survey of all the "vacant" city-owned properties in NYC. They discovered the city owned 660 acres of unused land spread over 1,800 properties, most of which were fenced-in plots full of garbage. Not surprisingly, the majority of the vacant sites were in low-income areas where most of the residents were people of colour. 596 Acres developed an interactive map of each location and then posted notices on the fences surrounding each property informing residents that it was possible to turn the garbage-strewn vacant lot into a green space, a community garden, or children's playground. Residents responded by setting up local committees. They reached out to others in the community, found political allies, and today scores of those formerly vacant lots provide valuable green space and, in some cases, an urban farm.

You might think that 596 Acres could hardly put a dent in the problem posed by urban food deserts. You would be wrong. Will Allen, a Milwaukee resident and owner of a one-hundred acre hobby farm on the outskirts of Milwaukee, was driving through one of the city's poorest neighbourhoods when he spotted a vacant piece of land. The lot was located between two freeways, five blocks from a large public-housing project, and four miles from the nearest grocery store. He bought the lot with the intent of using it to sell produce from his hobby farm. After two years of operation, he decided to turn the business into a non-profit organization and use it to teach children and their parents how to grow healthy food. Today, his three-acre Milwaukee operation grows forty tons of food from 150 different crops, enough to feed ten thousand people. He has opened twenty more urban farms around the United States, employing hundreds of urban farm workers. Allen was awarded a MacArthur Foundation grant for his work.

In New Jersey, an old steel mill was turned into the world's largest indoor vertical farm using a system called aeroponics. The process does not use soil to grow the produce but instead sprays the bare roots with nutrients, without the use of pesticides and herbicides. The plants are grown on mats laid out in trays stacked vertically, from floor to ceiling. The facility produces two million pounds of produce in a year. The only drawback to the AeroFarms project is the involvement of investment bankers Goldman Sachs, but that can be overcome by repurposing old factories, schools, and warehouses using a co-operative or non-profit model.

In many ways, these urban farms are a microcosm of the very best in social movement unionism. They bring together community activists, environmentalists, and community leaders to provide fresh vegetables at minimal cost to those in need. They can have a knock-on effect, inspiring residents and their children to set up urban gardens in their own backyards.

The Canadian labour movement would do well to volunteer to map out all of the vacant urban spaces in our cities and towns, and provide the seed money to community organizations to start up new urban farms in low-income areas and food deserts. Urban farms, community gardens, and children's playgrounds could be joint ventures with faith groups, poverty activists, or city hall. Pilot projects like these give back to the community. They put the labour movement in contact with local farmers, environmentalists, poverty activists, faith groups, young people, and parents. It doesn't get much better than that from a movement-building perspective.

Common Cause: The NDP

The 1950s were not a good decade for the Co-operative Commonwealth Federation (CCF). First, they failed to achieve an electoral breakthrough in Ontario, either in the 1951 or 1953 provincial elections. And then both Major James Coldwell, the party leader, and party stalwart Stanley Knowles went down to defeat in the 1958 federal election, as John Diefenbaker's Conservatives swept the country on their way to a historic majority in the House of Commons. "Something had to be done," wrote CCF MP (and later NDP leader) Donald C. MacDonald in his memoir, *The Happy Warrior*. That something turned out to come from ongoing informal discussions between CCF national chairman David Lewis and trade union leaders about the possibility of forming a new political party. By 1955, the discussions had progressed to the point where there was agreement in principle, but the deal could not be finalized until warring factions within the labour movement put their differences aside. The Canadian Congress of Labour (CCL) and the Trades and Labour Congress of Canada merged to form the Canadian Labour Congress in 1956. Then the Canadian labour movement could turn its attention to the state of working-class politics in Canada. At the CLC convention in Winnipeg in 1958, they introduced a resolution to form a new political party:

> The time has come for a fundamental re-alignment of political forces in Canada. There is a need for a broadly based people's political movement, which embraces the CCF, the labour movement, farm organizations, professional people and other liberal-minded persons interested in basic social reform and reconstruction through our parliamentary system of government.*

In July 1961, at the CCF convention in Ottawa, 2,200 delegates from unions, farm organizations, and progressive community organizations gathered together to breathe life into this vision. The new political party was to be called the New Democratic Party. It was meant to give political expression to the principles of a strong and united labour movement. At the time, it seemed like the dawn of a brave new day.

---

* Quoted in Donald C. MacDonald, *The Happy Warrior: Political Memoirs* (Toronto: Dundurn Press, 1998), 105.

Jack Layton, NDP leader, and me, the NDP candidate for Oshawa, during the 2004 federal election campaign.

Fast-forward to today. The audacious project that was born in Winnipeg all those years ago has collapsed under the weight of intra-union squabbles and, in some cases, the pernicious effect of untrammelled self-interest. The CLC no longer openly supports the NDP, the party it co-founded in 1961. When election campaigns require their intervention, the movement's leaders hide their half-hearted support behind meaningless slogans. In 2015, their slogan was, "Vote for the Better Choice," which was the CLC's way of saying vote Liberal if necessary, or NDP if the way is clear; anything to stop a Conservative from winning. In other words, the CLC adopted the Unifor/CAW model of strategic voting. They ditched fifty-seven years of labour history and did it without first consulting their membership. There was never an open discussion about the pros and cons of strategic voting within the fifty-four unions affiliated to the CLC. The closest labour came to having such a debate was at the November 2017 OFL convention in Toronto, when a motion to amend the OFL's Action Plan called upon the labour movement to mobilize its one million members in support of the provincial NDP in the next provincial election.

From left: Howard Hampton, Ontario NDP leader; Ed Broadbent, former NDP leader; and me, NDP candidate for Oshawa, during the 2003 provincial election campaign.

The amendment elicited a predictable and fierce response from Unifor, which spearheaded an unsuccessful attempt to defeat the amendment and derail support for the Ontario NDP.

The hostility of Unifor/CAW toward the NDP has a history. Much of the animus can be traced back to when Hargrove draped former prime minister Paul Martin in a CAW jacket at a CAW convention during the 2006 general election. Hargrove was expelled from the Ontario NDP for his actions. The following year Hargrove went after Ontario NDP leader Howard Hampton in the middle of the Ontario general election:

> Howard Hampton and the NDP has "lost complete touch" with the people of the province. "They are

Federal election, Oshawa, 2006. Left to right: Sheila Ryan, me, Jack Layton, and Olivia Chow.

> worse than they've ever been. I see absolutely no reason to vote NDP," said Hargrove. Hargrove lavishly praised Premier Dalton McGuinty's record, claiming the "Liberals have been more left than the NDP over the last four years" and predicting left-leaning voters will vote Liberal on Oct. 10.*

The NDP election platform was hardly the right-wing agenda that Hargrove tried to portray it as, and the CAW's support of strategic voting had far more to do with the evolution of Hargrove's personal politics than it did with the lack of progressivism by the NDP. Nonetheless, the idea of strategic voting appealed to a number of unions who saw it as the panacea for all of labour's electoral woes. The Canadian and Ontario Building Trades, nurses, and some teacher unions including CAW/Unifor bought into the strategy and formed a loose organization that called itself the Working Families Coalition. They pooled their financial resources, purchased TV and radio ads that

* Linda Diebel, "Hargrove: 'No Reason to Vote NDP,'" *Toronto Star*, October 5, 2007.

attacked the Tories, and were silent on the salient subject of Liberal attacks on workers' rights. By omission, at the very least, they became promoters of the neo-liberal agenda.

There is no study or empirical evidence that suggests strategic voting works. There is, however, strong evidence to the contrary. A case in point was my own experience during the 2004 Federal election campaign in Oshawa. The Oshawa riding is always hotly contested between the Tories and the NDP; the Liberals are rarely much of a factor. In 2004, I lost to the Conservative, Colin Carrie, by 463 votes. (Conservative, Colin Carrie, 15,815 votes; NDP, Sid Ryan, 15,352 votes; Liberal, Louise Parkes, 14,510 votes.)

A CBC/Environics poll across several ridings was conducted to ascertain whether strategic voting played a role in the final vote. People were asked: "Would you describe yourself as someone who seriously considered voting NDP but are now voting Liberal because you are concerned the Conservatives might form a government and you want to try and stop that from happening?" Thirty-four percent answered yes; 64 percent answered no. In other words, if the majority of the 34 percent had stuck with their first choice, I would have won in a landslide. People switched their NDP vote to the Liberal candidate and ended up electing the Conservative, the very outcome they were trying to avoid. Why did so many Oshawa voters believe that a Liberal vote would have the desired effect? The answer is that voters get to see only nationwide polling numbers in federal election campaigns. The NDP were running at about 17 percent nationally, according to the polls, and so the voters in Oshawa had no way of knowing I was running at close to 40 percent, with a couple of days left in the campaign.

The unions advocating strategic voting are, I believe, less interested in achieving an NDP victory than they are in currying favour with the Liberals. Over the years, CAW/Unifor has managed to twist the arms of federal and provincial Liberal governments to pump billions of taxpayers' dollars into the enormously profitable auto corporations, thus preserving union jobs at the expense of investing in social programs. The Building Trades, likewise, were granted favourable union organizing rights that

With Jagmeet Singh, leader of the NDP, at the Vaisakhi religious festival in Misssissauga, May 2012.

were denied to the rest of the labour movement by the Ontario Liberals. And recently, SEIU, another strategic voting union, was granted similar rights by the Ontario Liberals. Coincidence? I don't think so.

The Canadian labour movement is divided along several lines. A minority of unions exclusively support the NDP; the majority support both the Liberals and the NDP; while a small number sit on the sidelines and ignore electoral politics altogether. Missing from the equation is an honest debate within the house of labour about our relationship to the NDP. It appears one private-sector union is driving the debate and the CLC acquiesces to their demands in order to keep the peace. The current leader of the CLC has reached the mandatory retirement age for CLC officers; therefore, an election will be held in 2020. It is an opportunity for leadership candidates to address these pressing issues of our time. We must talk about the inevitable transition away from a carbon-based economy. We must take the coming revolution in artificial intelligence seriously. (We ignore this at our peril. Major corporations, from Ford to Google, are plotting a future in which robots operate factories and cars drive themselves.) We must ask ourselves which political party is more likely to protect the interest of workers during and after that transition. As a movement, we must take a long-term view of labour's prospects.

We are in danger of finding ourselves fighting a losing, rearguard action to mitigate the massive job losses that are coming. We need to be in a position to convince governments to invest in training and retraining programs — ideally by using the subsidies previously shovelled to the extractive industries. The EI program will need to be completely overhauled and opened up to accommodate workers transitioning to new jobs. Denmark has a program they call "flexicurity," where laid-off workers go back to school or community college to learn a new trade or skill set while earning up to 90 percent of previous earnings. The labour movement has to be in the vanguard of the revolution to complete Tommy Douglas's dream for a truly free and universal healthcare system including pharma, dental, home, and hospital care. The healthcare professions are among the fastest-growing components of the U.S. and Canadian economies. The sector provides highly skilled and good-paying green jobs that are mostly unionized. The same can be said for the education sector and social services sectors.

We need to be brutally honest about the role both the Liberals and the NDP have played in government, at both the federal and provincial levels. The Rae government screwed up with their Social Contract, but Rae inflicted no lasting damage and passed quite a lot of good policy around employment equity, pay equity, anti-scab legislation, rent controls, welfare, and public housing. The Liberals, meanwhile, took a meat cleaver to health, education, and social program transfer payments in the mid-1990s. As finance minister, Paul Martin delighted in promising to slash the deficit, "come hell or high water." The damage he caused was permanent. We can see it today in the number of homeless people on the streets, the shortage of hospital beds, and the grotesque cost of post-secondary tuition. The Liberals also have accelerated the negotiation and signing of free trade agreements with multiple countries, including the hated CETA and TPP, which labour opposes on paper. Most recently, the Liberals broke their main election promise to reform the electoral system. They said the 2015 election would be the last "first past the post" Canadian election. They lied. And still, some unions in the house of labour conveniently overlook Liberal attacks on workers' rights and social programs to curry favour for their pet causes. We need to have this debate at the 2020 CLC convention.

A COMMON VISION

Labour needs to come together to hammer out a common vision. It is only through this exercise that labour will be able to discover for themselves and show the world what they stand for. Canada's labour movement is at that point in history where they need to take stock of their accomplishments down through the decades — and there have been many — and look ahead to what the future holds for our children and grandchildren. Will they be thankful that we shifted our economy away from the disastrous path of environmental destruction we were on? Will they be glad that they have access to clean air and water? Will they marvel at the ease and speed of the super-fast electric trains on which they commute to work in Toronto, Montreal, Vancouver, or Calgary? Will they have an ample and cheap supply of electricity thanks to the solar panel mounted on the roof? Will they be relieved that the nuclear- and fossil-fuelled generating stations have been closed down?

Or will they curse our lack of vision and call us Luddites for refusing to more fully embrace the new technologies of the twenty-first century? Will they decry our stupidity when an oil tanker spills one million barrels of crude oil into the Burrard Inlet off the British Columbia coast? Will they be asking union leaders what happened to the retraining programs that were promised, as they sit at home, unable to collect the EI they paid into because the Liberals and Tories used it to give tax cuts and subsidies to the fossilized oil and gas industry?

This is the debate waiting to be had inside Canada's labour movement. In 1956 Claude Jodoin, the first CLC president, faced a similar situation. He had a divided labour movement and a political party that was struggling in the polls. He called for unity in the labour movement and united two factions behind one common vision. In 1961 the CLC and CCF made history by forming the NDP. It is no secret that their relationship is dysfunctional today. It can be fixed, but only if the CLC confronts the issues that divide us. Strategic voting, for a start, undermines the long-term interests of union members. It has to end. The

Liberals' persistent devotion to CETA and TPP alone is reason enough to oppose them. Are the CLC and the others who turn a blind eye to the Liberals' anti-union policies doing so wilfully — or is there something else at play?

The only way to answer these questions is through open debate. I hope the CLC will set aside one day at the 2020 convention to hammer out consensus on all of these pressing issues; but above all, an agreement must be reached on the relationship between labour and the NDP. The CLC can no longer run milquetoast electoral campaigns that offer token support to NDP candidates while nodding, winking, and nudging real support for the Liberals. The message we send when we do this is a message of weakness: it says we stand for what we can grab in the short term and let the devil take the hindmost — leaving behind a world of privatized public services, effective governance by transnational corporations, and lost benefits — which amounts to a betrayal of our forebears. We stand on the shoulders of previous generations of workers, men and women who sweated blood to build a political party that would fight for the interest of workers. We cannot allow their long-term vision to be trampled on because of short-term gains and petty grievances. In the words of Tommy Douglas, "Courage, my friends; 'tis not too late to build a better world."

CONCLUSION

The OFL convention that opened on November 23, 2015, would be my twenty-third and final union convention as chair. As usual, Antoni knocked on my hotel room door thirty minutes before the start. I had decided that, for this convention, I was going to break with tradition: I would leave the duty of opening the convention to Nancy Hutchison and Irwin Nanda and make my appearance a little later. When I did step into the convention hall, about thirty minutes after the start, I was met with total bedlam.

A motion was made requesting that time be set aside for the candidates seeking elected office to both address the delegates and answer questions from the floor. Incredibly, the leadership of the pink paper unions, now joined by ETFO leader Sam Hammond and Unifor, opposed the motion. Perhaps they were afraid delegates might ask tough questions about the unethical and undemocratic practice of withholding per capita payments from the OFL, but whatever their reason, they were turning the convention into a shambles. I watched from the sidelines for about twenty minutes as Nancy Hutchison was repeatedly challenged with points of order that she was unable to handle.

Hassan Yussuff's executive assistant, Chris MacDonald, shouted interventions at her from the sidelines, and in confusion and exasperation, she inappropriately handed the chair over to MacDonald. Not only did MacDonald lack experience at chairing a convention but also, as a CLC staff person, he had no constitutional right to be in the chair. He quickly found himself in trouble, too. Those on the convention floor are always quick to sense weakness, and they exploited the situation by raising numerous points of order. MacDonald was flummoxed and lost control of the room.

Finally, I'd seen enough. I walked onto the stage to a huge cheer from the crowd. MacDonald gripped the podium with both hands as if to say, *I'm not leaving*. I gave him a look that said, *Buddy, step back*, as I gently nudged him away. It took me about five minutes to restore order, and eventually the motion was voted on and defeated. In its place, each candidate was given five minutes to read a prepared speech but delegates would not be allowed to ask questions. The OFL is by far the largest federation of labour in the country, representing more than one million workers, and yet some prominent union leaders counselled their members to vote against a motion that would have allowed their delegates to ask a few questions of the three candidates running for elected office. Sam Hammond of ETFO and Tony DePaulo of USW both actively spoke against the motion on the microphones themselves. The unmistakable message to the new OFL officers from these union leaders was "we put you into office and we can take you out of office." The muzzling of the new leadership was played out on the convention floor before they were elected into office.

This was not a good start. At 10:00 a.m., I gave my president's report after Fred Hahn gave me a fantastic introduction, recounting a brief synopsis of my career. Sheila; two of my daughters, Lisa and Amanda; and my granddaughter Ava were on stage with me. As I approached the podium, the delegates rose for a prolonged standing ovation. I was overcome with emotion, and for the first time it struck home that this would be the last convention I would chair. I thought about the makeup of the twelve hundred delegates in the hall. I knew Unifor had pumped up their numbers to 450-plus, and the pink paper unions had mobilized as well, just in case I changed my mind at the last minute and decided to run. But I also knew that I had a large swath of support from the rank and file within all the unions, if only I could find the words to reach them.

I figured some of the union leaders in the hall were expecting me to deliver a scorched-earth speech and to go after my political rivals, but they underestimated my love and respect for the membership and the well-being of the movement as a whole.

Instead, I started by heaping genuine, heartfelt praise on the district labour councils of Ontario for their incredible work and loyalty. They were my rock and the engine for mobilization and action in Ontario, and I wanted to acknowledge that the labour councils are the reason we can accomplish so much together.

I decided to touch only briefly on the dues strike, mentioning the withholding of $1.2 million per year or 25 percent of the OFL's total budget, by some unions. Then I said,

> I was going to castigate those leaders [who withheld the per capita tax] during this speech, but last night my better angels spoke to me after I read a few verses of Seamus Heaney's poem "The Cure at Troy," in which Heaney talks about healing. As I read his words, it struck me like a bolt of lightning that what our movement needs more than anything right now is a whole lot of healing. And so, we will move on and begin that healing process, safe in the knowledge that people already know what came down, but that does not mean we will forget. The Irish have long memories [I joked] — we still talk about the murderous invasion of Ireland by Oliver Cromwell in the 1650s as if it were yesterday.

It was enough. I moved on to the heart of my speech. I went into what I felt the labour movement needed to do in order to become more relevant in the lives of workers who do not belong to unions, developing many of the themes I have since described as social movement unionism. I chastised the leadership for not doing enough to reach out to people of colour and young workers. What follows is a part of the speech I delivered.

> Let us talk about the kind of union movement we want. I am proud to say the OFL is on the cutting edge of building a new kind of labour movement that puts equity and equality for all at the heart of everything we do. If the labour movement is to survive and meet the challenges of white privilege and systemic racism, then we have to stop electing middle-aged white men — like me — to lead. Toronto is a city of almost three million people, where over 50 percent of the population are people of colour. Look around, brothers and sisters, what percentage of Indigenous workers and workers of colour are in this convention hall today?
>
> Some unions, like Unite Here, are already organizing within the growing pool of precarious workers and are moving workers of colour up the union ranks. But we're moving far too slowly. The growth of precarious work far outstrips our ability to respond. Over the course of this convention you will hear over and over about the need to address precarity head-on with improved labour and employment standard laws that remove the roadblocks to union organizing. But we also need to address systemic discrimination within our unions. That means we need to remove the barriers that advantage some groups over others. Indigenous workers and workers of colour need to see their race, language, and culture reflected in the union that wants their vote. If we refuse to take strong and immediate steps now, our density levels will continue to fall, particularly in the private sector.

We also need to call upon the NDP to put employment equity back on the agenda at Queen's Park and in Ottawa. I am calling upon the unions that make up our movement to show leadership by developing employment equity plans within your own unions and sharing your best practices with the CLC and OFL. By 2030 this convention hall should be at least 50 percent Indigenous workers and workers of colour. We need to stand with these communities when they're battling fundamental human rights abuses like carding, missing Native women, and the police use of force. This creates trust and a basis for other aspects of collaboration.

The type of collaboration I'm talking about is the kind that inspired the creation of the Ontario Common Front to address rising inequality and defend the interests of the next generation. The Common Front has become the province's largest labour-community alliance since the Mike Harris era, with over ninety community-based organizations affiliated. The recent OFL anti-poverty summit and the Common Front have mobilized against austerity cuts and released groundbreaking research on inequality written by Natalie Mehra, president of the Ontario Health Coalition, and one of our Common Front partners. We take great pride in an OFL that understands that if unions are to repel right-wing attacks and grow as a movement, we need to undermine the politics of envy by fighting for all working people.

How do we strengthen our unions in an age of systematic anti-unionism? We link arms with other progressives. We seize our responsibility to fight for and protect the interests of the next generation. We take that responsibility and build an inclusive Common Front with all workers, and with other activists who haven't always considered labour a natural ally. On meagre resources, the Common Front has become a model of organization that encouraged similar coalitions in London, Oshawa, Ottawa, Kitchener-Waterloo, Guelph, and Toronto. Common Front activists have travelled to the Northwest Territories to help them establish a Common Front coalition. The Common Front represents a new kind of labour movement organization, one that opens our structures to the participation of non-unionized workers and the unemployed. It provides a bigger and stronger movement and allows us to imagine and work toward equality, a green economy, free tuition, retirement security, universal pharmacare, and a guaranteed minimum income.

Everything about building a new labour movement and fighting for the Ontario we want must be backed up by mass mobilization. We need to show corporations and governments that we are serious and that we are prepared to come out in numbers to demonstrate our commitment. We need to achieve the type of Common Front we recently witnessed in Quebec, where students came together with social partners to stage massive province-wide protests in defence of public education and social services. We need to represent all workers regardless of whether they're unionized or not, employed or not. We have to go where movements start: local communities.

Today Ottawa and Queen's Park are so overrun by corporate lobbyists and controlled by an entrenched party establishment that squelches any hope for true social democratic change in the short run. Truly successful movements in Canadian history have always started at the grassroots level, not in the insulated halls of elite power. Because the hard truth is this: we can only win with an ideological movement that captures

Canadians' hearts and minds. The values of equality, fair treatment, open democratic participation, and economic security extended to all working people. We can't be just seen as fighting for wages and benefits — these are the backbone of what we stand for, but they can't be the only things we stand for. And if you didn't already know it, right-wing think tanks, the media, and corporate Canada have painted a picture of our movement as greedy and self-serving. Too often we have allowed ourselves to be cut off from the big issues that define a nation and, indeed, that define our movement.

Our movement should be leading by example with the might of our combined power. Not just quietly helping, but visibly providing leadership on this issue. For example, we should be out front on the question of Syrian refugees. Canadian workers are united in our sympathy and solidarity for the recent victims of the Paris bombings. In the coming days, Canadians may be tempted to revert to the divisive politics of Stephen Harper, but racism and Islamophobia will not solve our international problems. The commitment to receive twenty-five thousand Syrian refugees before the end of 2015 is a promise that must be kept. These refugees need our assistance.

We must not allow ourselves to be drawn into supporting the cycle of violence created by revenge. Bombing always creates collateral damage. What Syria and other places of conflict really need is diplomacy instead of bombs. Conflict resolution must replace power politics. We need peace-creators and peacekeepers. We need political leaders with the courage to stop exports from the multi-billion arms-creating industries so we can "give peace a chance." We can honour the dead by promoting peace, not war, and by welcoming refugees, not fearing them.

I want to assure you, brothers and sisters, that we stand ready for the challenges ahead. In fact, the Ontario Federation of Labour has never been more ready. We build on a history of solid leadership and the bold activism of past generations. We have nurtured and grown a solid foundation, and we are ready to lead a broader, bolder movement. We have the necessary community partnerships including the "We Are Ontario" Common Front, and we continue to be an important educational resource to labour affiliates, our friends in civil society, and the broader community. We have the capacity to fight back. We cannot allow any government to destroy the social safety net that labour helped build. We cannot ignore politicians who threaten to take away our right to act collectively. We cannot sit idly by while the proponents of austerity continue to advance their divisive and destructive agendas.

No, sisters and brothers, I have a real sense that people from across the land are rising; labour is rising; civil society is rising; the progressive guardians of fairness and justice are rising; and we are ready to take back our province and take back our country.

Brothers and sisters, we should be invigorated by the challenge before us, content in the knowledge we have the collective solidarity of our union movement behind us and the support of millions of Canadians outside this hall, and comforted by the words of Martin Luther King: "Let us realize that the arc of the moral universe is long, but it bends toward justice."

Let us seize the moment. Let us come together from all corners of this province, unions, students, racialized communities, First Nations Peoples, let us come together as one and let us meet this challenge.

I thanked everyone and paused for a moment as the applause filled the room. Delegates from every union in the hall got to their feet and filled the air with whistles, hoots, and applause, several of the CUPE members in front of the podium were in tears, and for those few moments, the Ontario Federation of Labour was taking the first steps in believing, as Seamus Heaney said, that "further shore is reachable from here." I pumped my fist several times in the air, hugged Sheila, Lisa, and Amanda, and walked off the stage to chants of "Sid! Sid! Sid!"

The family. From left: Callum, held by Dave Morgan; Lisa (my daughter); me; Sheila (my wife); Amanda (my daughter); and Susie (my daughter). In front, from left: Ava and Kiyara (granddaughters).

ACKNOWLEDGEMENTS

I began to write this book ten years ago in 2009. I decided to spend time in Ireland to immerse myself in the culture and surroundings of the country of my birth in order to bring those memories flooding back into my consciousness. It was an emotional and cathartic experience for me as I delved into my youth and childhood years. I could not have written the book without the lifetime support and love from Sheila and our three daughters, Lisa, Susie, and Amanda. My life's work has taken me away from them on far too many important occasions. Over the years I have been embroiled in many high profile controversies and skirmishes with governments and numerous organizations but through it all my family have been my solid rock of support.

I almost gave up on the book several times but hung in there because of the patience and encouragement of Jonathan Webb, who brilliantly guided me through the process and edited the early drafts of the book. I owe a great deal of gratitude to the entire team at Dundurn Press: Elena Radic, project editor, Michelle Melski, publicity manager, Tabassum Siddiqui, publicist, and Laura Boyle, artistic director, all of whose lives

I made a misery with my constant stream of emails and phone calls. Without them this book would never have seen the light of day.

I thoroughly enjoyed working with editor Kate Unrau, who expertly edited and pulled apart each chapter and at the same time maintained my voice. I was blown away by the thoroughness of copy editor Laurie Miller's work, especially his keen eye for detail. Any mistakes or errors are strictly of my own making and I promise to fix them in any future reprints.

I also want to thank my good friends and comrades Antoni Shelton and Edgar Godoy for their steadfast support and invaluable advice over the years but in particular their insights for this book. Likewise, I want to thank James Behan for constantly reminding me of the good and bad times growing up in Dublin during the fifties, sixties, and seventies. Lastly, I am grateful to all those who are mentioned throughout the book who have so enriched my life beyond my wildest dreams. I hold a very special place in my heart for CUPE and the entire membership of the union who have been so good to me from almost the first day I arrived in this beautiful country of Canada.

IMAGE CREDITS

Al McConnell: 10, 11
Christy Burgess: 28
Courtesy of the author: 26, 30, 31, 33, 79, 80
Canadian Union of Public Employees Ontario: 102, 105, 115, 116, 117, 141, 195, 222, 246
Jim Woodward, CUPE Ontario: 125, 211
Joel Duff, Ontario Federation of Labour: 17, 232, 254, 260, 278
Meghan Appleton: 164, 168
Nate Thompson: 290
Ontario Federation of Labour: 192, 265
Stella Yeadon, CUPE Ontario: 18, 21, 172, 178, 201, 274, 275, 276
Unattributed: 249
William Smith: 114

INDEX

Page numbers in italics represent photos.